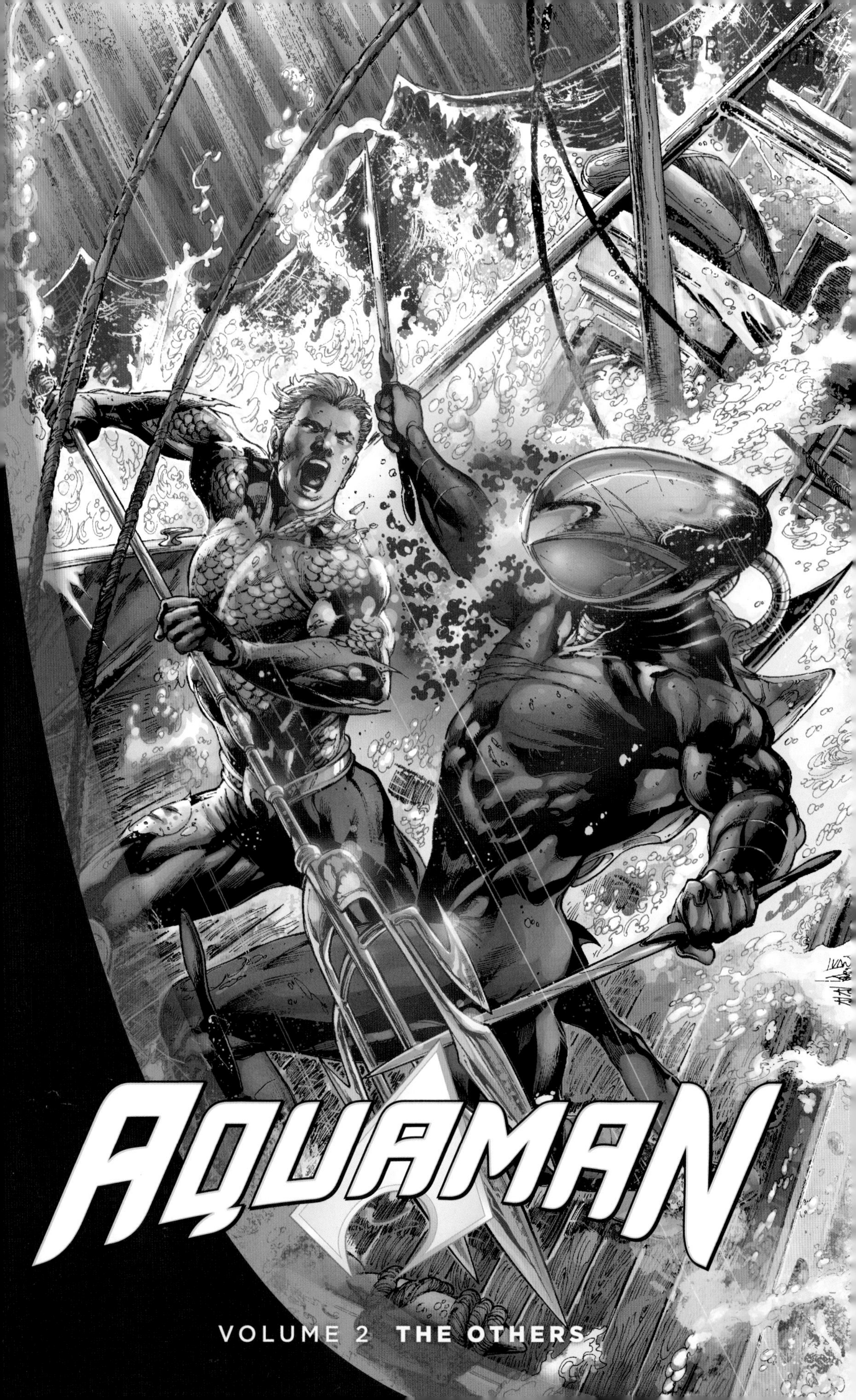
AQUAMAN
VOLUME 2 THE OTHERS

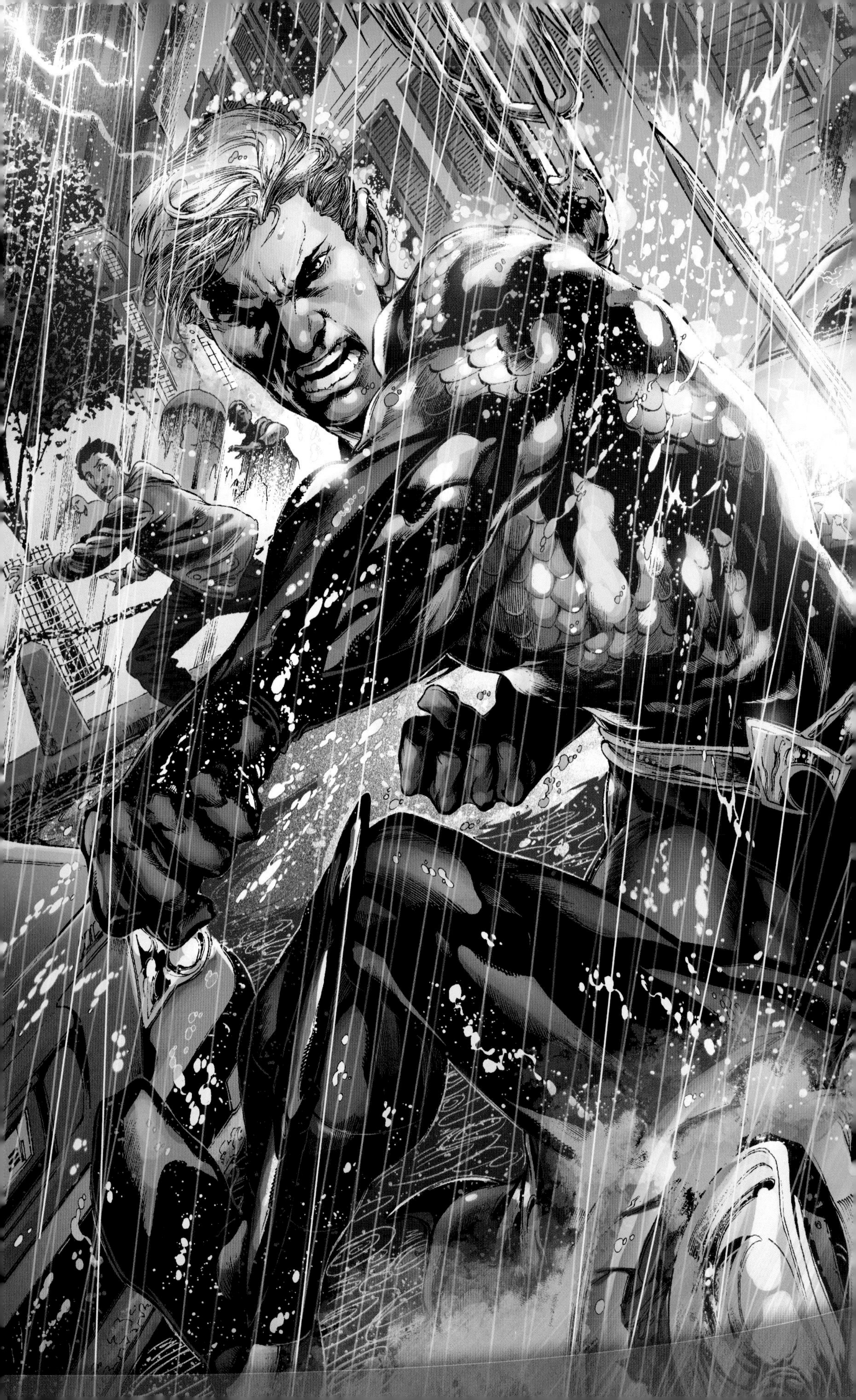

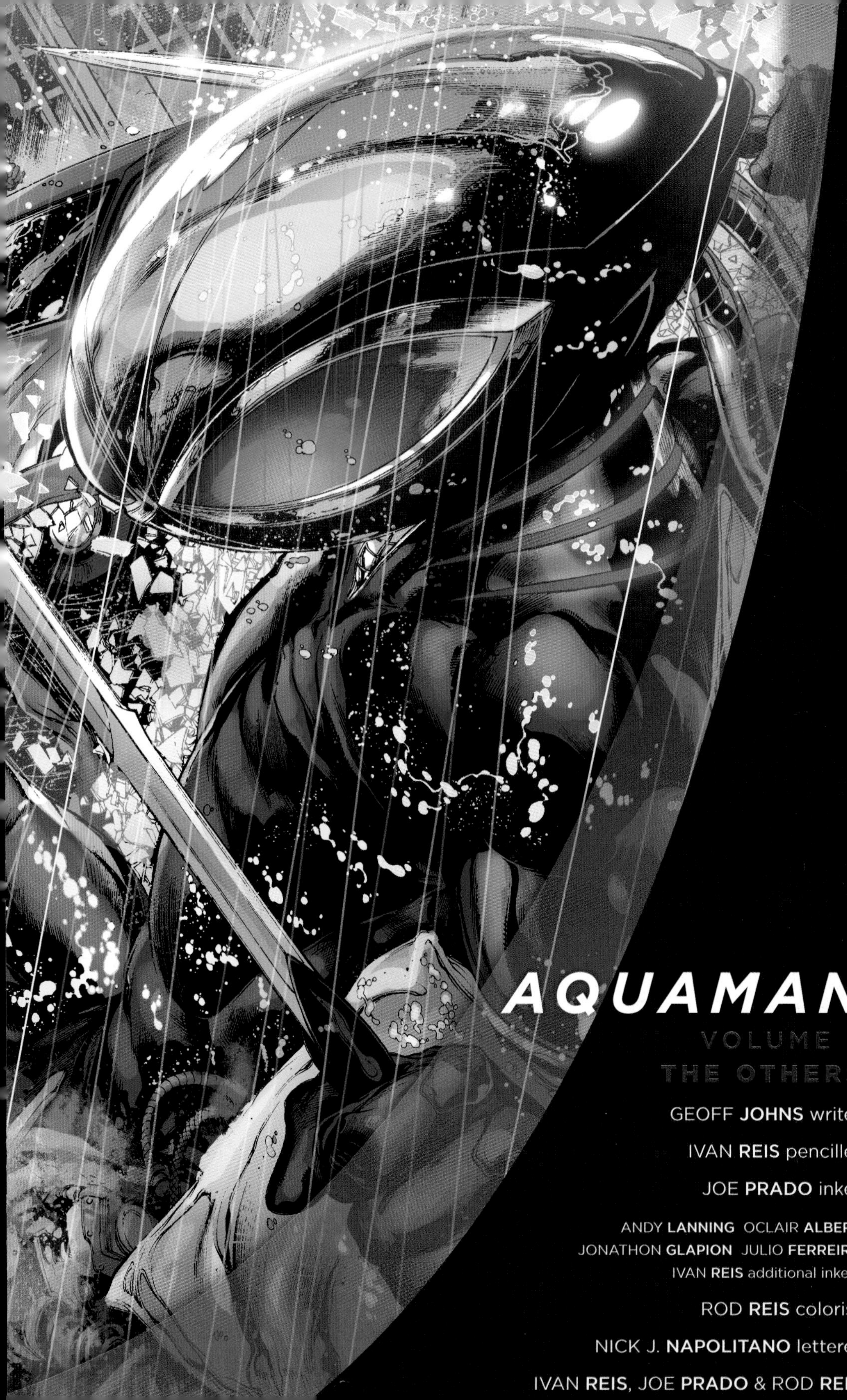

AQUAMAN

VOLUME 2
THE OTHERS

GEOFF **JOHNS** writer

IVAN **REIS** penciller

JOE **PRADO** inker

ANDY **LANNING** OCLAIR **ALBERT**
JONATHON **GLAPION** JULIO **FERREIRA**
IVAN **REIS** additional inkers

ROD **REIS** colorist

NICK J. **NAPOLITANO** letterer

IVAN **REIS**, JOE **PRADO** & ROD **REIS**

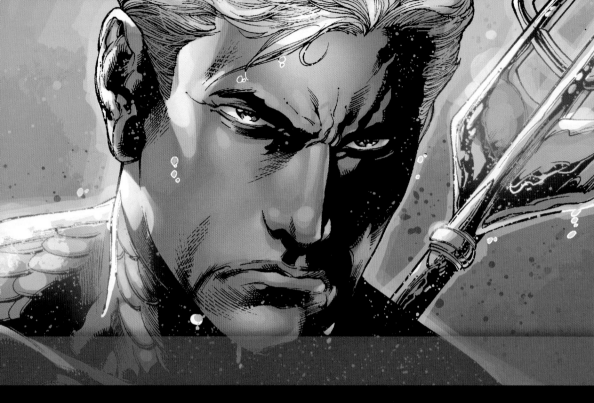

PAT McCALLUM Editor – Original Series CHRIS CONROY Associate Editor – Original Series
SEAN MACKIEWICZ Assistant Editor – Original Series ROBIN WILDMAN Editor
ROBBIN BROSTERMAN Design Director – Books ROBBIE BIEDERMAN Publication Design

BOB HARRAS VP – Editor-in-Chief

DIANE NELSON President DAN DIDIO and JIM LEE Co-Publishers
GEOFF JOHNS Chief Creative Officer
JOHN ROOD Executive VP – Sales, Marketing and Business Development
AMY GENKINS Senior VP – Business and Legal Affairs NAIRI GARDINER Senior VP – Finance
JEFF BOISON VP – Publishing Operations MARK CHIARELLO VP – Art Direction and Design
JOHN CUNNINGHAM VP – Marketing TERRI CUNNINGHAM VP – Talent Relations and Services
ALISON GILL Senior VP – Manufacturing and Operations HANK KANALZ Senior VP – Digital
JAY KOGAN VP – Business and Legal Affairs, Publishing JACK MAHAN VP – Business Affairs, Talent
NICK NAPOLITANO VP – Manufacturing Administration SUE POHJA VP – Book Sales
COURTNEY SIMMONS Senior VP – Publicity BOB WAYNE Senior VP – Sales

AQUAMAN VOLUME 2: THE OTHERS

DC Comics, 1700 Broadway, New York, NY 10019
A Warner Bros. Entertainment Company.
Printed by RR Donnelley, Salem, VA, USA. 4/12/13. First Printing.

HC ISBN: 978-1-4012-4016-5
SC ISBN: 978-1-4012-4295-4

Library of Congress Cataloging-in-Publication Data

Johns, Geoff, 1973- author.
Aquaman. Volume 2, The Others / Geoff Johns, Ivan Reis, Joe Prado.
pages cm
"Originally published in single magazine form in AQUAMAN 7-13."
ISBN 978-1-4012-4016-5
1. Graphic novels. I. Reis, Ivan, illustrator. II. Prado, Joe, illustrator. III. Title. IV. Title: Others.
PN6728.A68J65 2013
741.5'973—dc23
2012050773

SUSTAINABLE Certified Chain of Custody

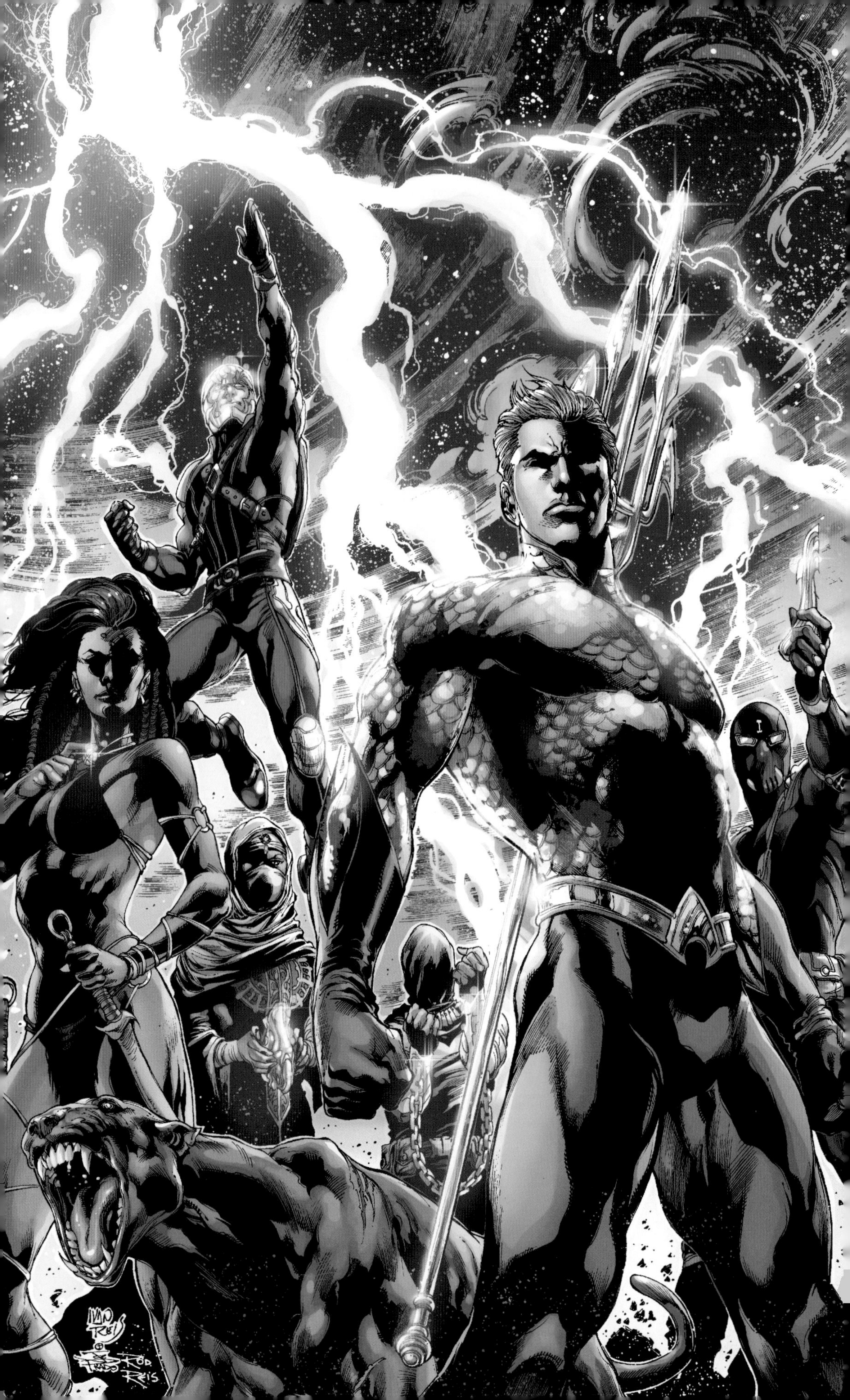

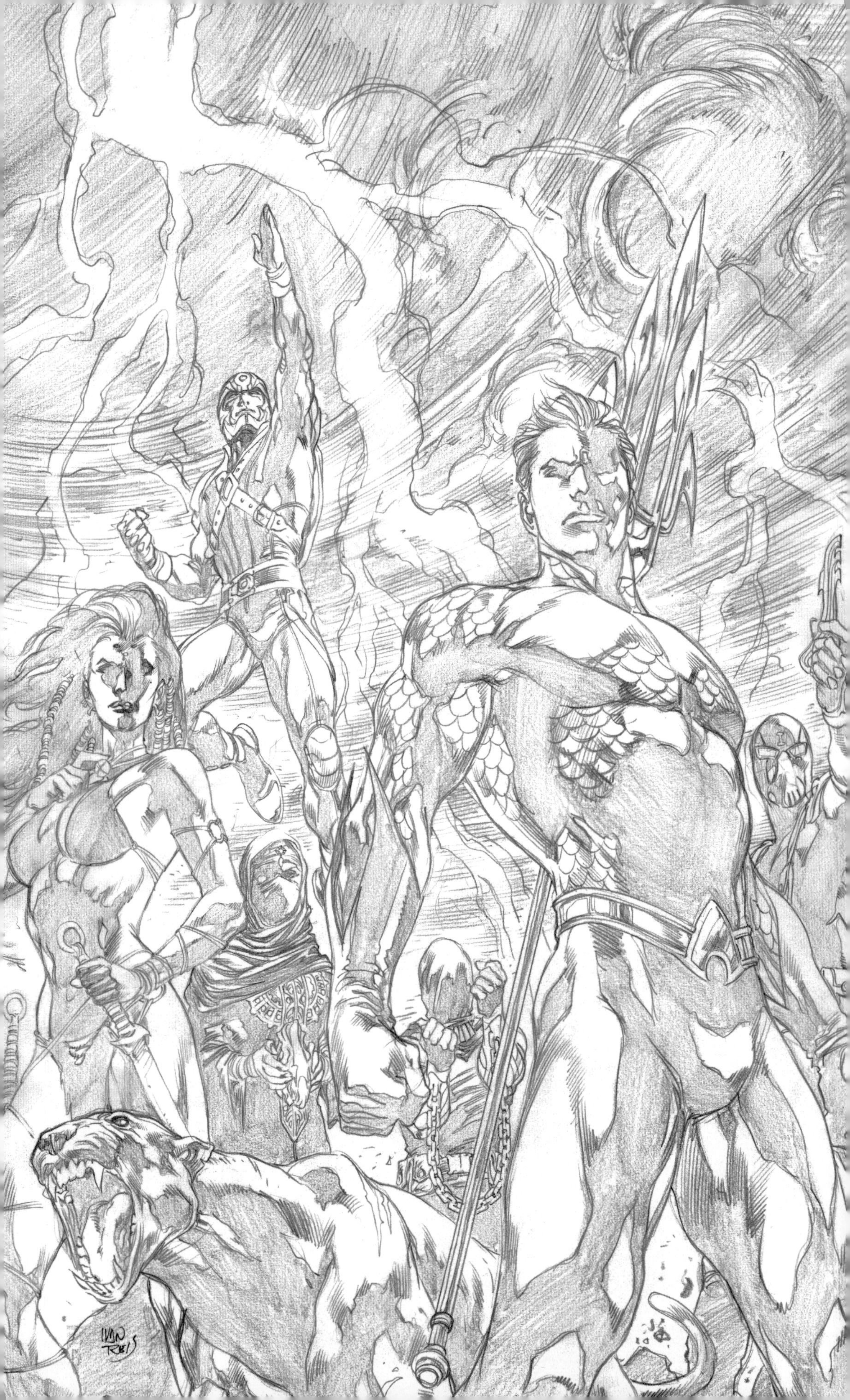

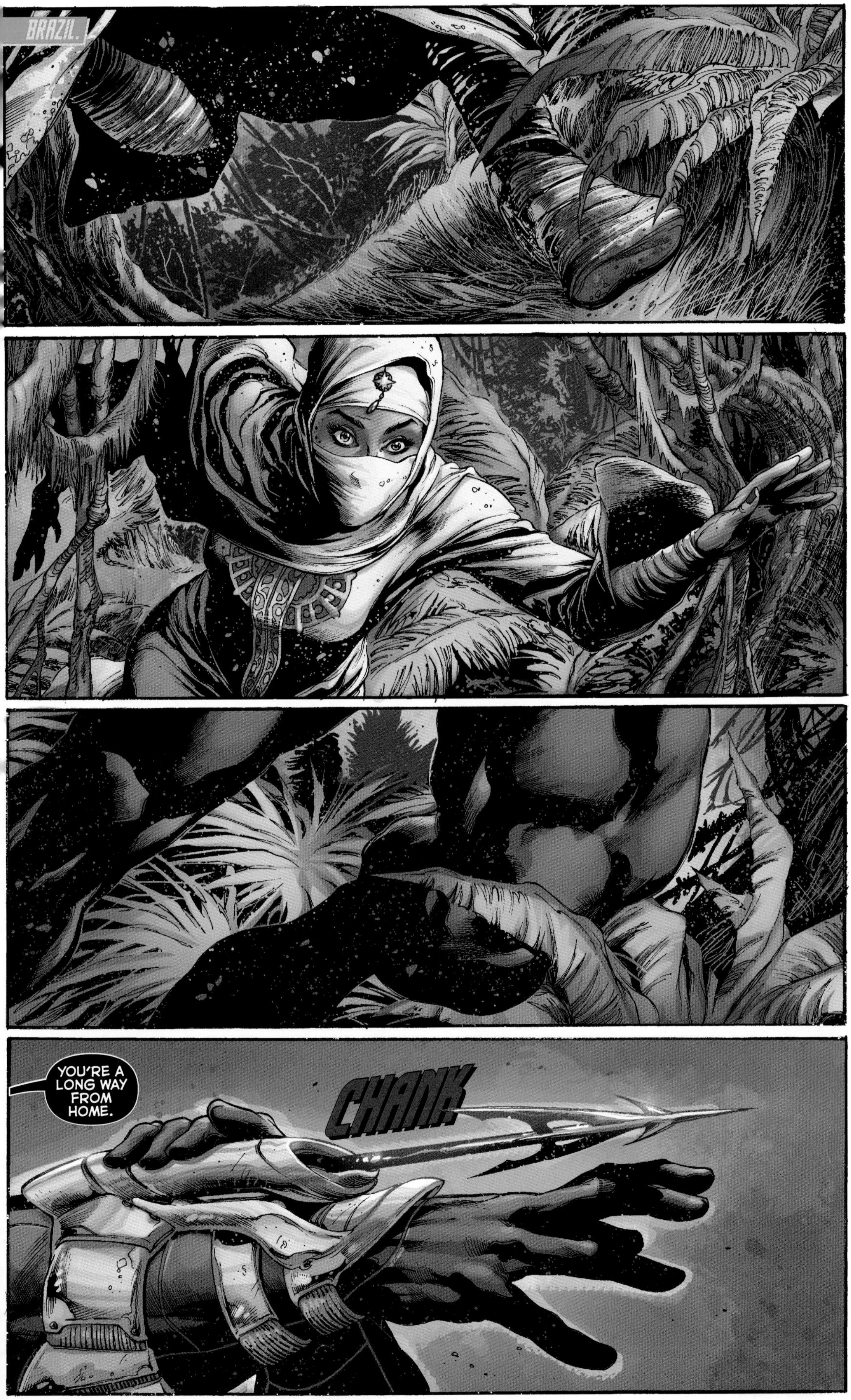
BRAZIL.
YOU'RE A LONG WAY FROM HOME.
CHANK

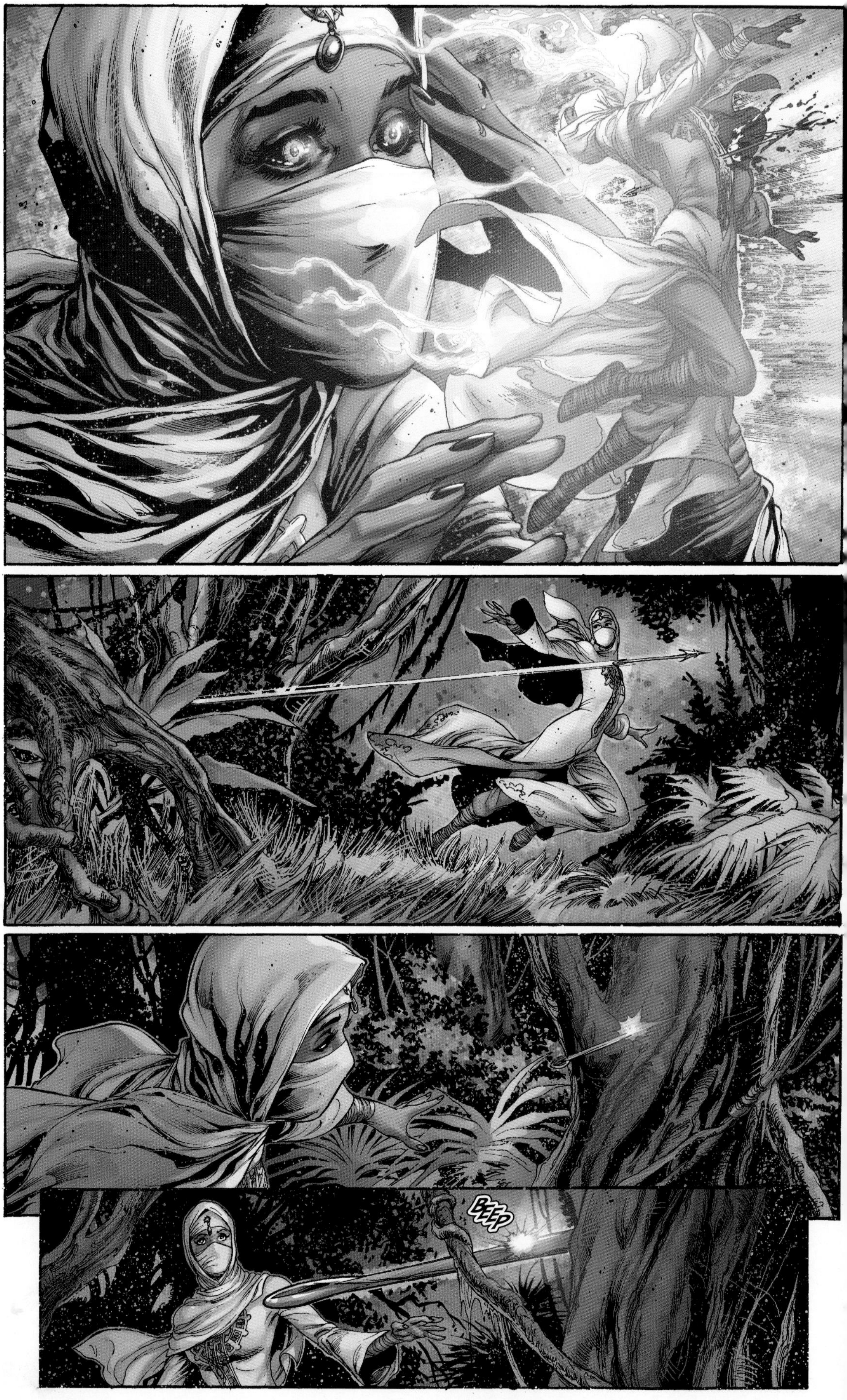
BEEP

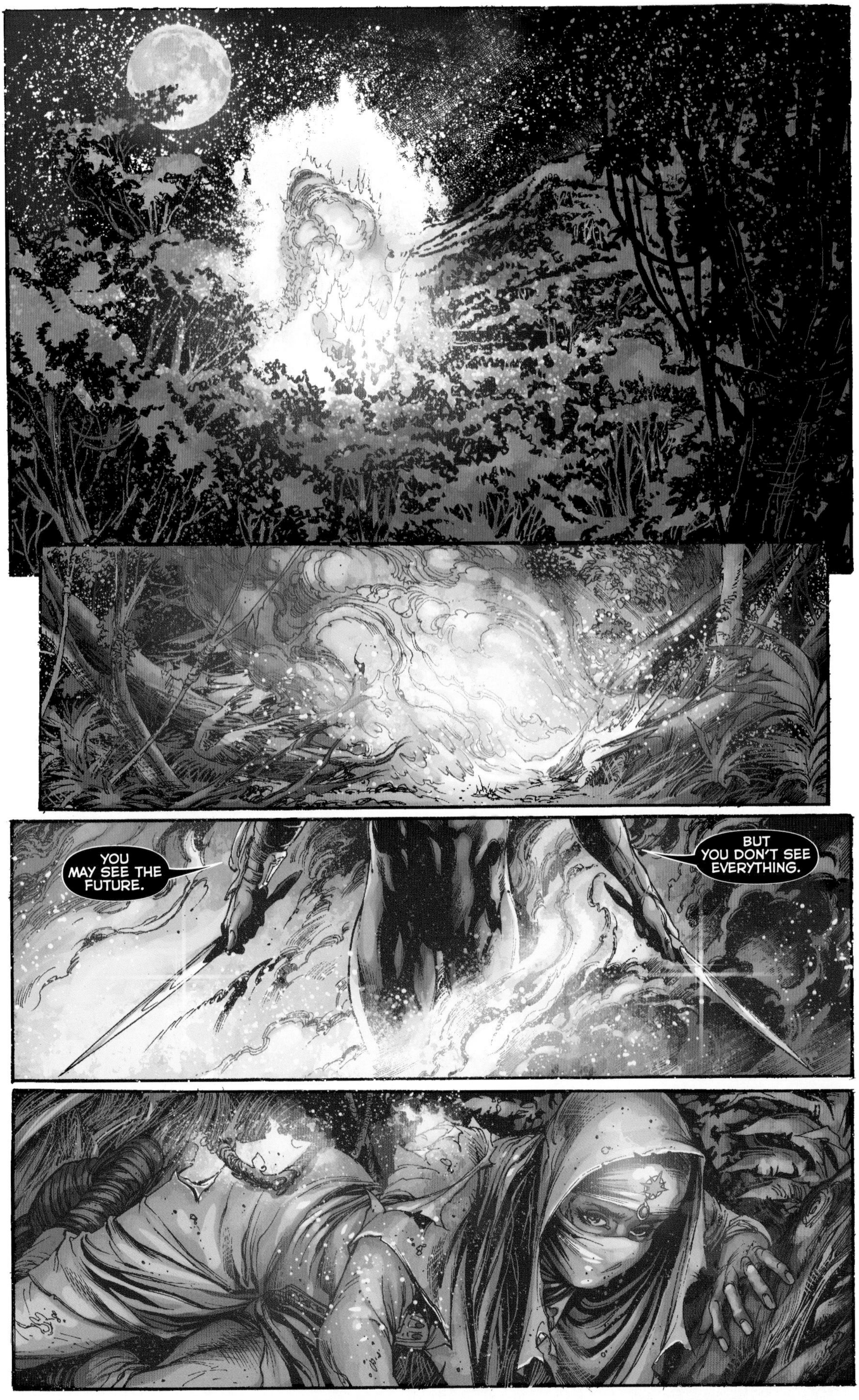
YOU MAY SEE THE FUTURE.
BUT YOU DON'T SEE EVERYTHING.

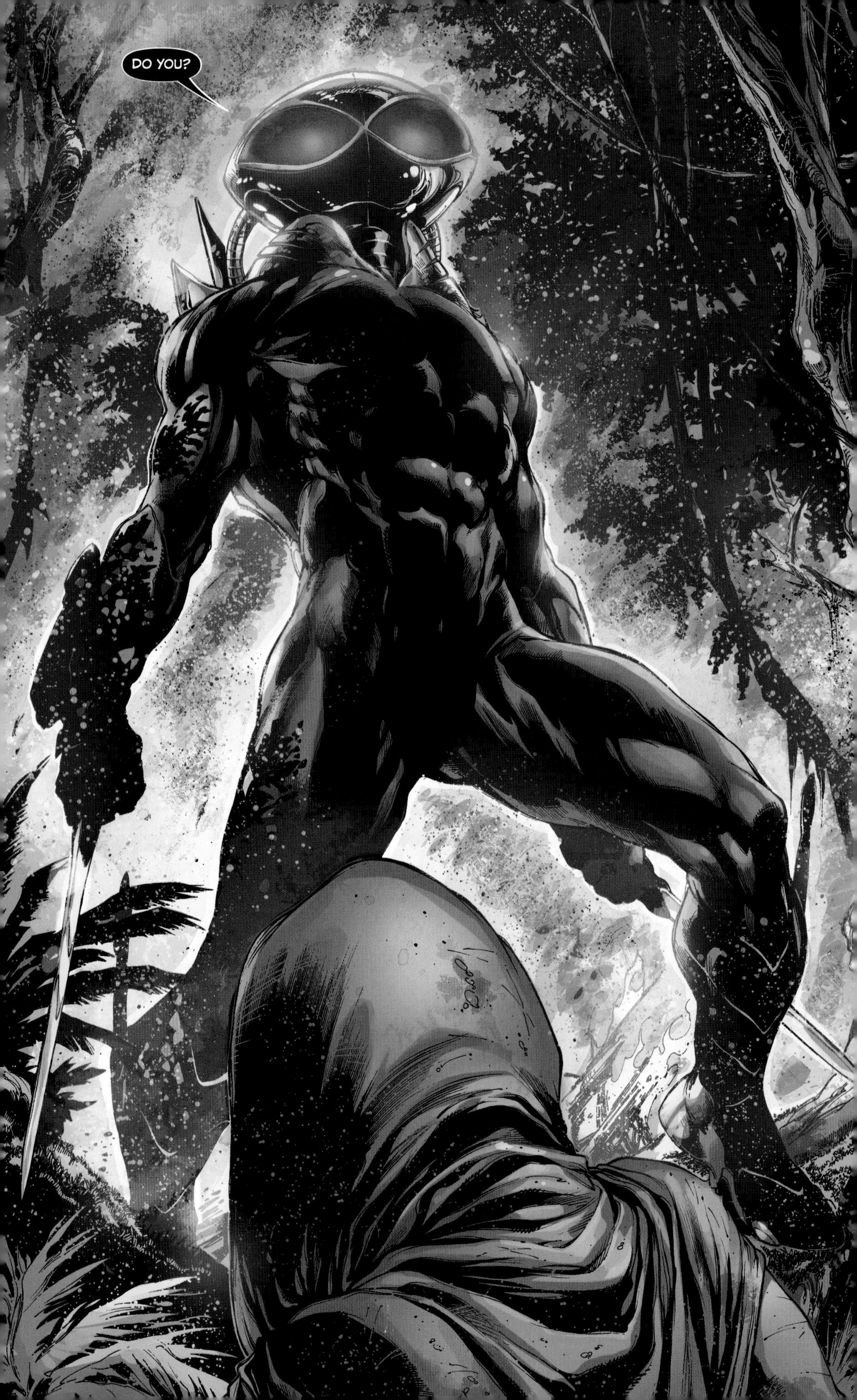
DO YOU?

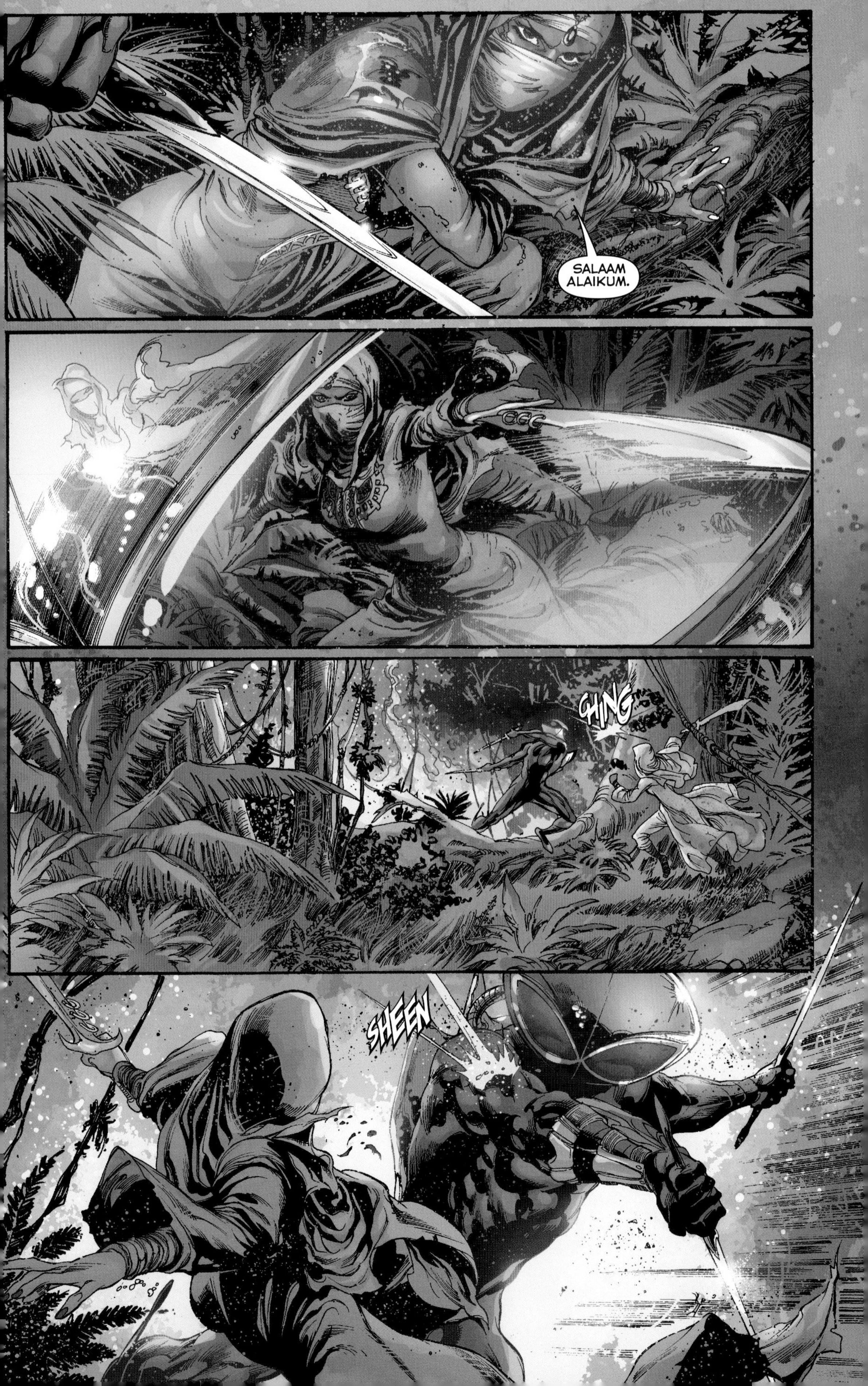
SALAAM ALAIKUM.
CHING
SHEEN

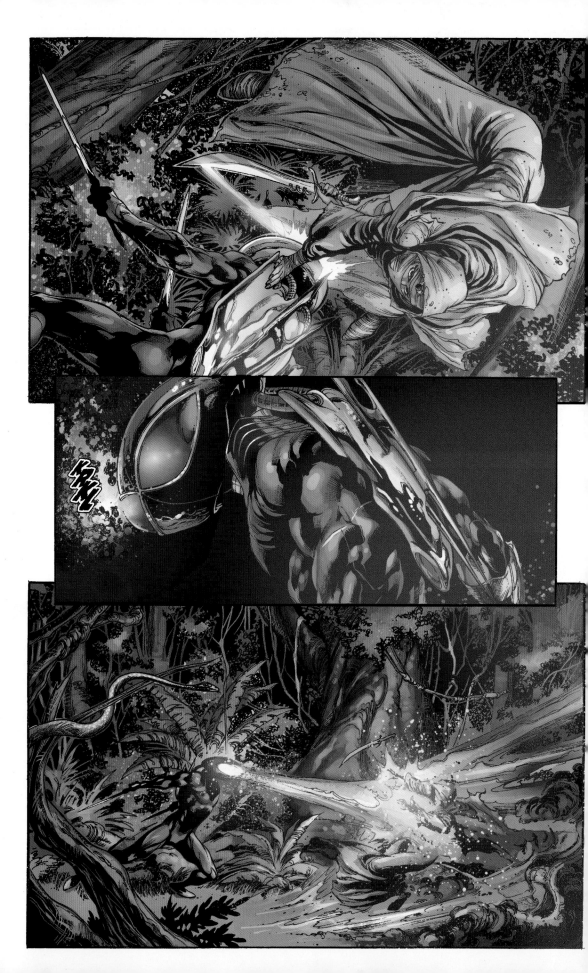

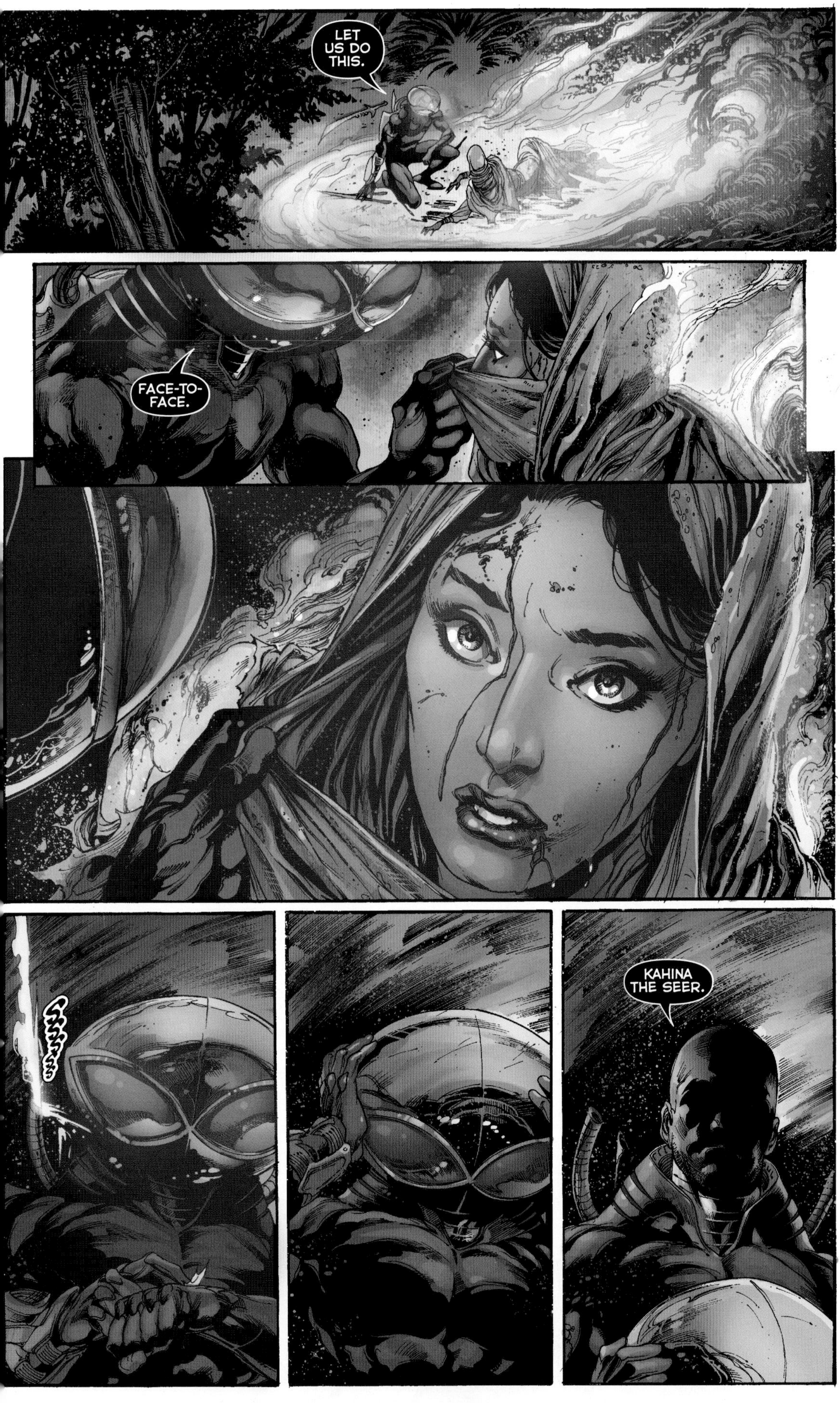
LET US DO THIS.
FACE-TO-FACE.
KAHINA THE SEER.

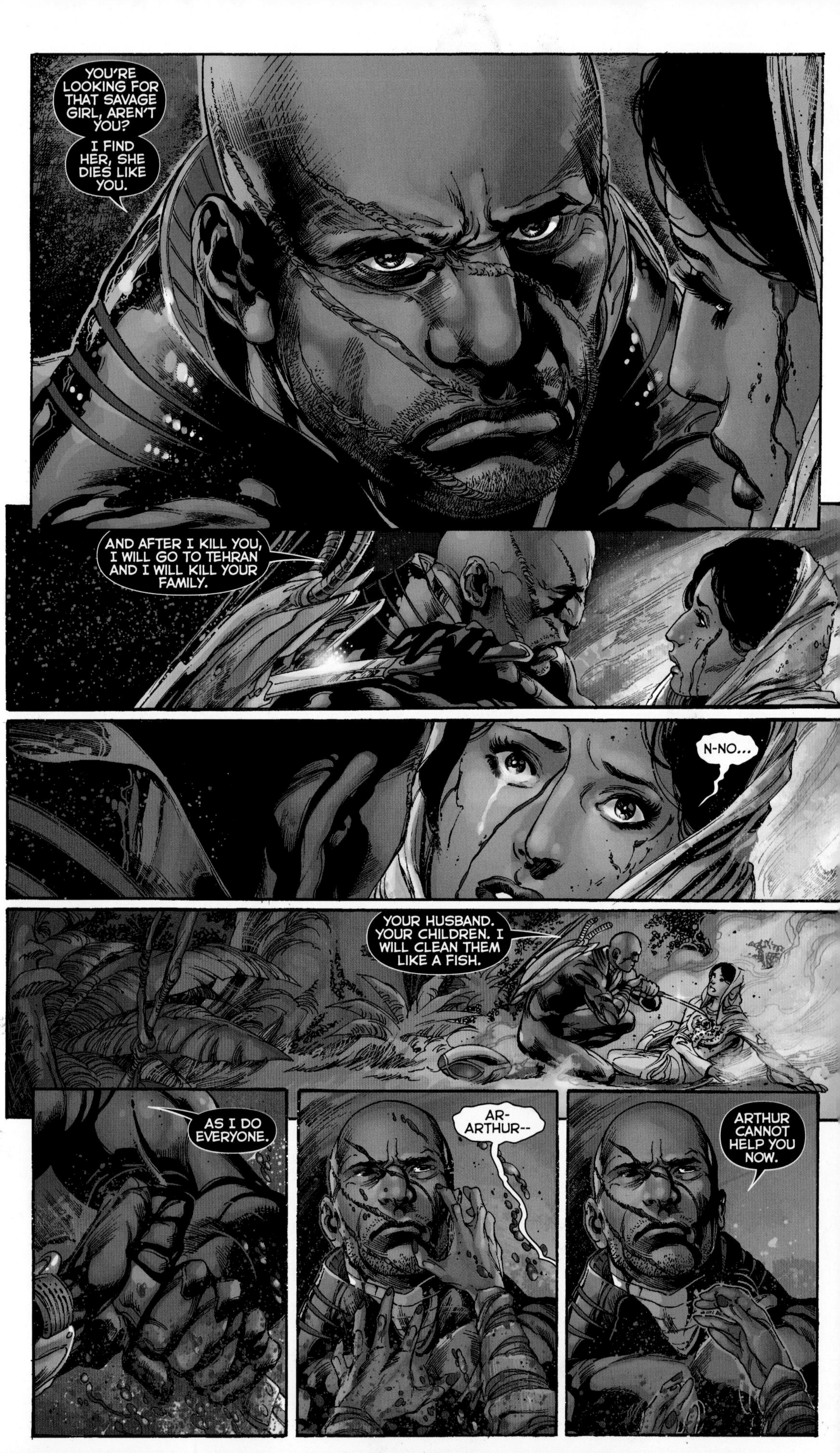

YOU'RE LOOKING FOR THAT SAVAGE GIRL, AREN'T YOU?
I FIND HER, SHE DIES LIKE YOU.
AND AFTER I KILL YOU, I WILL GO TO TEHRAN AND I WILL KILL YOUR FAMILY.
N-NO...
YOUR HUSBAND. YOUR CHILDREN. I WILL CLEAN THEM LIKE A FISH.
AS I DO EVERYONE.
AR- ARTHUR--
ARTHUR CANNOT HELP YOU NOW.

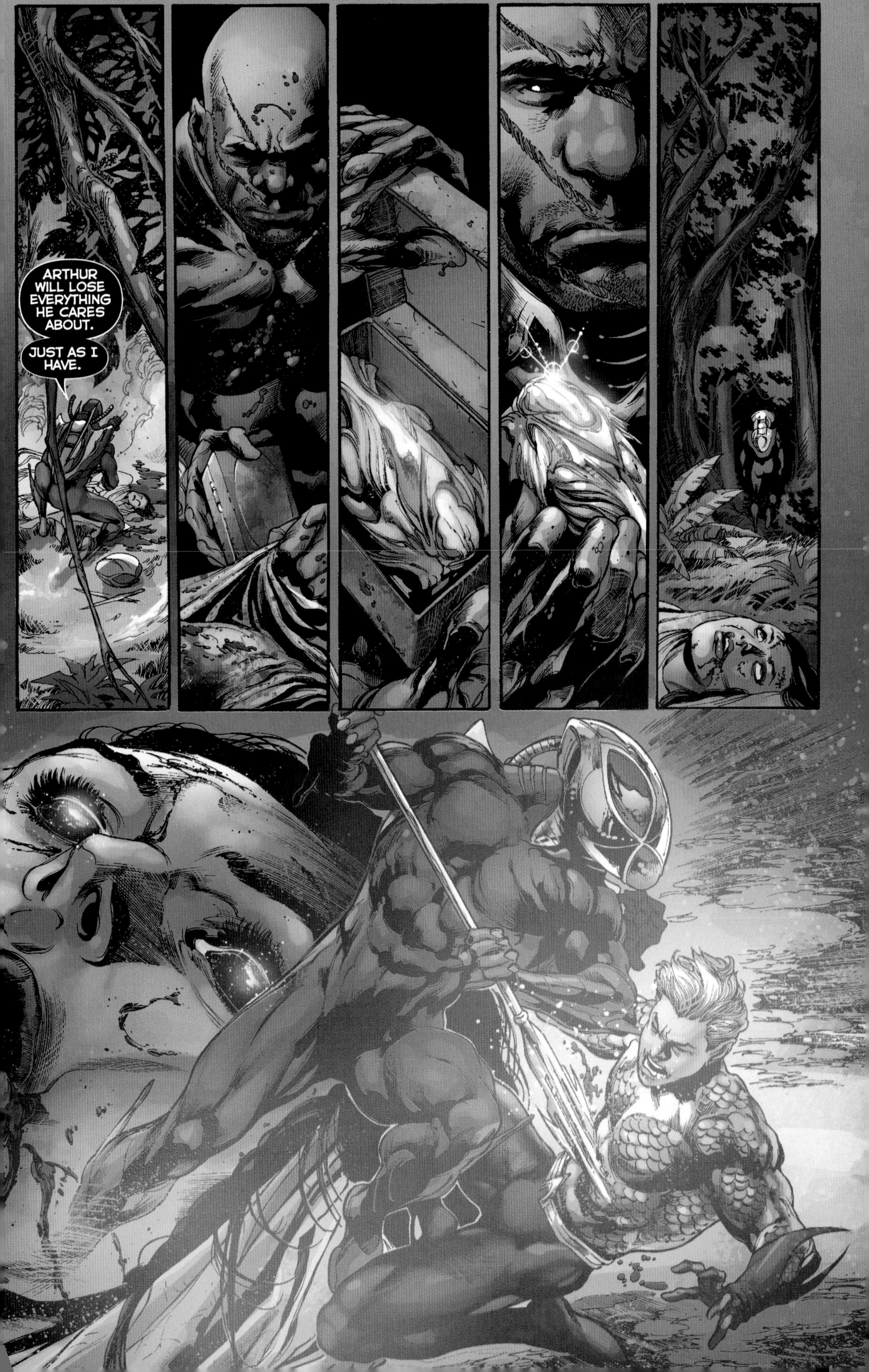
ARTHUR WILL LOSE EVERYTHING HE CARES ABOUT.
JUST AS I HAVE.

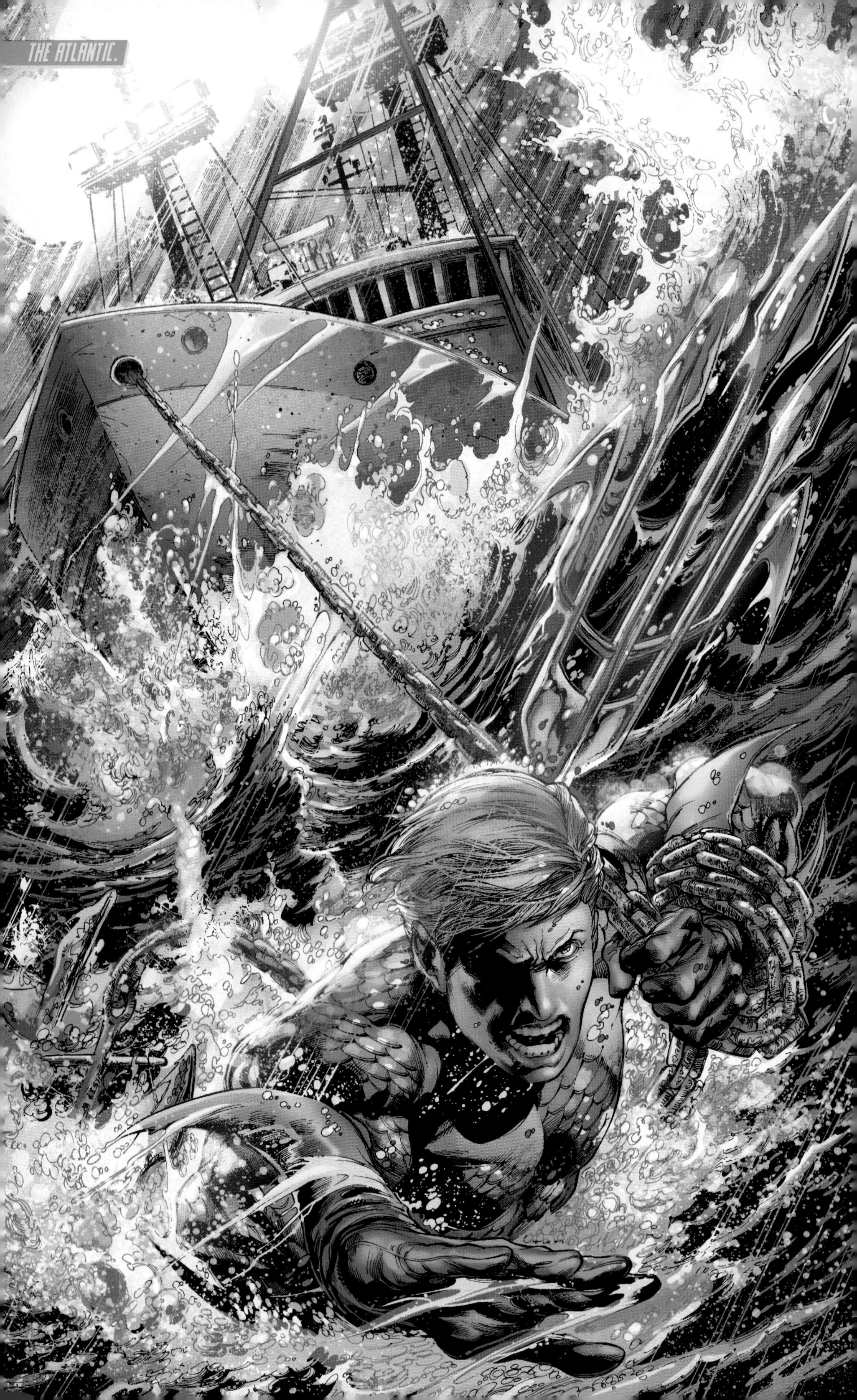
THE ATLANTIC.

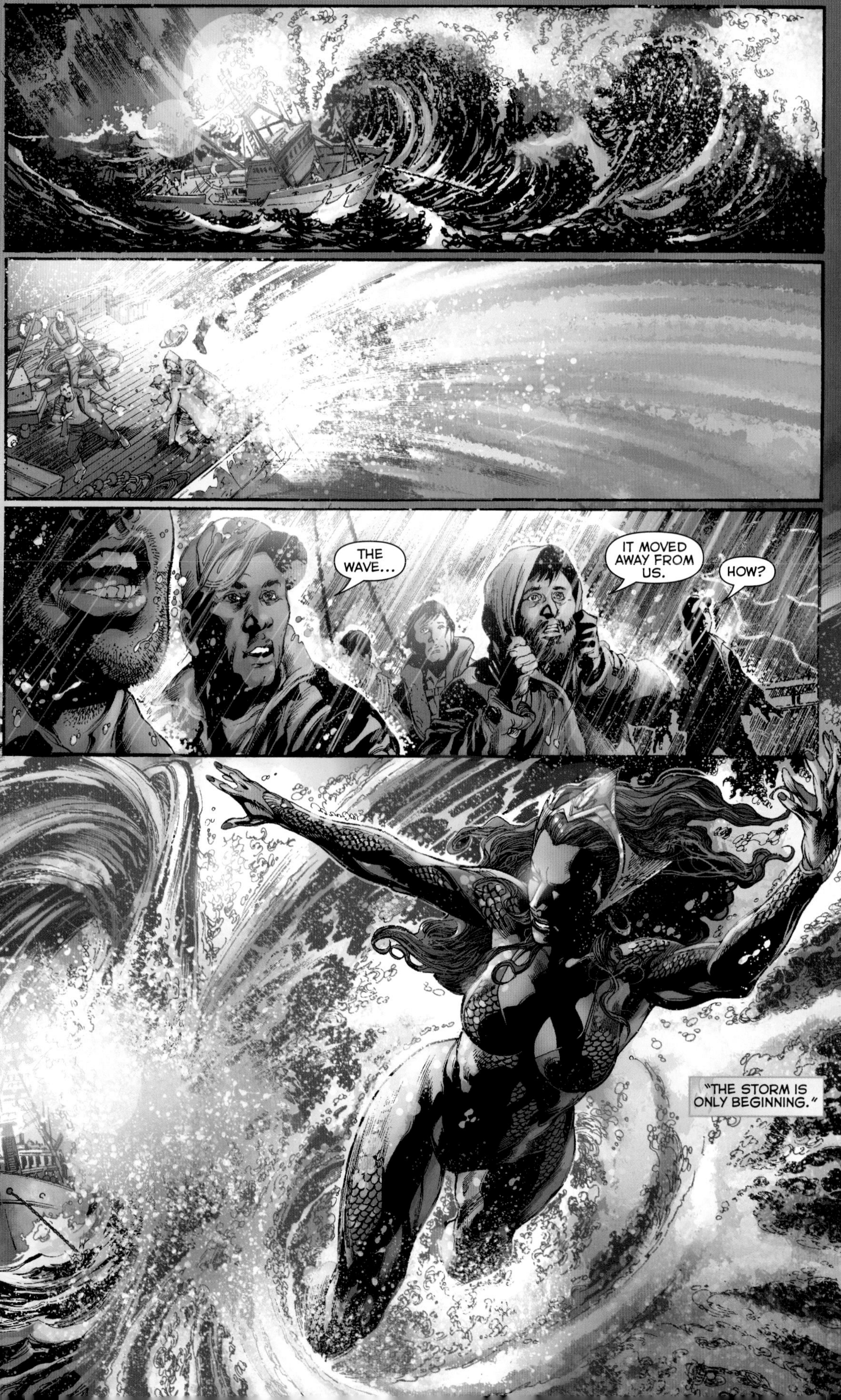
THE WAVE...
IT MOVED AWAY FROM US.
HOW?
"THE STORM IS ONLY BEGINNING."

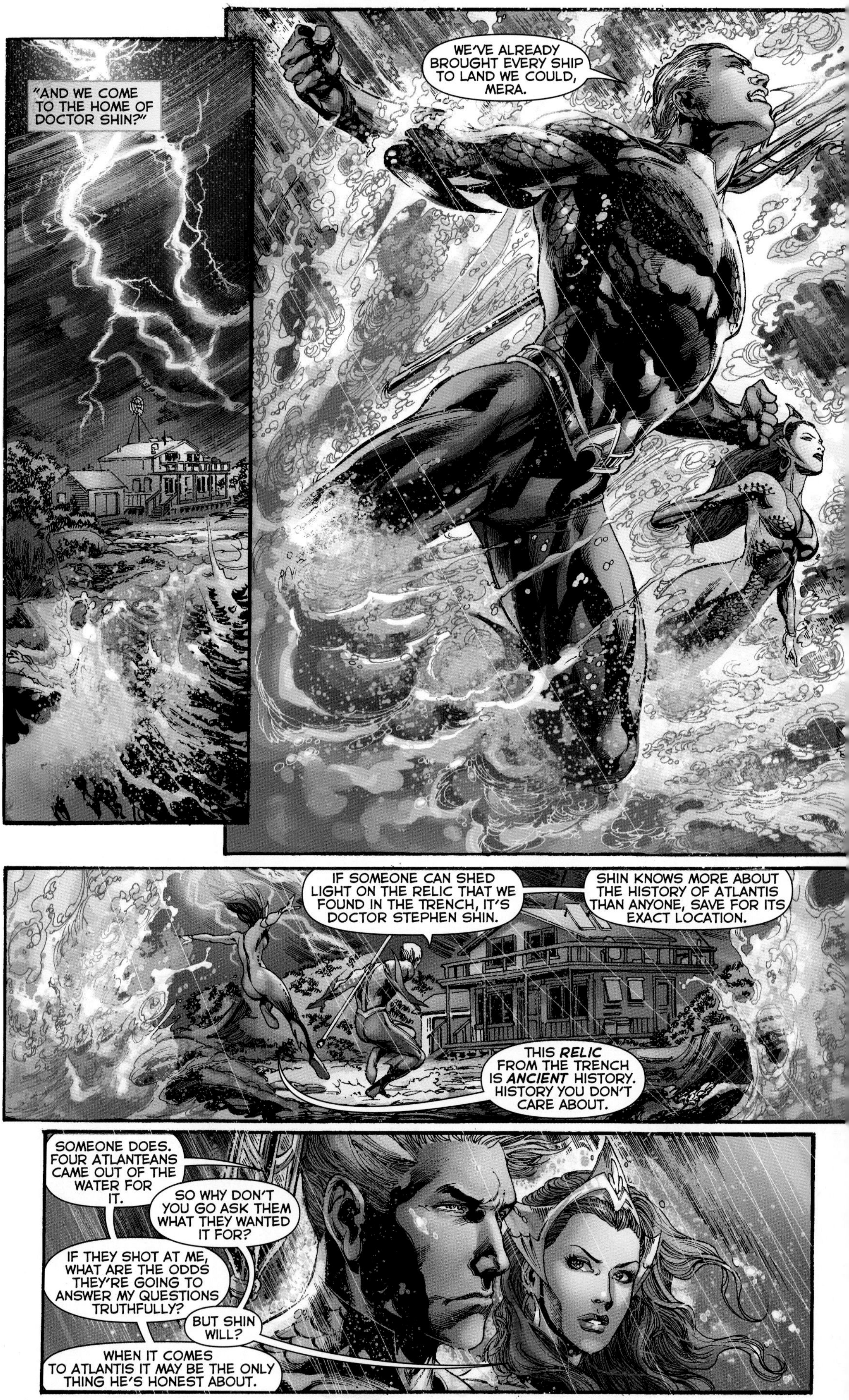
"AND WE COME TO THE HOME OF DOCTOR SHIN?"
WE'VE ALREADY BROUGHT EVERY SHIP TO LAND WE COULD, MERA.
IF SOMEONE CAN SHED LIGHT ON THE RELIC THAT WE FOUND IN THE TRENCH, IT'S DOCTOR STEPHEN SHIN.
SHIN KNOWS MORE ABOUT THE HISTORY OF ATLANTIS THAN ANYONE, SAVE FOR ITS EXACT LOCATION.
THIS RELIC FROM THE TRENCH IS ANCIENT HISTORY. HISTORY YOU DON'T CARE ABOUT.
SOMEONE DOES. FOUR ATLANTEANS CAME OUT OF THE WATER FOR IT.
SO WHY DON'T YOU GO ASK THEM WHAT THEY WANTED IT FOR?
IF THEY SHOT AT ME, WHAT ARE THE ODDS THEY'RE GOING TO ANSWER MY QUESTIONS TRUTHFULLY?
BUT SHIN WILL?
WHEN IT COMES TO ATLANTIS IT MAY BE THE ONLY THING HE'S HONEST ABOUT.

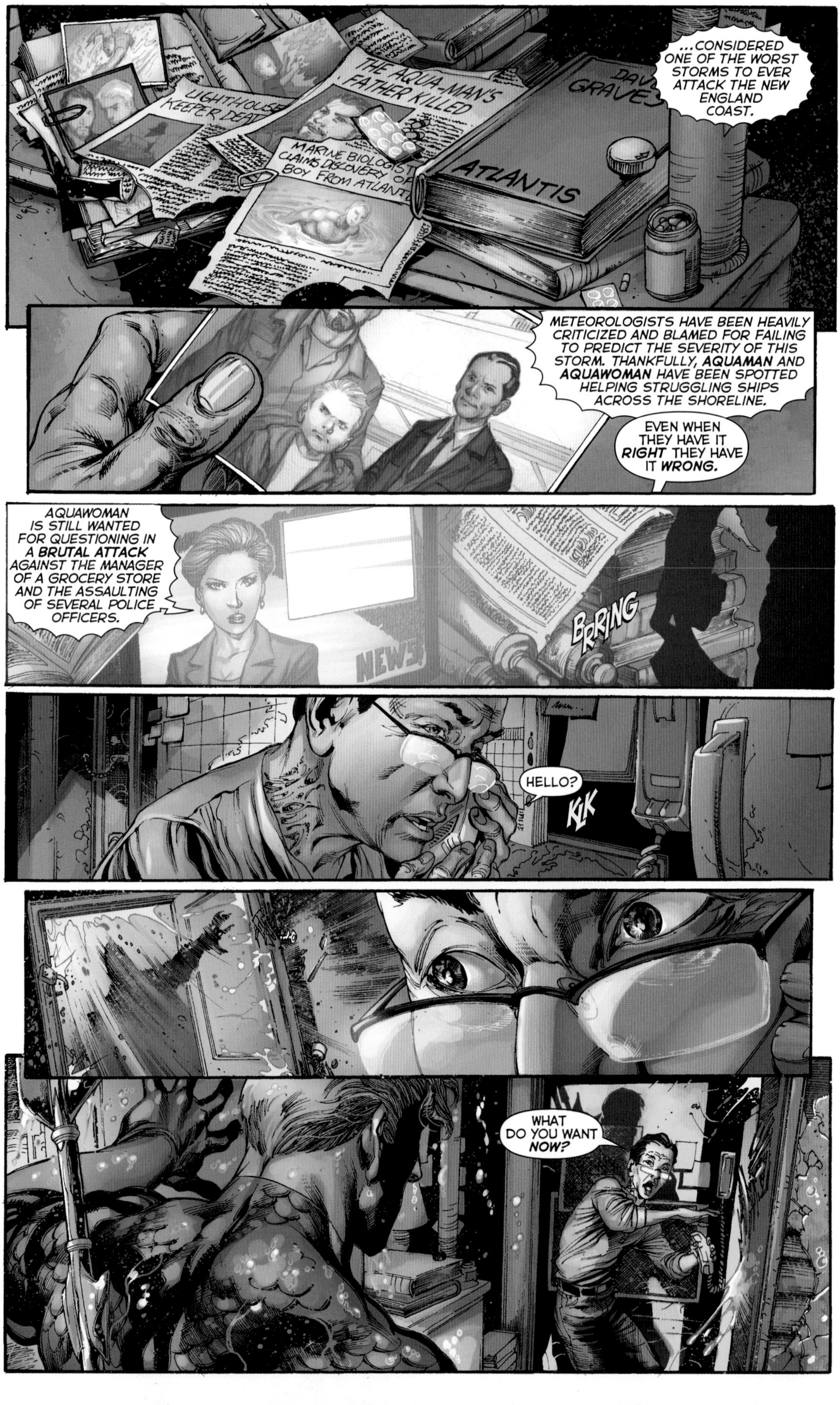
THE AQUA-MAN'S FATHER KILLED
ATLANTIS
...CONSIDERED ONE OF THE WORST STORMS TO EVER ATTACK THE NEW ENGLAND COAST.
METEOROLOGISTS HAVE BEEN HEAVILY CRITICIZED AND BLAMED FOR FAILING TO PREDICT THE SEVERITY OF THIS STORM. THANKFULLY, AQUAMAN AND AQUAWOMAN HAVE BEEN SPOTTED HELPING STRUGGLING SHIPS ACROSS THE SHORELINE.
EVEN WHEN THEY HAVE IT RIGHT THEY HAVE IT WRONG.
AQUAWOMAN IS STILL WANTED FOR QUESTIONING IN A BRUTAL ATTACK AGAINST THE MANAGER OF A GROCERY STORE AND THE ASSAULTING OF SEVERAL POLICE OFFICERS.
NEWS
BRRING
HELLO?
KLK
WHAT DO YOU WANT NOW?

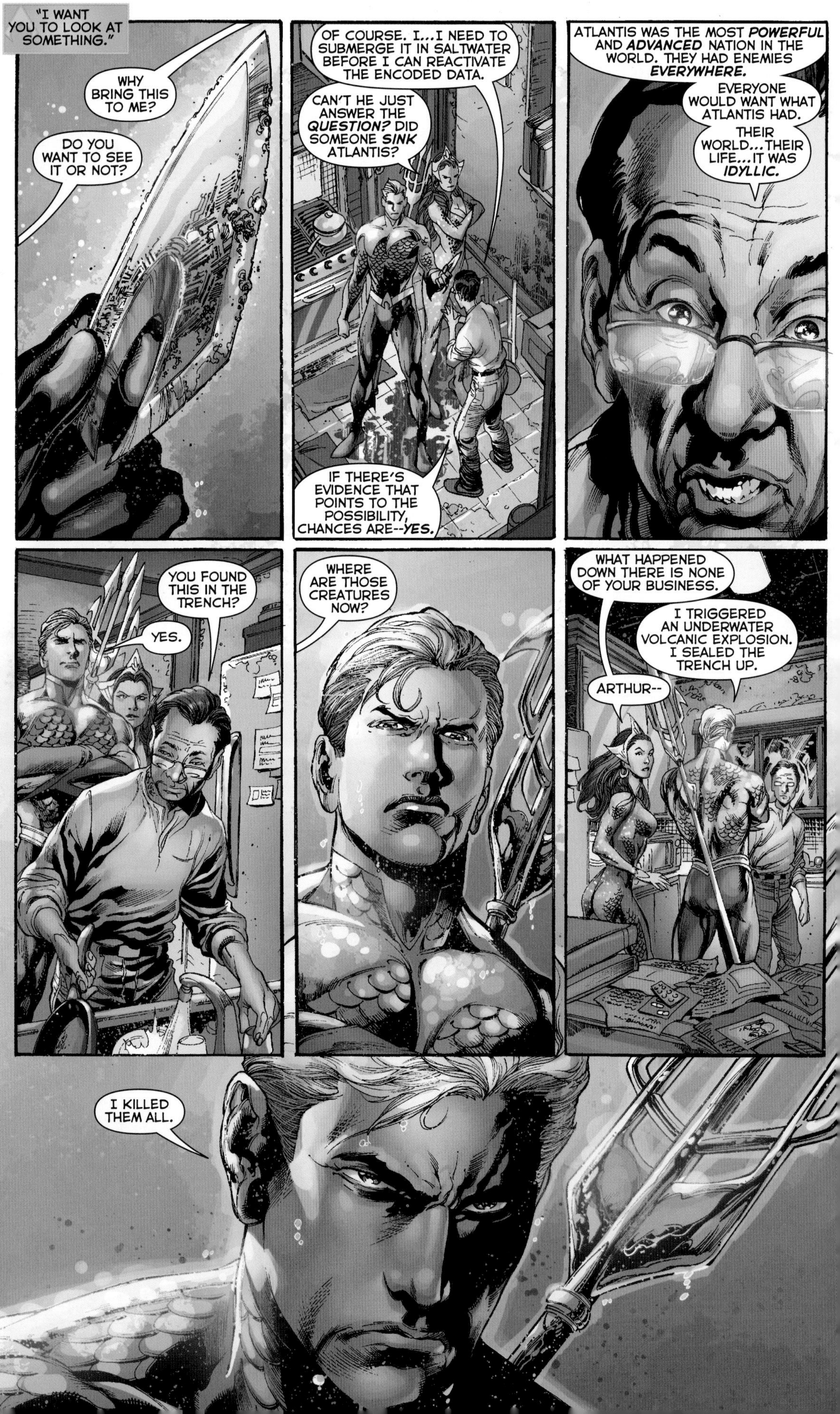
"I WANT YOU TO LOOK AT SOMETHING."
WHY BRING THIS TO ME?
DO YOU WANT TO SEE IT OR NOT?
OF COURSE. I...I NEED TO SUBMERGE IT IN SALTWATER BEFORE I CAN REACTIVATE THE ENCODED DATA.
CAN'T HE JUST ANSWER THE QUESTION? DID SOMEONE SINK ATLANTIS?
IF THERE'S EVIDENCE THAT POINTS TO THE POSSIBILITY, CHANCES ARE--YES.
ATLANTIS WAS THE MOST POWERFUL AND ADVANCED NATION IN THE WORLD. THEY HAD ENEMIES EVERYWHERE.
EVERYONE WOULD WANT WHAT ATLANTIS HAD.
THEIR WORLD...THEIR LIFE...IT WAS IDYLLIC.
YOU FOUND THIS IN THE TRENCH?
YES.
WHERE ARE THOSE CREATURES NOW?
WHAT HAPPENED DOWN THERE IS NONE OF YOUR BUSINESS.
I TRIGGERED AN UNDERWATER VOLCANIC EXPLOSION. I SEALED THE TRENCH UP.
ARTHUR--
I KILLED THEM ALL.

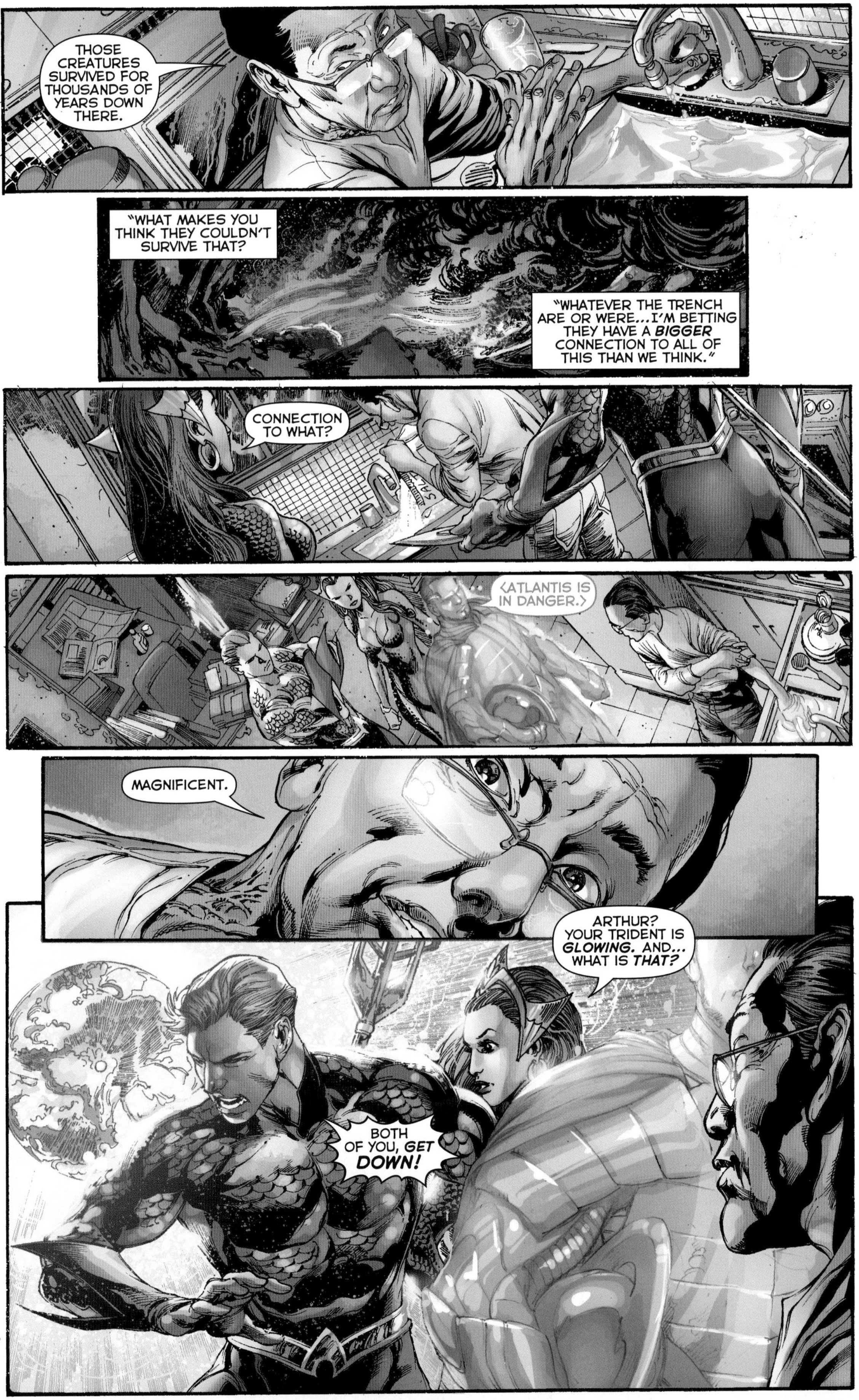
THOSE CREATURES SURVIVED FOR THOUSANDS OF YEARS DOWN THERE.
"WHAT MAKES YOU THINK THEY COULDN'T SURVIVE THAT?
"WHATEVER THE TRENCH ARE OR WERE...I'M BETTING THEY HAVE A *BIGGER* CONNECTION TO ALL OF THIS THAN WE THINK."
CONNECTION TO WHAT?
<ATLANTIS IS IN DANGER.>
MAGNIFICENT.
ARTHUR? YOUR TRIDENT IS *GLOWING.* AND... WHAT IS *THAT?*
BOTH OF YOU, *GET DOWN!*

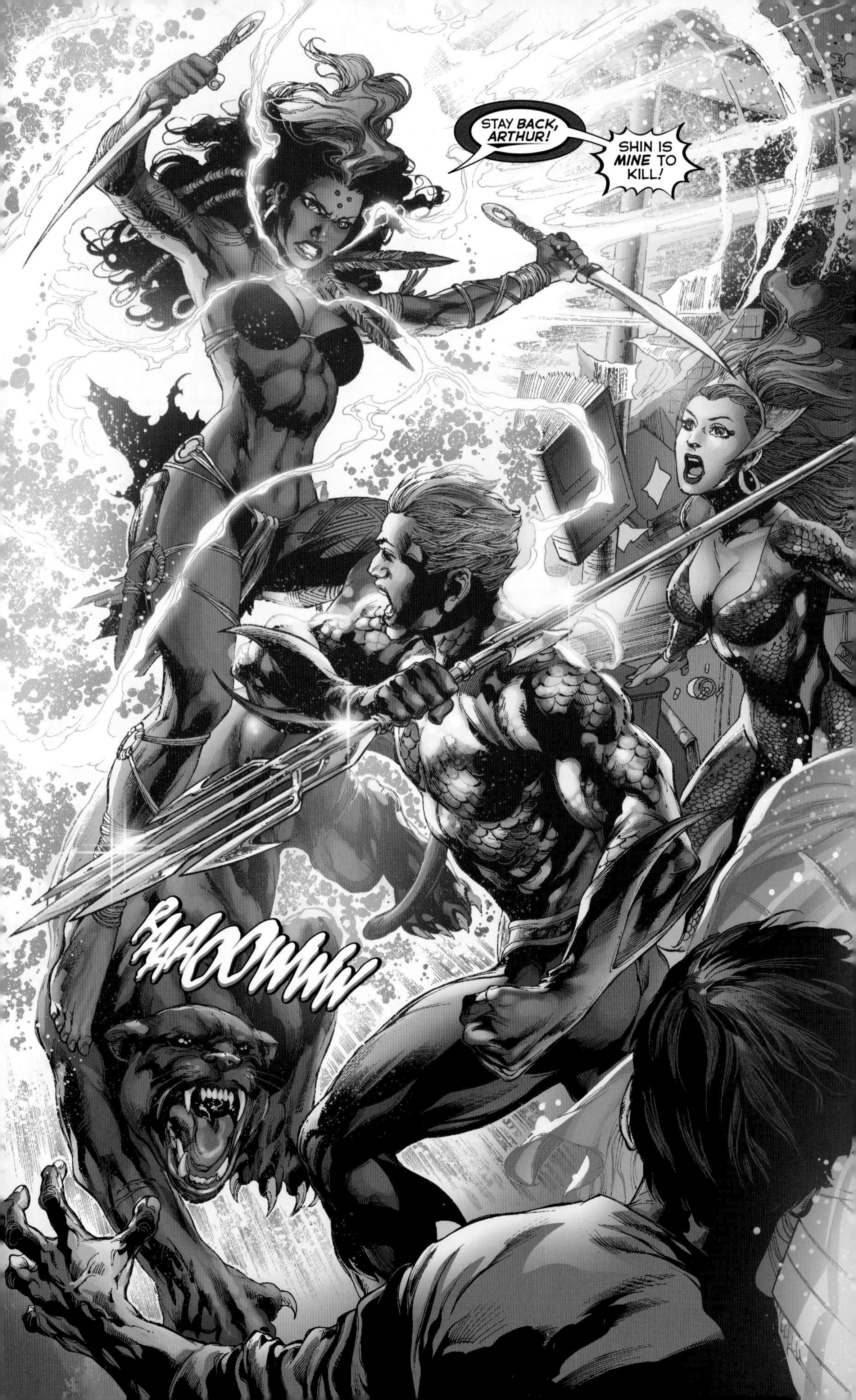
STAY BACK, ARTHUR!
SHIN IS MINE TO KILL!
RAAOOWWW

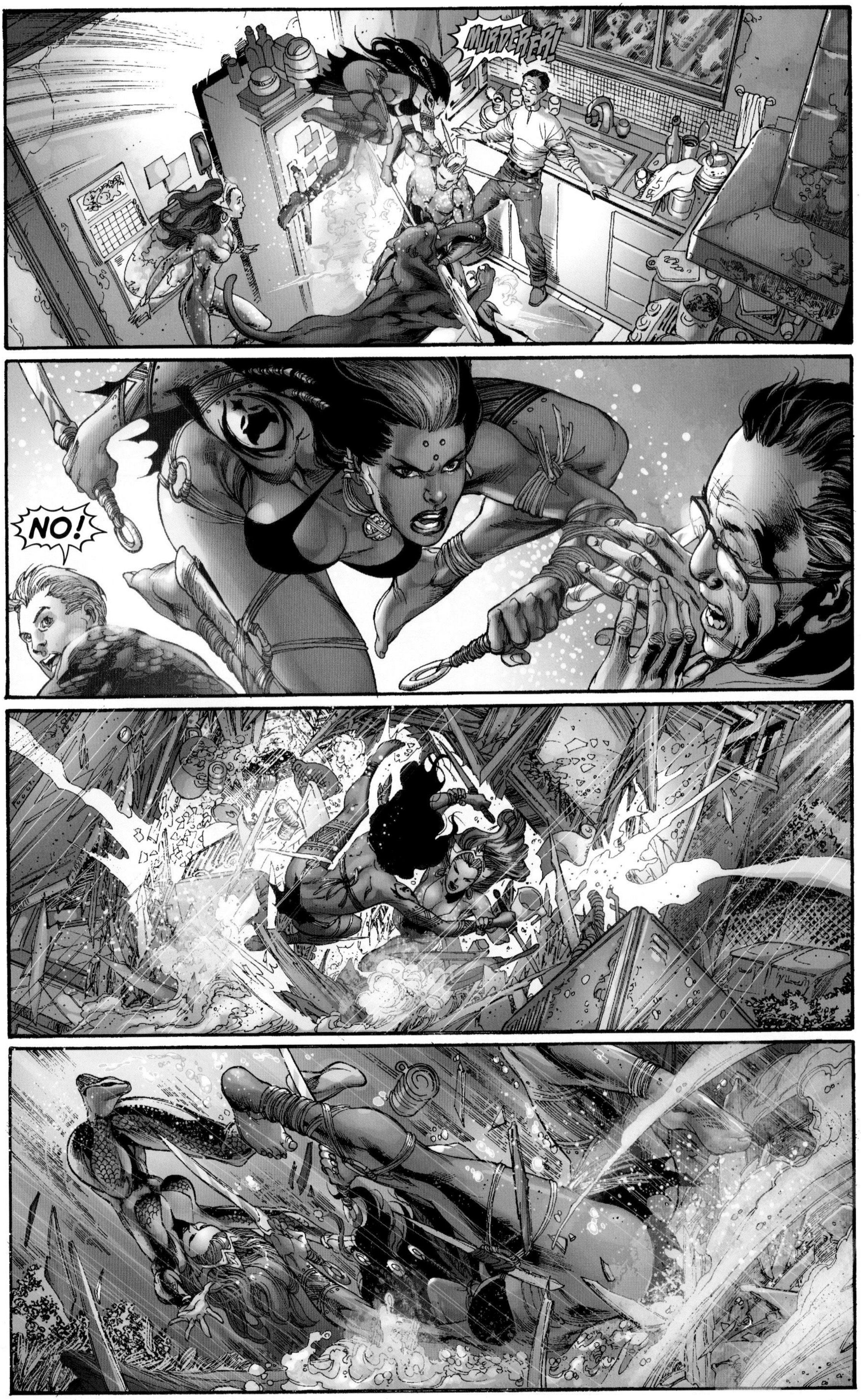
MURDERER!
NO!

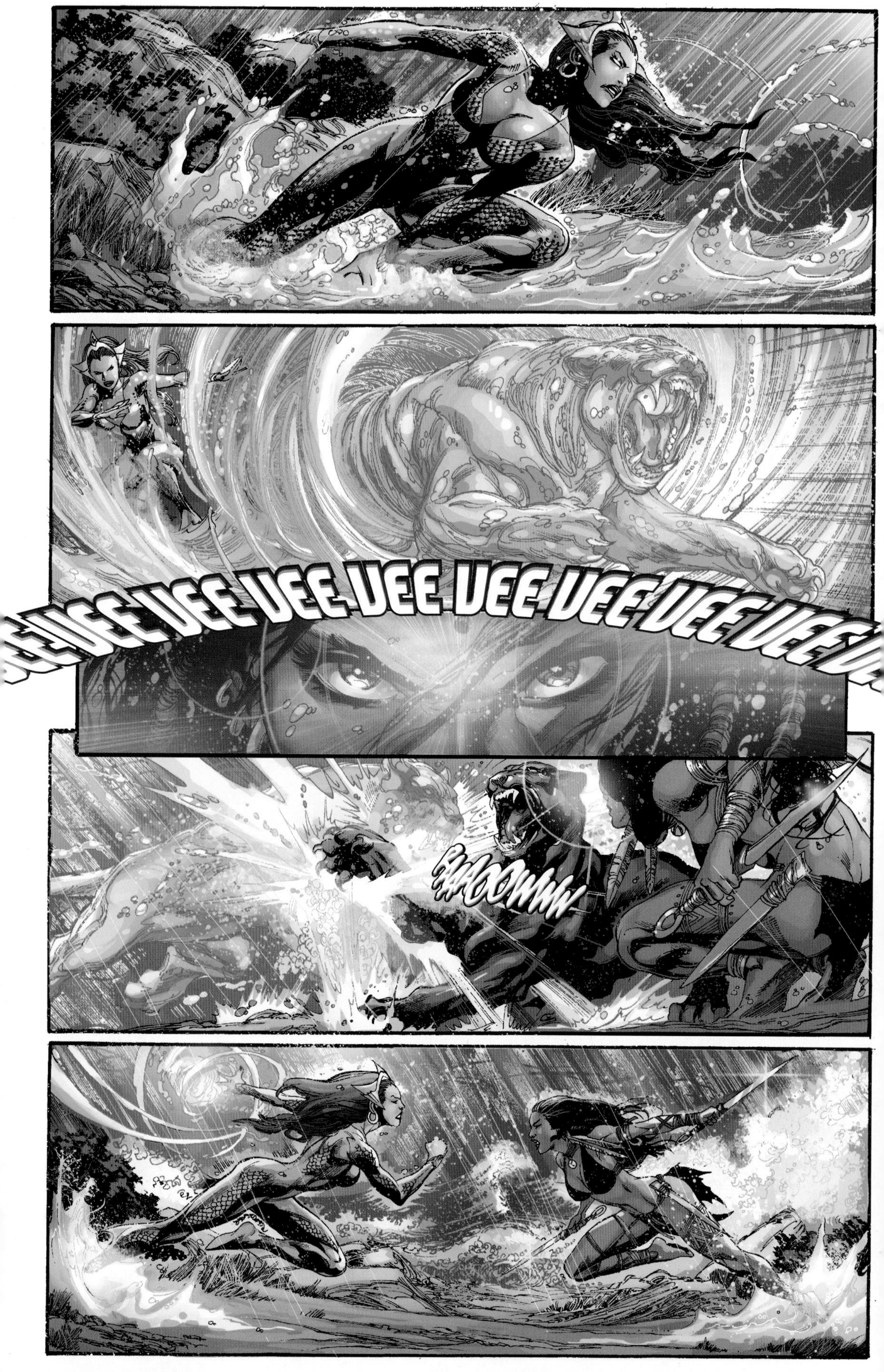
VEE VEE VEE VEE VEE VEE
RAAOWWW

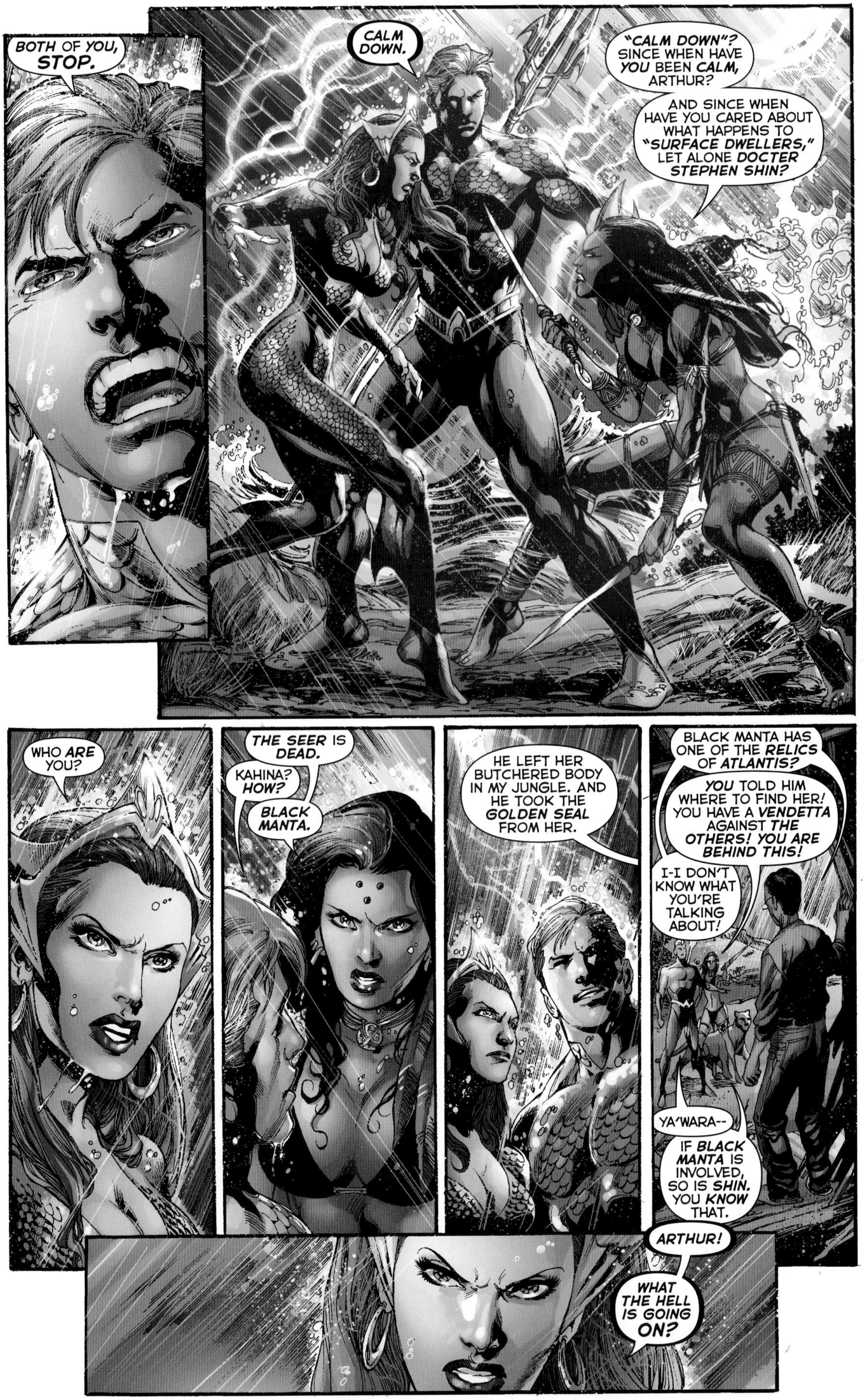
BOTH OF YOU, STOP.
CALM DOWN.
"CALM DOWN"? SINCE WHEN HAVE YOU BEEN CALM, ARTHUR?
AND SINCE WHEN HAVE YOU CARED ABOUT WHAT HAPPENS TO "SURFACE DWELLERS," LET ALONE DOCTER STEPHEN SHIN?
WHO ARE YOU?
THE SEER IS DEAD.
KAHINA? HOW?
BLACK MANTA.
HE LEFT HER BUTCHERED BODY IN MY JUNGLE. AND HE TOOK THE GOLDEN SEAL FROM HER.
BLACK MANTA HAS ONE OF THE RELICS OF ATLANTIS?
YOU TOLD HIM WHERE TO FIND HER! YOU HAVE A VENDETTA AGAINST THE OTHERS! YOU ARE BEHIND THIS!
I-I DON'T KNOW WHAT YOU'RE TALKING ABOUT!
YA'WARA--
IF BLACK MANTA IS INVOLVED, SO IS SHIN. YOU KNOW THAT.
ARTHUR!
WHAT THE HELL IS GOING ON?

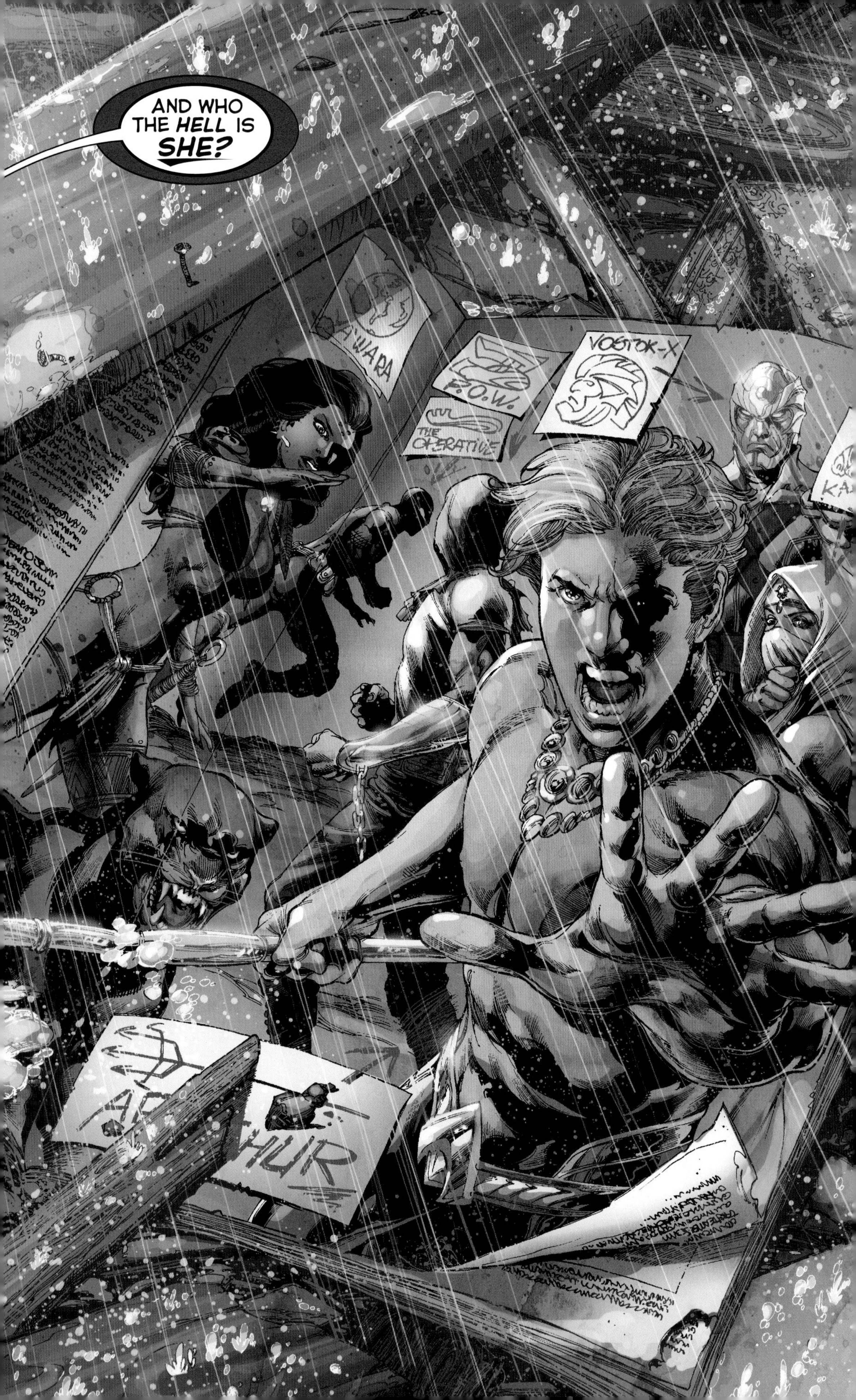
AND WHO THE HELL IS SHE?
VOSTOK-X
P.O.W.
THE OPERATIVE

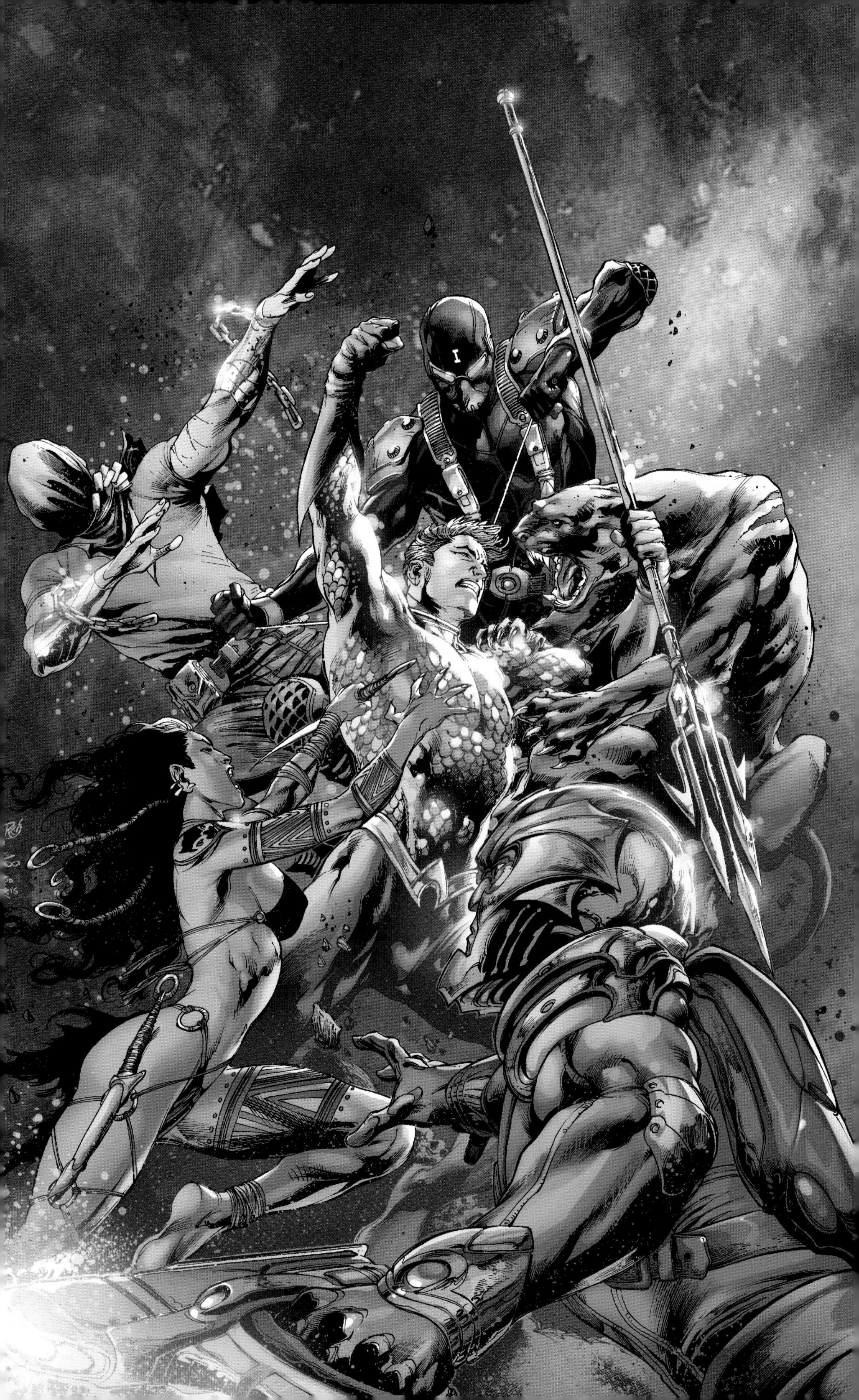

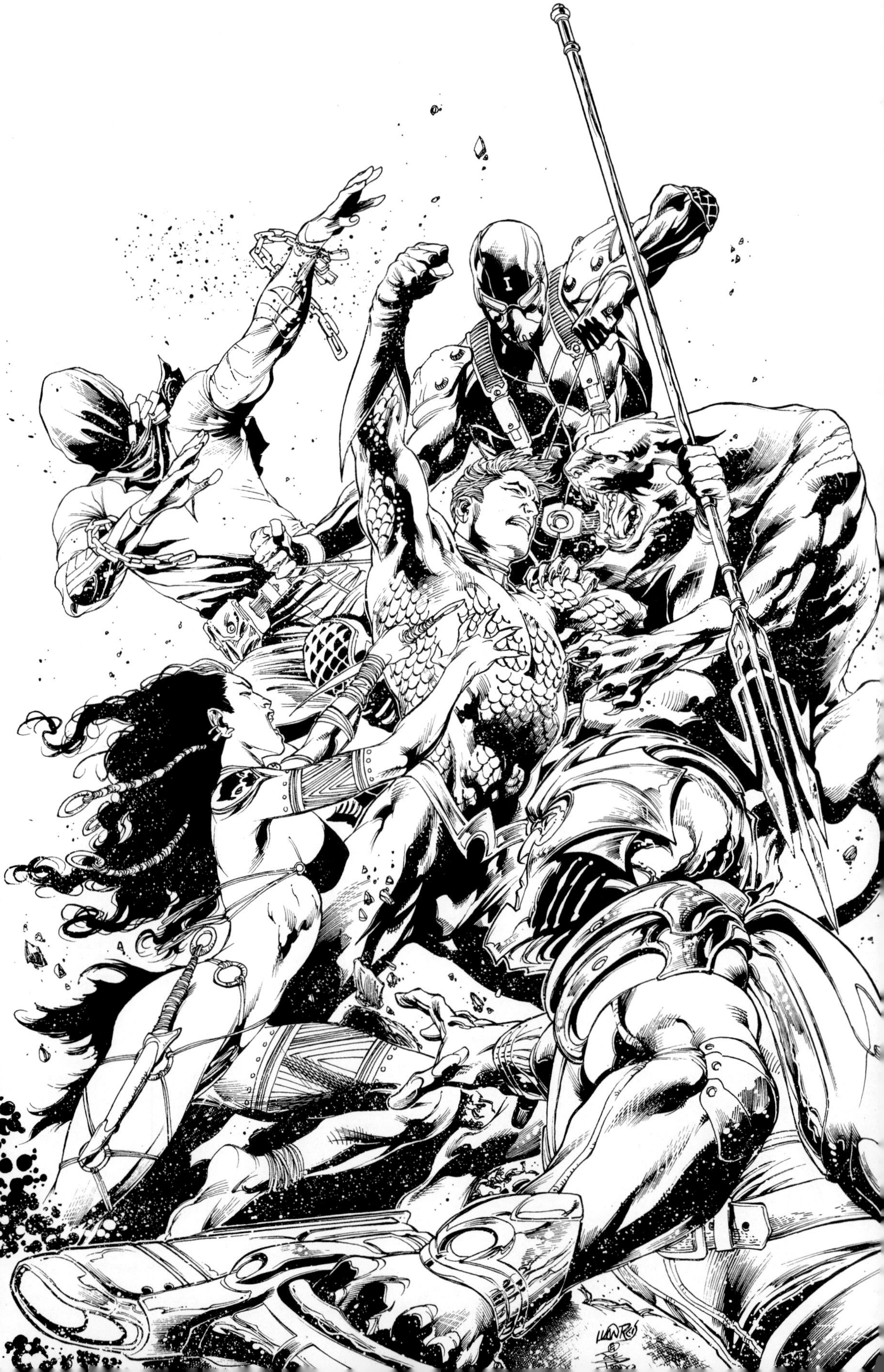

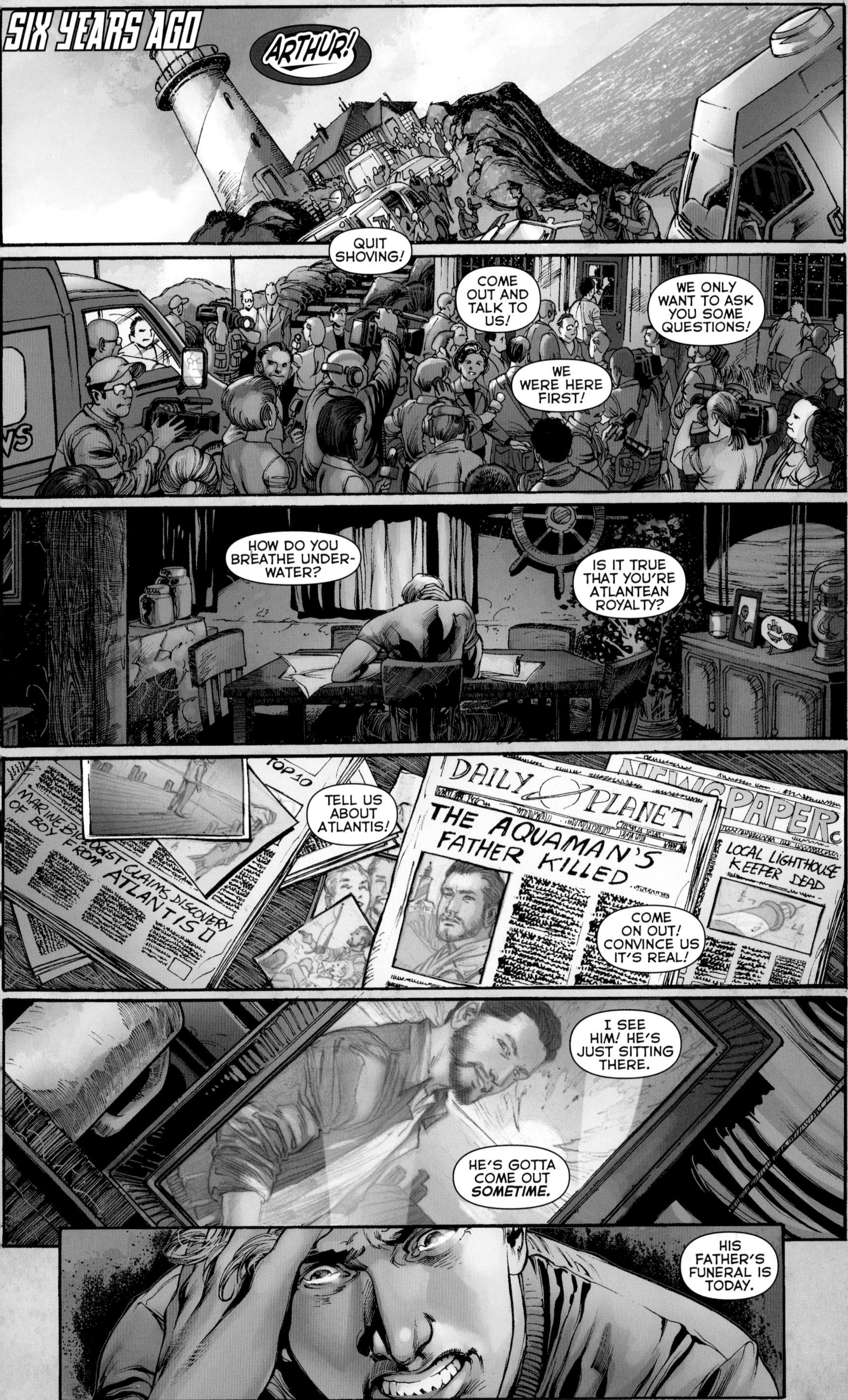
SIX YEARS AGO
ARTHUR!
QUIT SHOVING!
COME OUT AND TALK TO US!
WE ONLY WANT TO ASK YOU SOME QUESTIONS!
WE WERE HERE FIRST!
HOW DO YOU BREATHE UNDER-WATER?
IS IT TRUE THAT YOU'RE ATLANTEAN ROYALTY?
TOP 10
MARINE BIOLOGIST CLAIMS DISCOVERY OF BOY FROM ATLANTIS
TELL US ABOUT ATLANTIS!
DAILY PLANET
THE AQUAMAN'S FATHER KILLED
NEWSPAPER
LOCAL LIGHTHOUSE KEEPER DEAD
COME ON OUT! CONVINCE US IT'S REAL!
I SEE HIM! HE'S JUST SITTING THERE.
HE'S GOTTA COME OUT SOMETIME.
HIS FATHER'S FUNERAL IS TODAY.

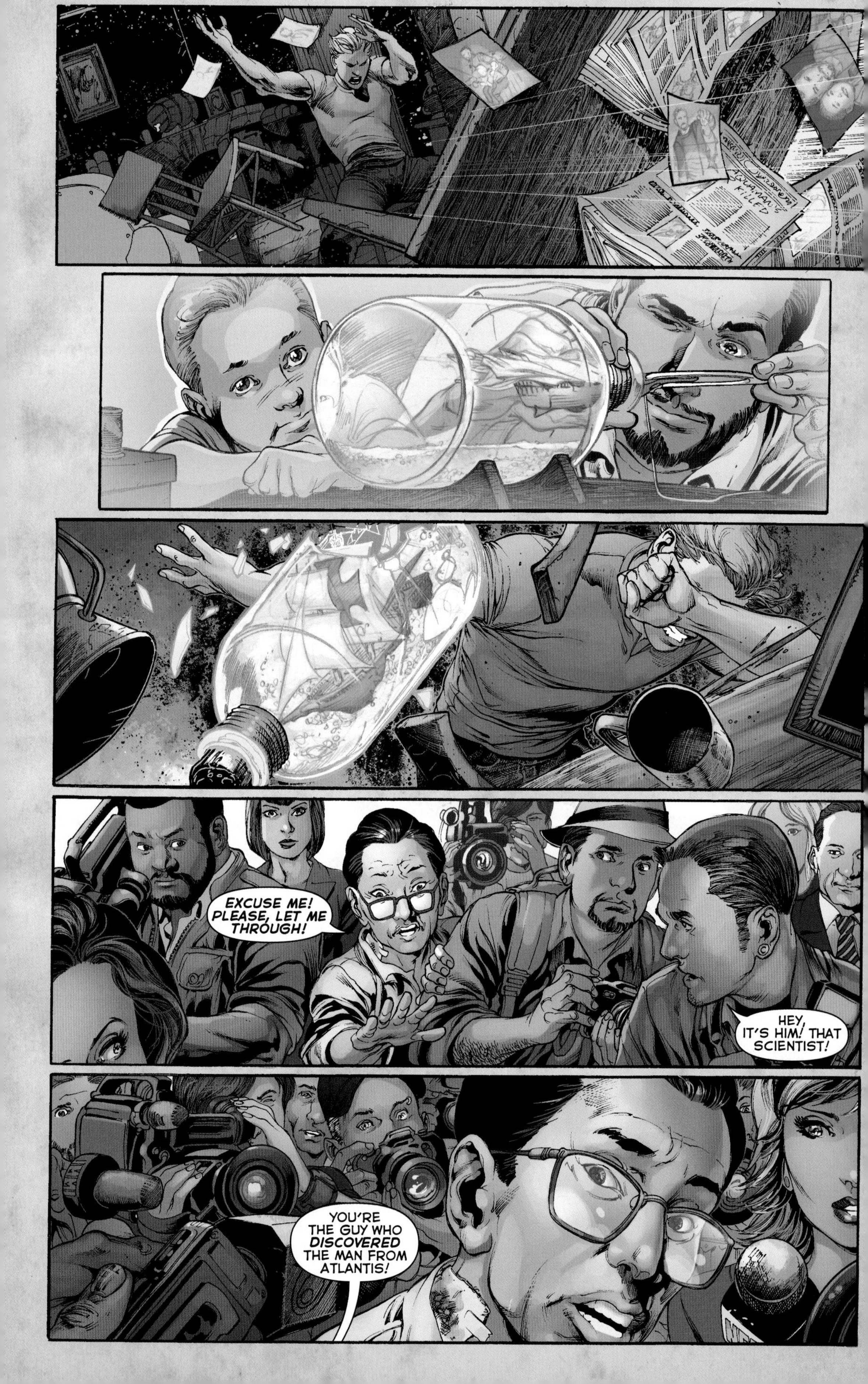
EXCUSE ME! PLEASE, LET ME THROUGH!
HEY, IT'S HIM! THAT SCIENTIST!
YOU'RE THE GUY WHO *DISCOVERED* THE MAN FROM ATLANTIS!

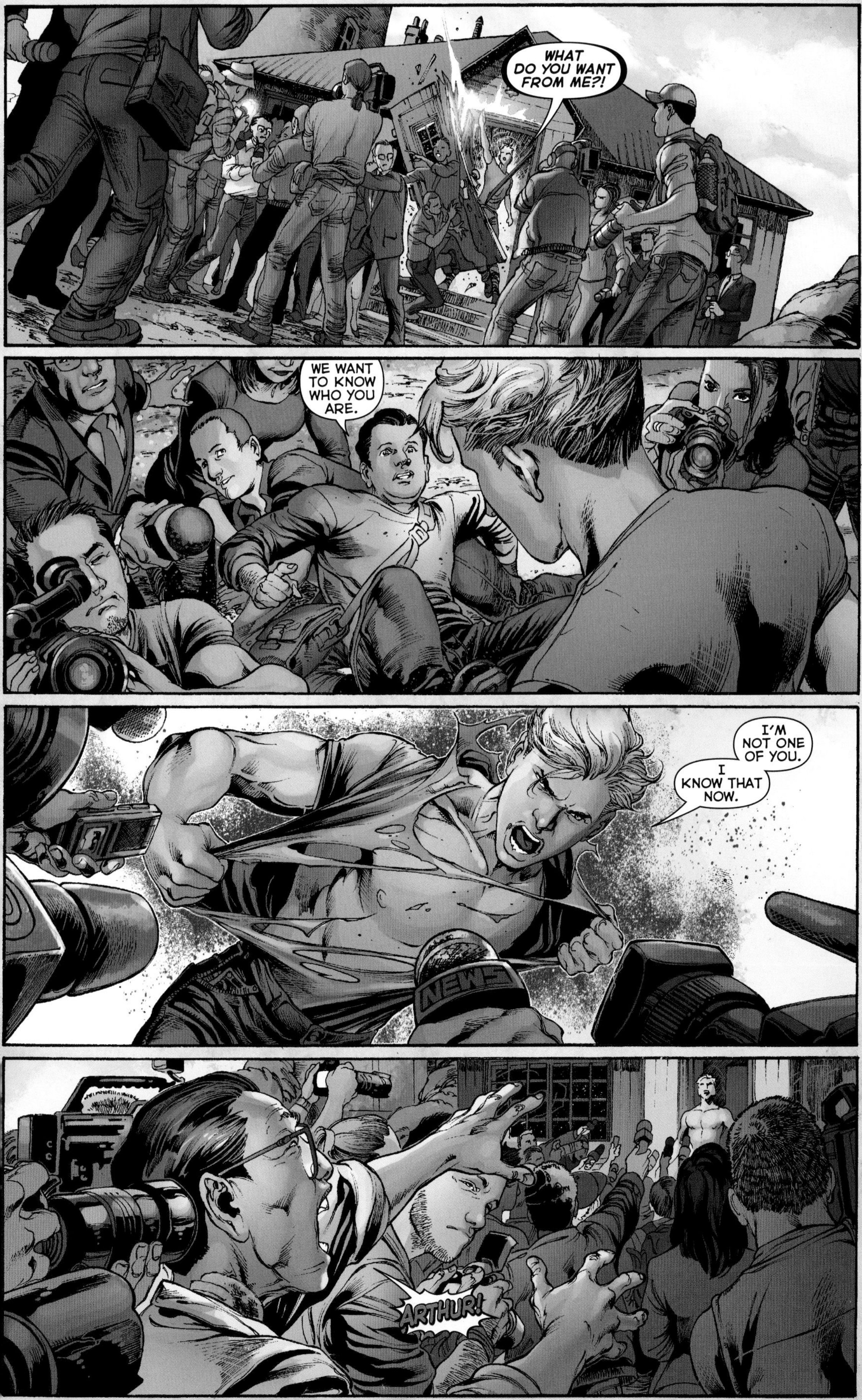

WHAT DO YOU WANT FROM ME?!
WE WANT TO KNOW WHO YOU ARE.
I'M NOT ONE OF YOU.
I KNOW THAT NOW.
NEWS
ARTHUR!

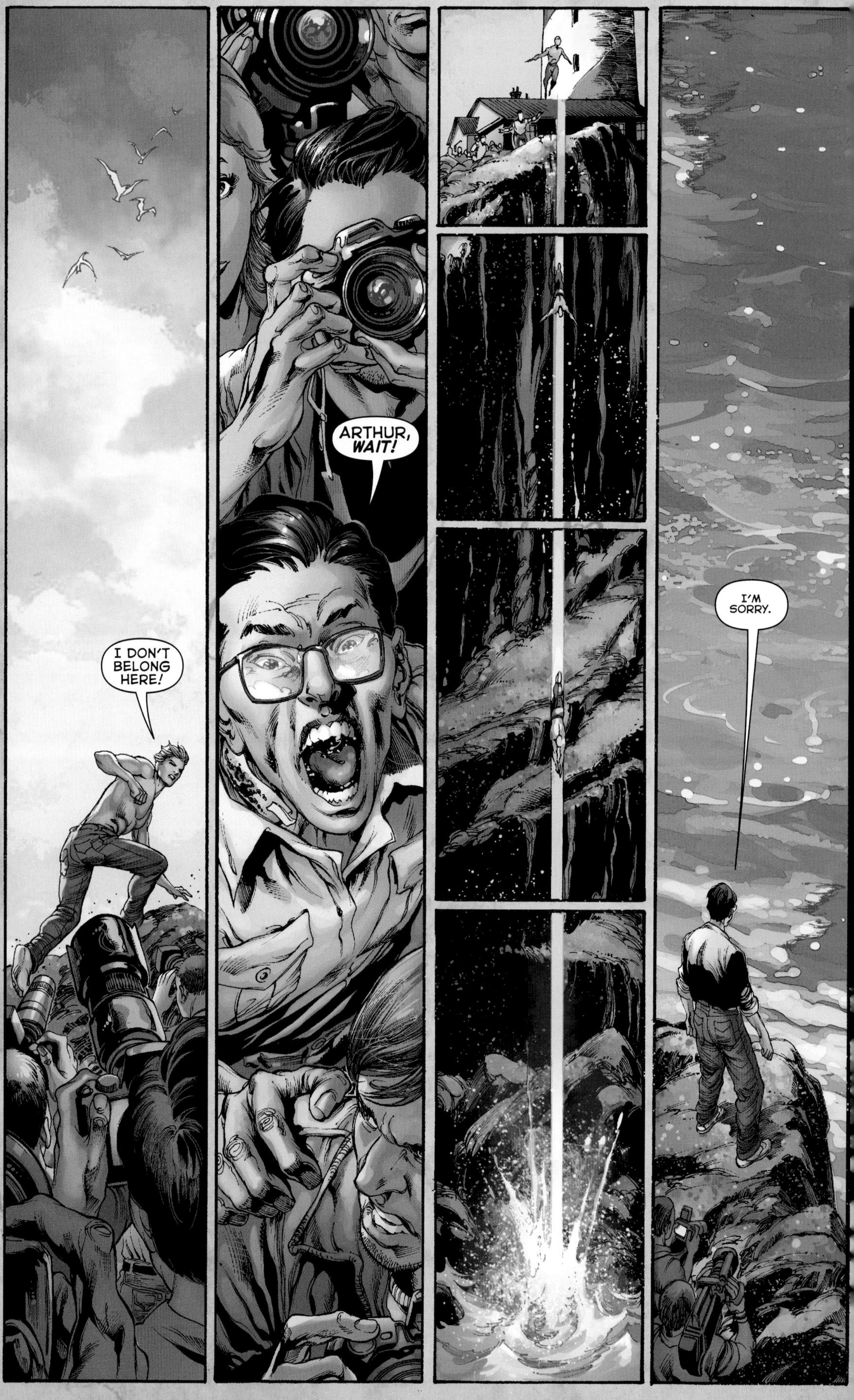
I DON'T BELONG HERE!
ARTHUR, WAIT!
I'M SORRY.

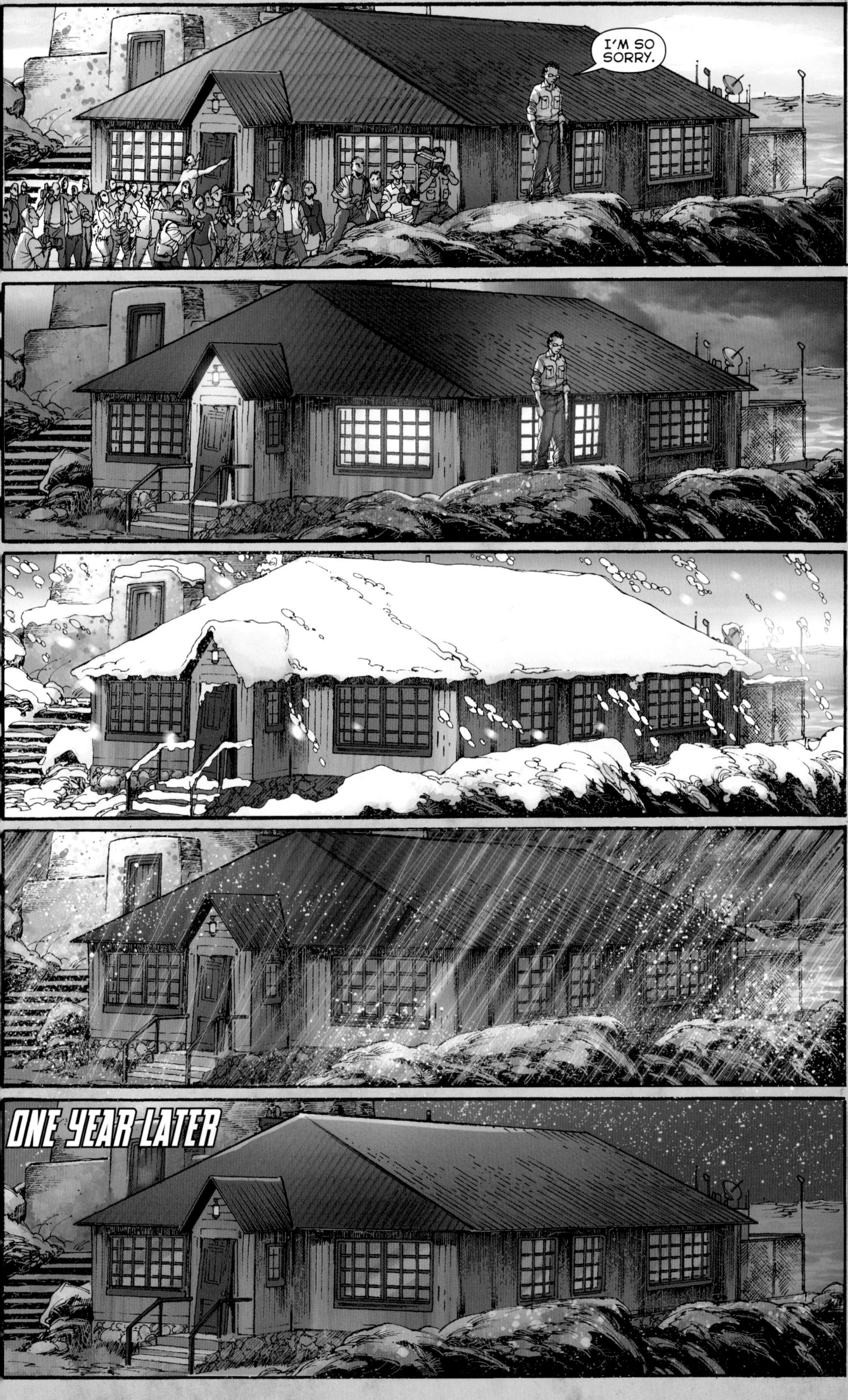
I'M SO SORRY.
ONE YEAR LATER

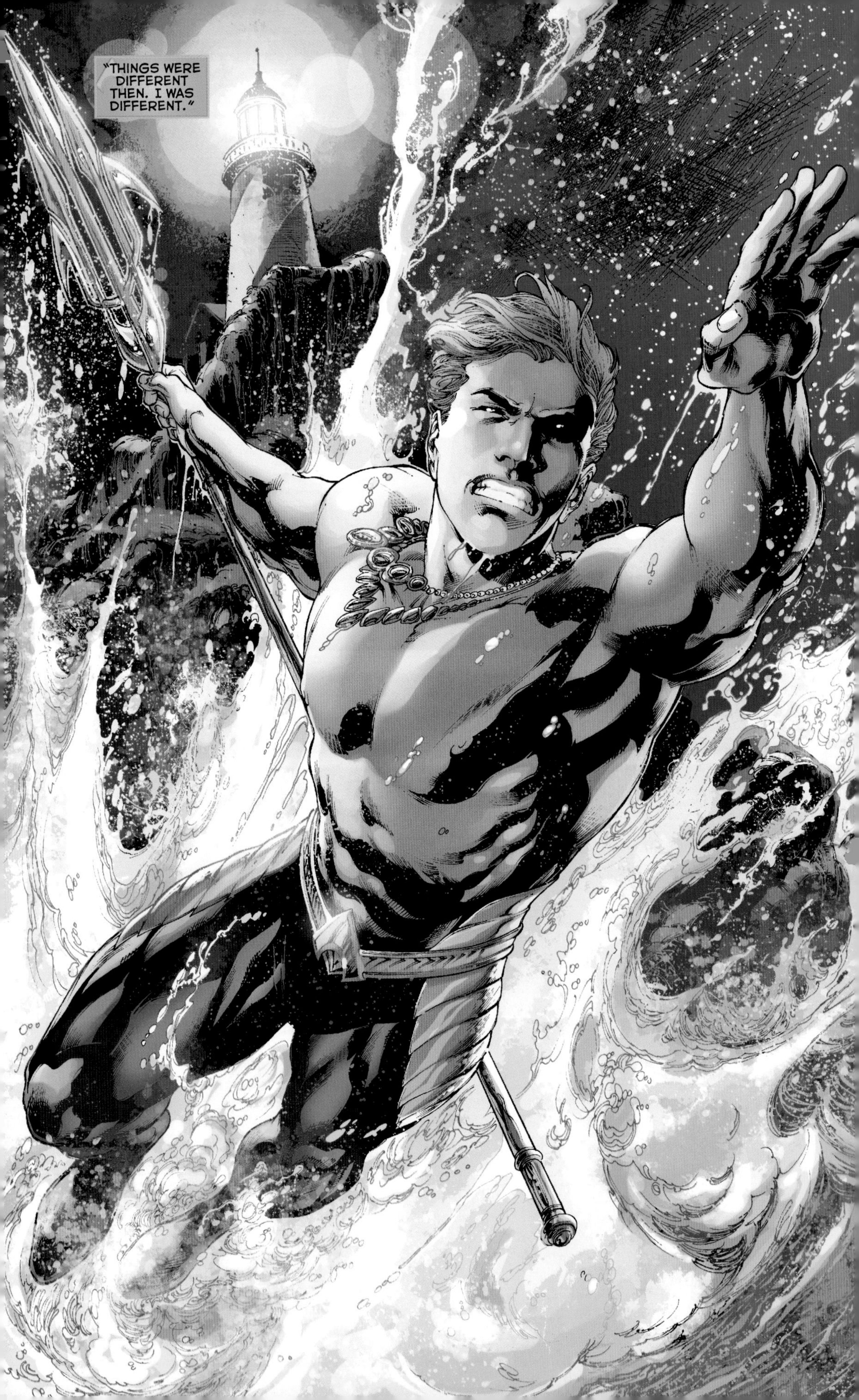
"THINGS WERE DIFFERENT THEN. I WAS DIFFERENT."

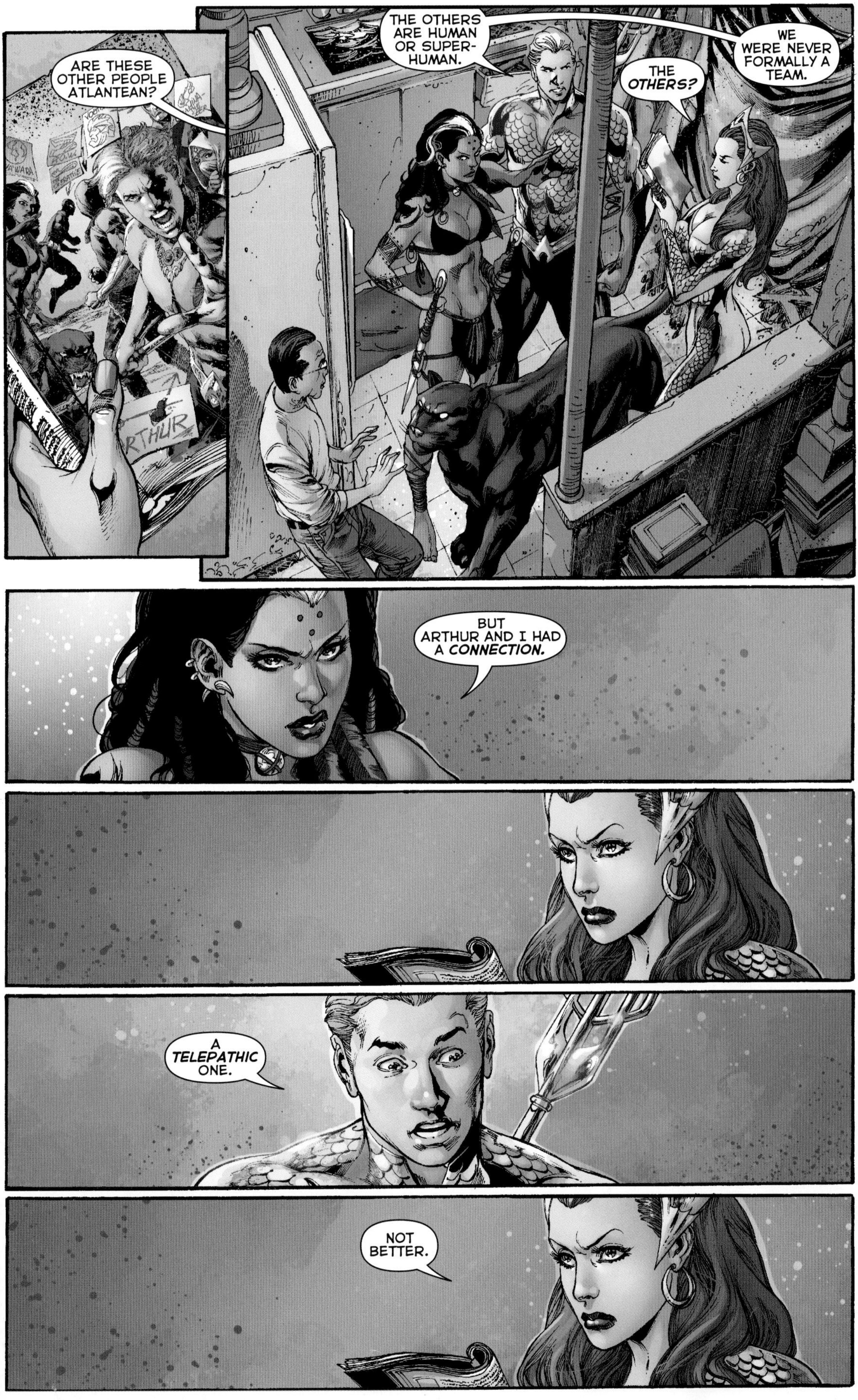

ARE THESE OTHER PEOPLE ATLANTEAN?
THE OTHERS ARE HUMAN OR SUPER-HUMAN.
WE WERE NEVER FORMALLY A TEAM.
THE *OTHERS?*
BUT ARTHUR AND I HAD A *CONNECTION.*
A *TELEPATHIC* ONE.
NOT BETTER.

THEY CAME TOGETHER BY NECESSITY, MERA. TO LOCATE THE *RELICS OF ATLANTIS* AND TO KEEP THEM FROM FALLING INTO THE WRONG HANDS.

THE *WRONG HANDS?* AS IF YOU KNEW ANYTHING ABOUT THAT.

KEEP THE JAGUAR UNDER CONTROL, YA'WARA. I NEED SHIN ALIVE.

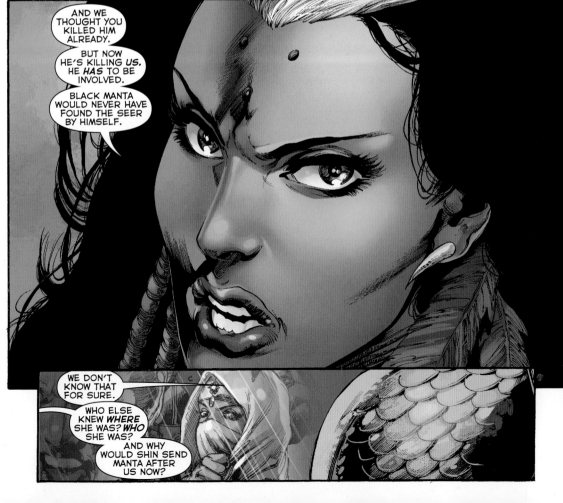

AND WE THOUGHT YOU KILLED HIM ALREADY.

BUT NOW HE'S KILLING *US.* HE *HAS* TO BE INVOLVED.

BLACK MANTA WOULD NEVER HAVE FOUND THE SEER BY HIMSELF.

WE DON'T KNOW THAT FOR SURE.

WHO ELSE KNEW *WHERE* SHE WAS? *WHO* SHE WAS?

AND WHY WOULD SHIN SEND MANTA AFTER US NOW?

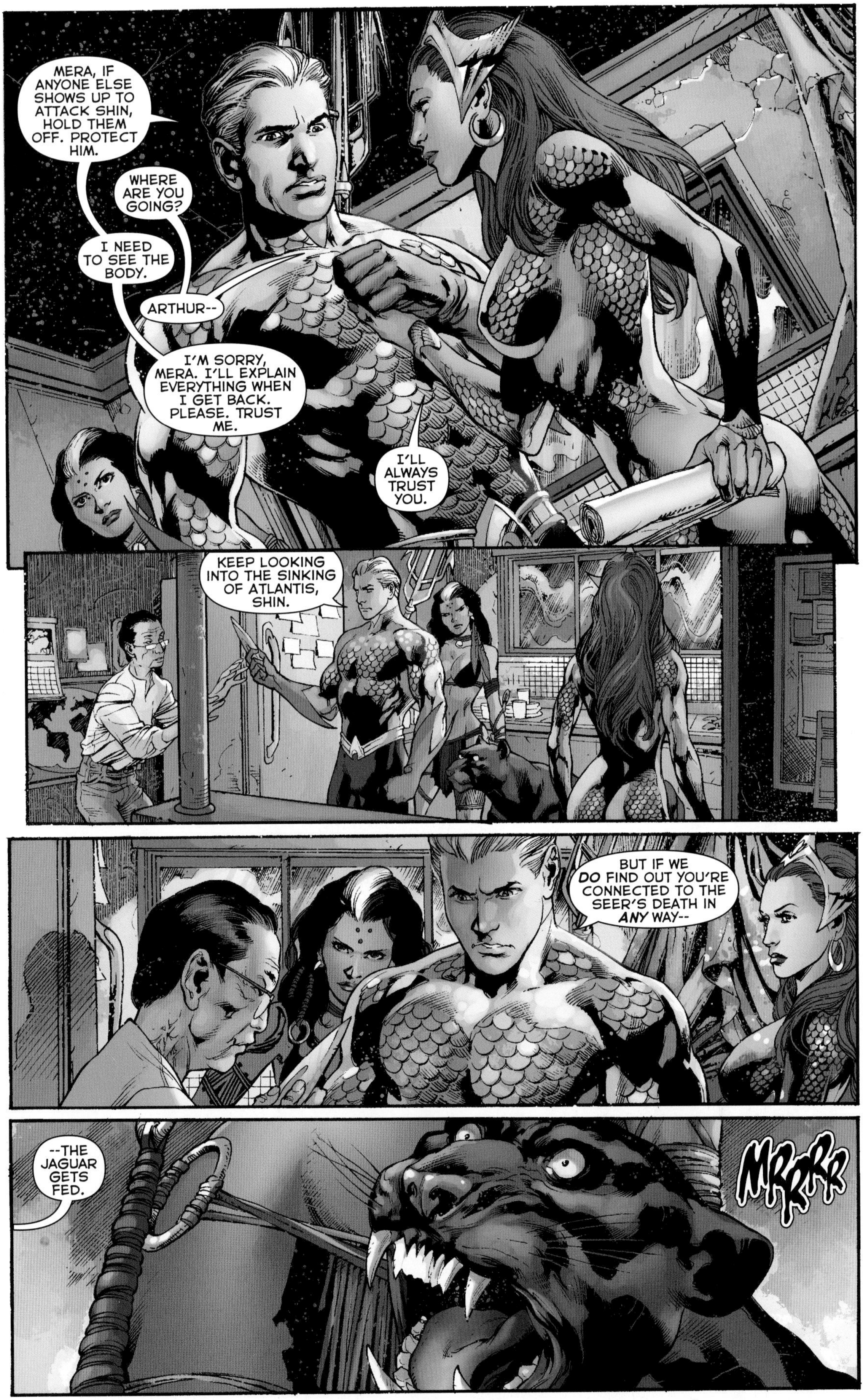
MERA, IF ANYONE ELSE SHOWS UP TO ATTACK SHIN, HOLD THEM OFF. PROTECT HIM.
WHERE ARE YOU GOING?
I NEED TO SEE THE BODY.
ARTHUR--
I'M SORRY, MERA. I'LL EXPLAIN EVERYTHING WHEN I GET BACK. PLEASE. TRUST ME.
I'LL ALWAYS TRUST YOU.
KEEP LOOKING INTO THE SINKING OF ATLANTIS, SHIN.
BUT IF WE DO FIND OUT YOU'RE CONNECTED TO THE SEER'S DEATH IN ANY WAY--
--THE JAGUAR GETS FED.
MRRRR

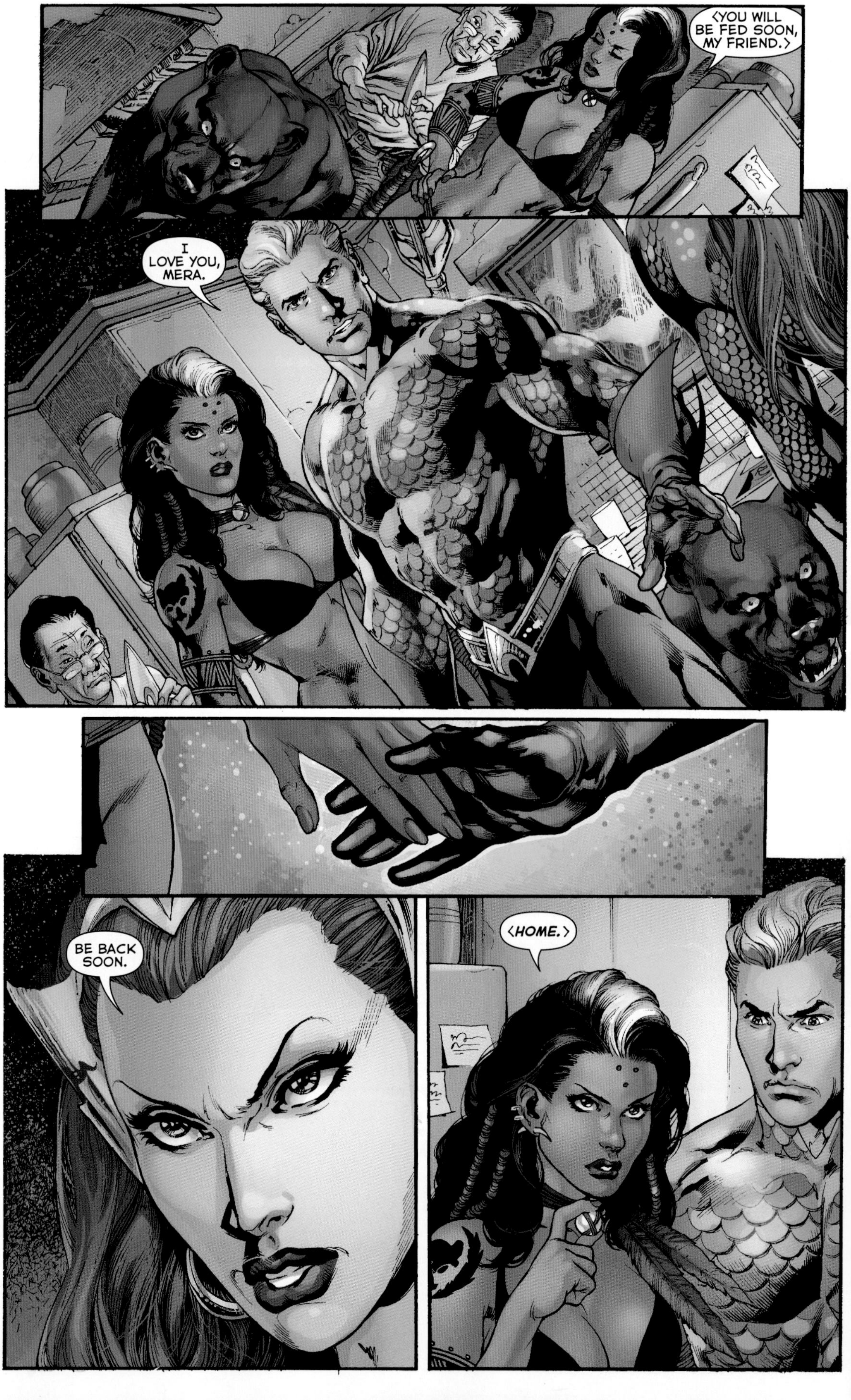
<YOU WILL BE FED SOON, MY FRIEND.>
I LOVE YOU, MERA.
BE BACK SOON.
<HOME.>

I...I SHOULD GET BACK TO THIS.

NO.

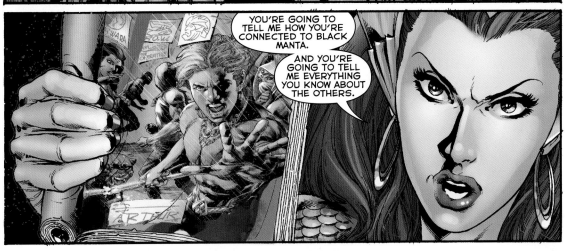

YOU'RE GOING TO TELL ME HOW YOU'RE CONNECTED TO BLACK MANTA.

AND YOU'RE GOING TO TELL ME EVERYTHING YOU KNOW ABOUT THE OTHERS.

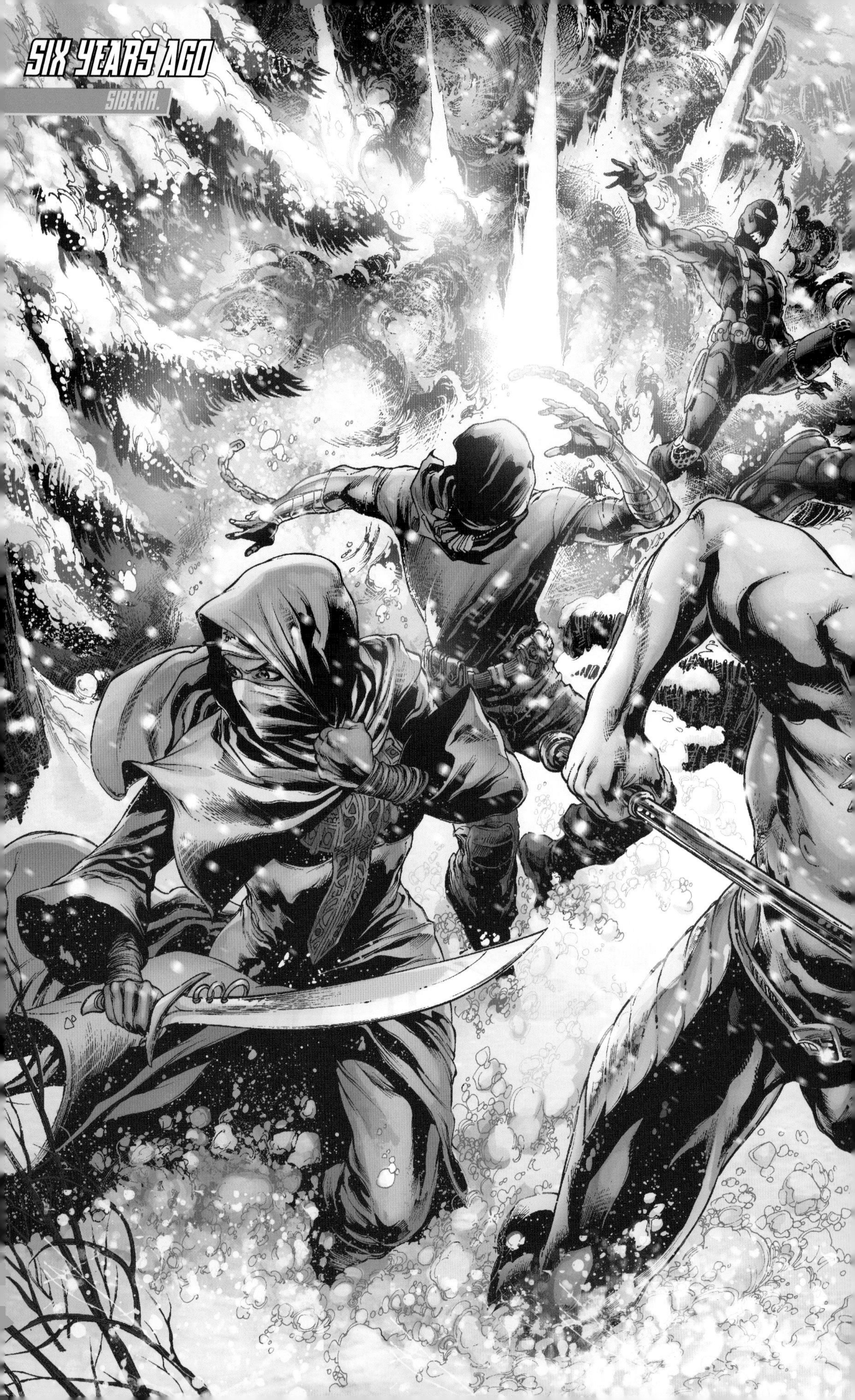
SIX YEARS AGO
SIBERIA.

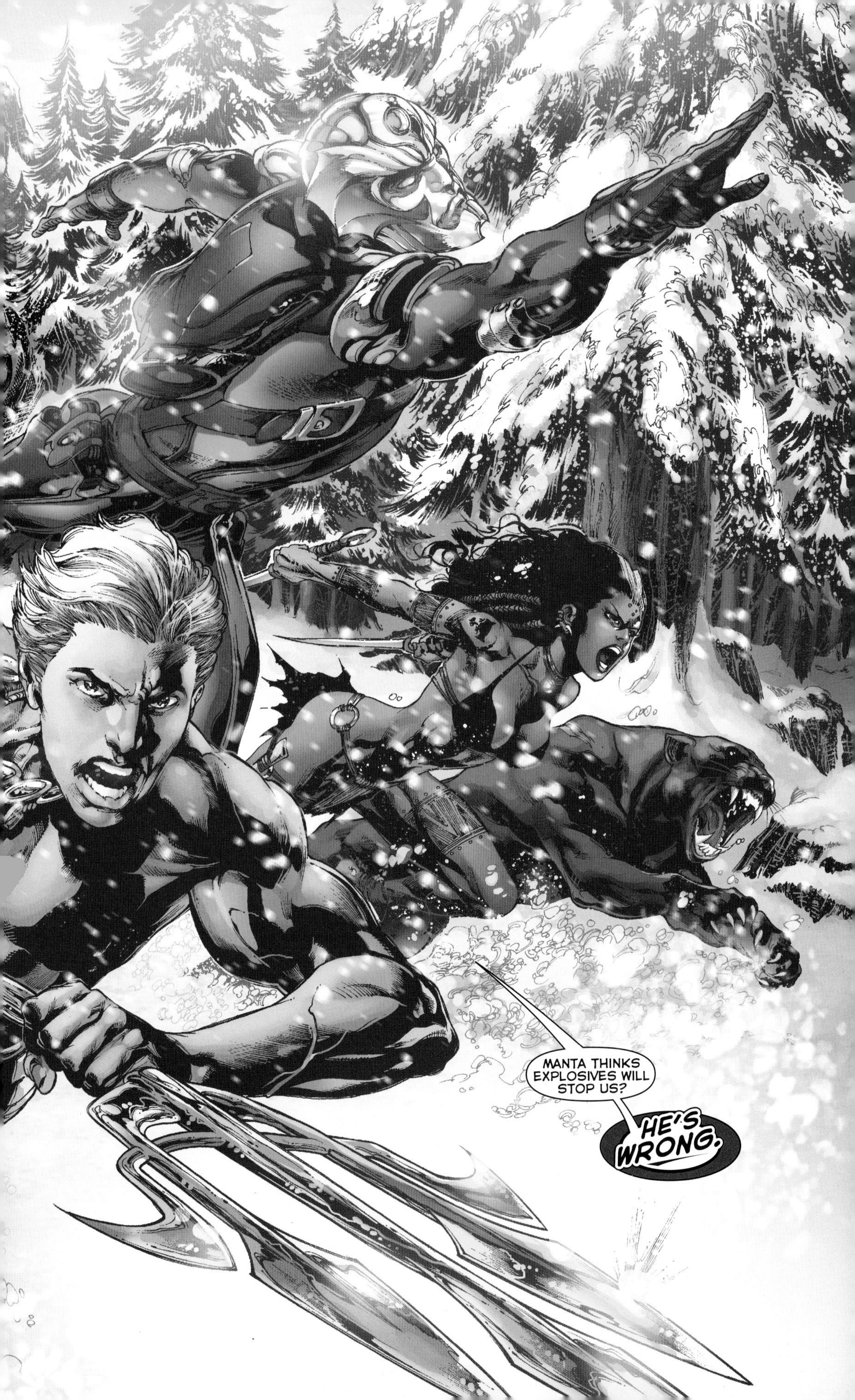
MANTA THINKS EXPLOSIVES WILL STOP US?
HE'S WRONG.

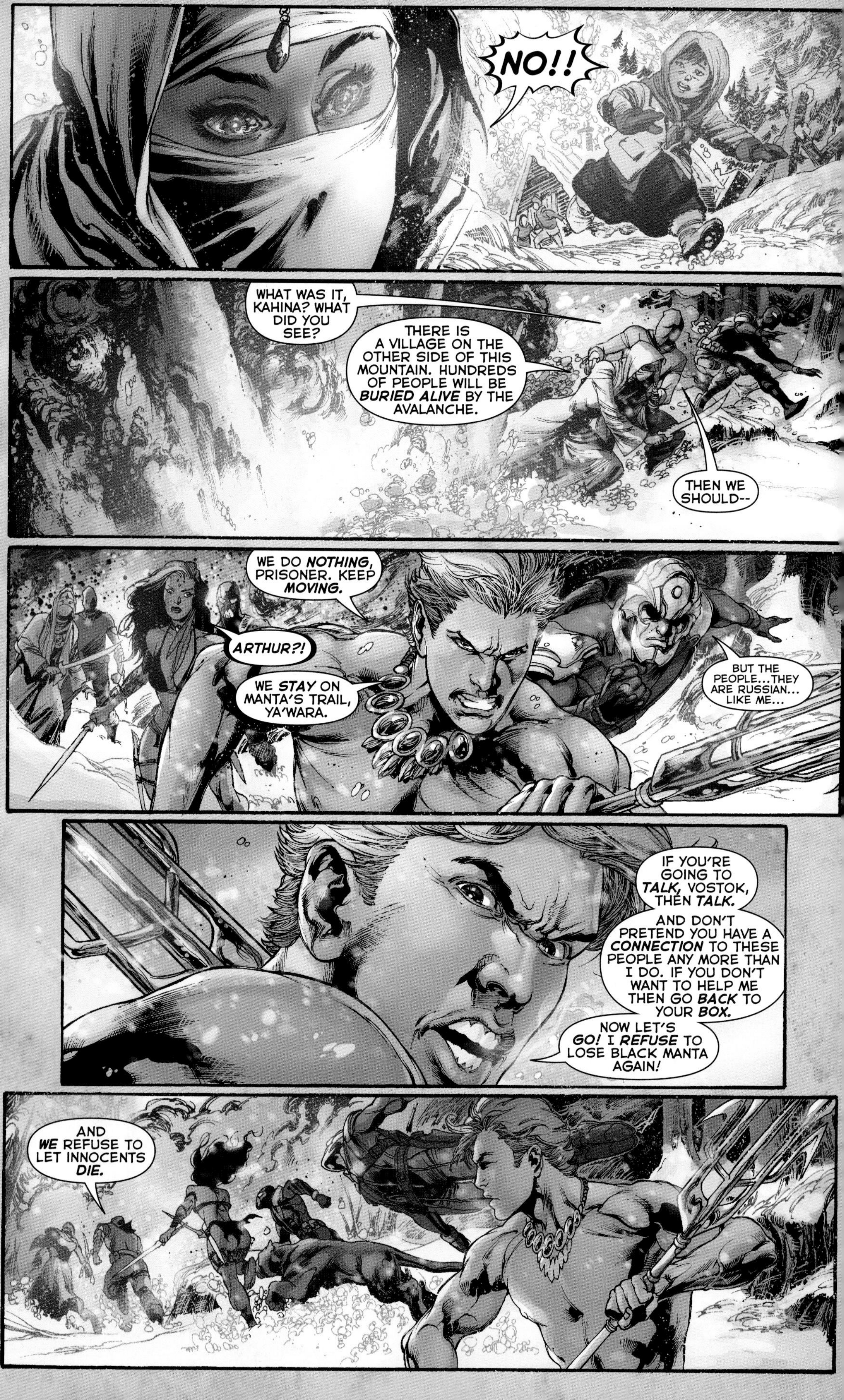
NO!!
WHAT WAS IT, KAHINA? WHAT DID YOU SEE?
THERE IS A VILLAGE ON THE OTHER SIDE OF THIS MOUNTAIN. HUNDREDS OF PEOPLE WILL BE BURIED ALIVE BY THE AVALANCHE.
THEN WE SHOULD--
WE DO NOTHING, PRISONER. KEEP MOVING.
ARTHUR?!
WE STAY ON MANTA'S TRAIL, YA'WARA.
BUT THE PEOPLE...THEY ARE RUSSIAN... LIKE ME...
IF YOU'RE GOING TO TALK, VOSTOK, THEN TALK.
AND DON'T PRETEND YOU HAVE A CONNECTION TO THESE PEOPLE ANY MORE THAN I DO. IF YOU DON'T WANT TO HELP ME THEN GO BACK TO YOUR BOX.
NOW LET'S GO! I REFUSE TO LOSE BLACK MANTA AGAIN!
AND WE REFUSE TO LET INNOCENTS DIE.

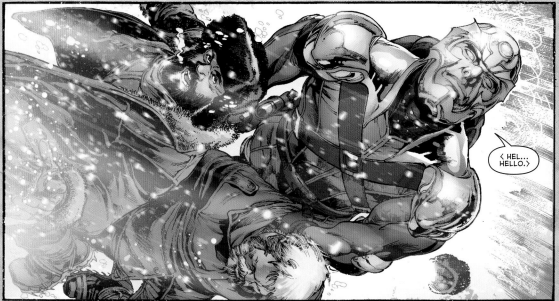

‹HEL...
HELLO.›

IT'S COMING TOO FAST.
WE NEED TO SAVE
WHO WE CAN.

NO,
OPERATIVE.

WE SAVE...
EVERYBODY.

OR I DIE
WITH THEM
THIS TIME.

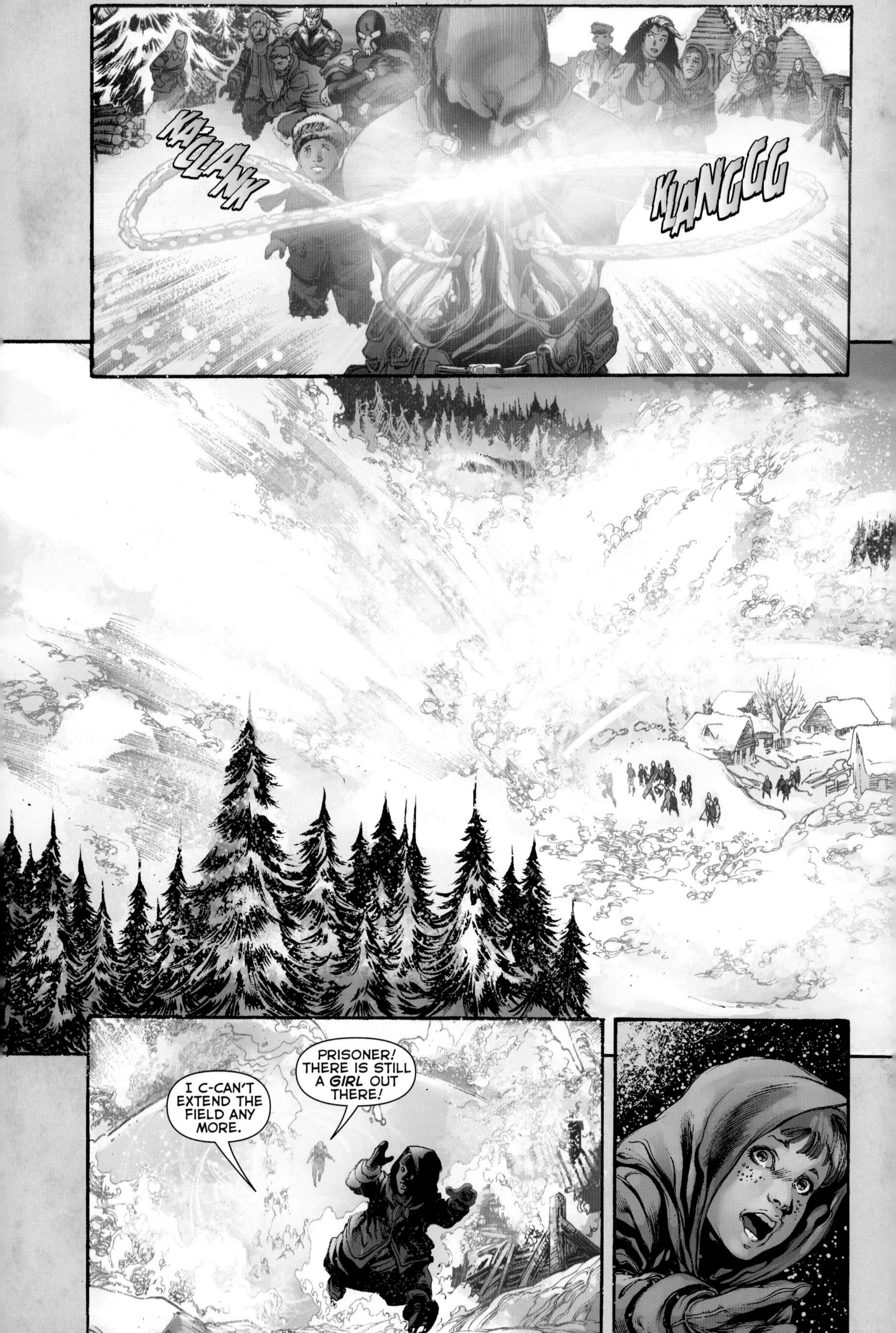
KA-CLANK
KLANGGG
I C-CAN'T EXTEND THE FIELD ANY MORE.
PRISONER! THERE IS STILL A *GIRL* OUT THERE!

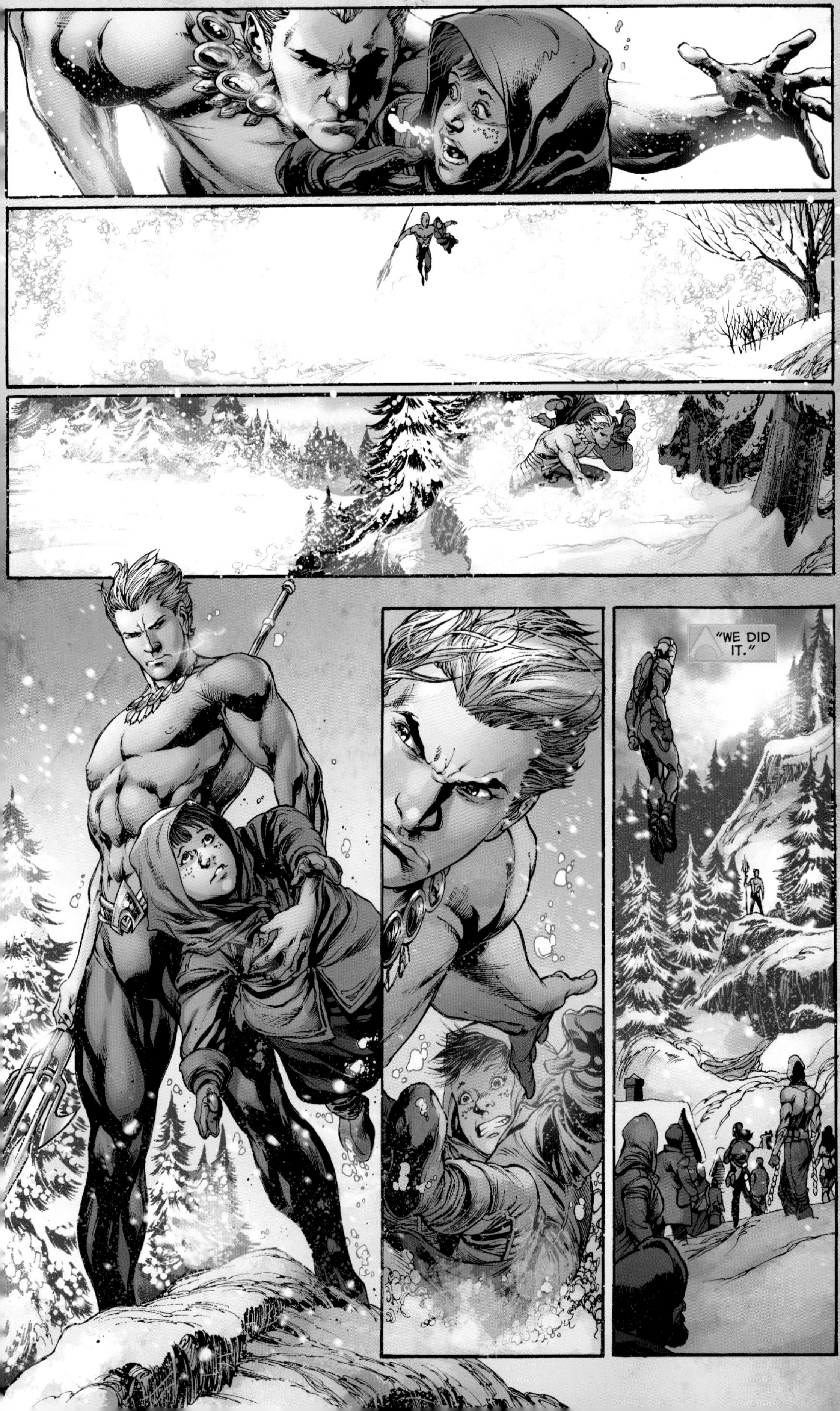
"WE DID IT."

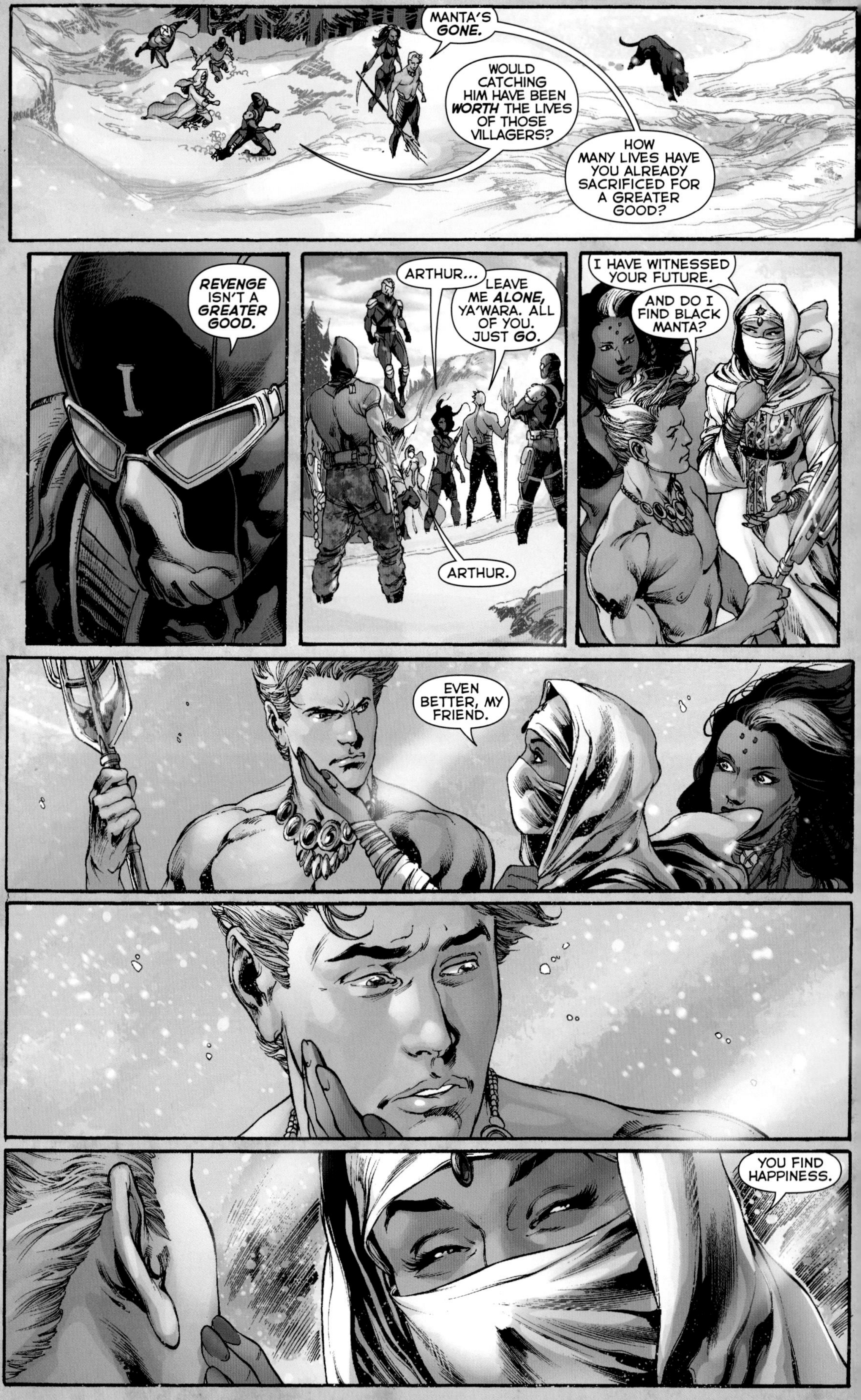
MANTA'S GONE.
WOULD CATCHING HIM HAVE BEEN WORTH THE LIVES OF THOSE VILLAGERS?
HOW MANY LIVES HAVE YOU ALREADY SACRIFICED FOR A GREATER GOOD?
REVENGE ISN'T A GREATER GOOD.
ARTHUR...
LEAVE ME ALONE, YA'WARA. ALL OF YOU. JUST GO.
ARTHUR.
I HAVE WITNESSED YOUR FUTURE.
AND DO I FIND BLACK MANTA?
EVEN BETTER, MY FRIEND.
YOU FIND HAPPINESS.

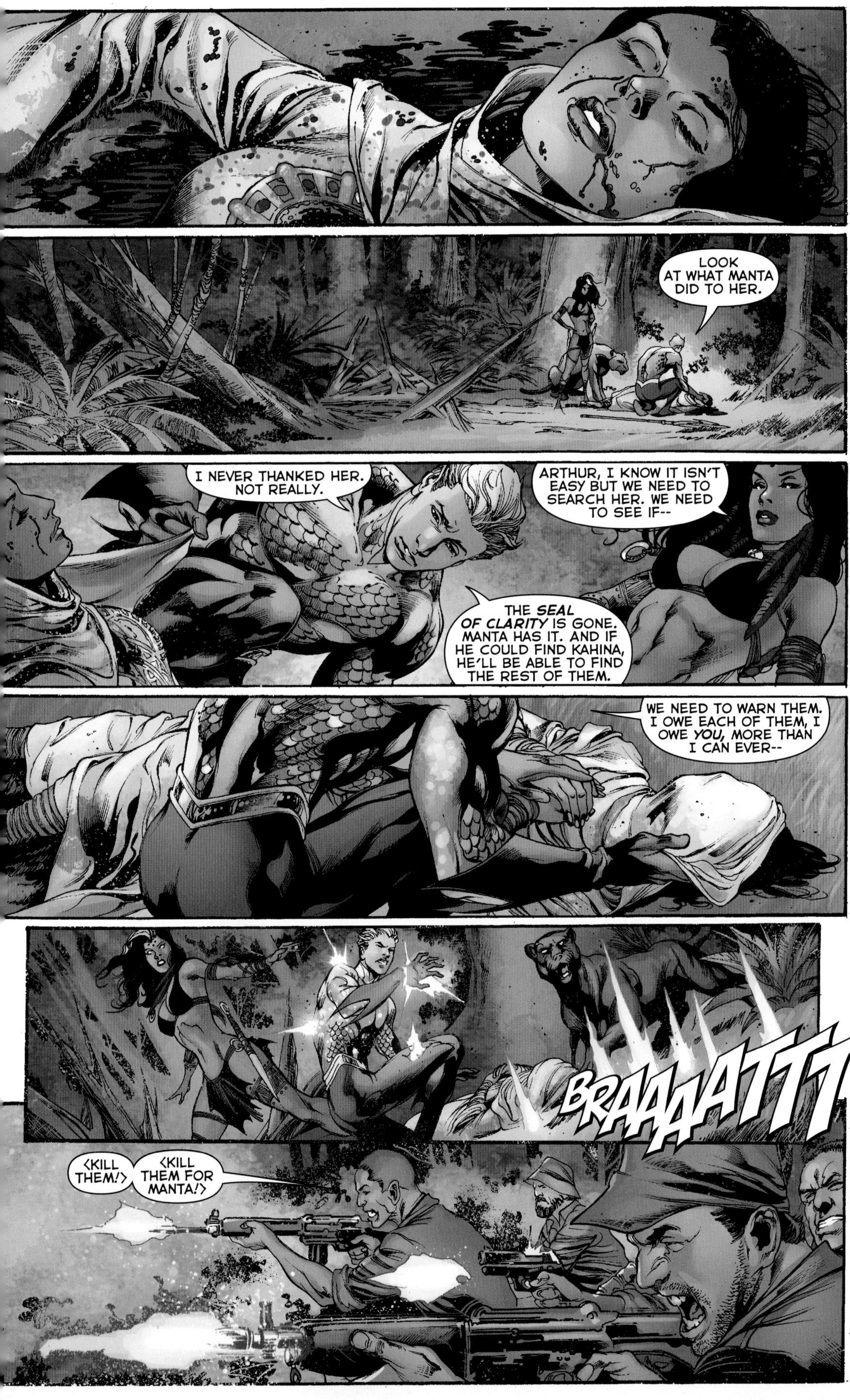

LOOK AT WHAT MANTA DID TO HER.
I NEVER THANKED HER. NOT REALLY.
ARTHUR, I KNOW IT ISN'T EASY BUT WE NEED TO SEARCH HER. WE NEED TO SEE IF--
THE SEAL OF CLARITY IS GONE. MANTA HAS IT. AND IF HE COULD FIND KAHINA, HE'LL BE ABLE TO FIND THE REST OF THEM.
WE NEED TO WARN THEM. I OWE EACH OF THEM, I OWE YOU, MORE THAN I CAN EVER--
BRAAAAATTT
<KILL THEM!>
<KILL THEM FOR MANTA!>

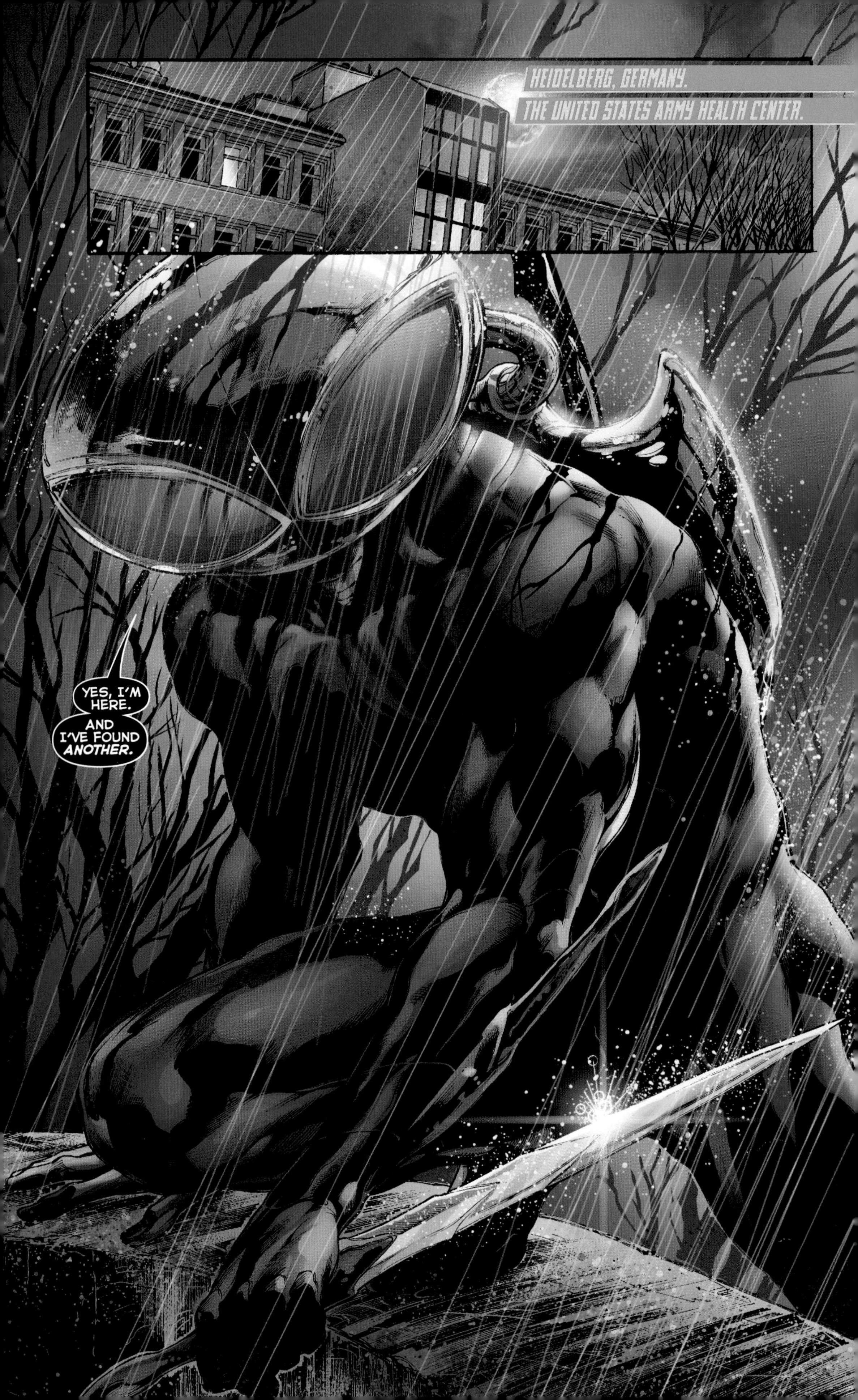
HEIDELBERG, GERMANY.
THE UNITED STATES ARMY HEALTH CENTER.
YES, I'M HERE.
AND I'VE FOUND *ANOTHER*.

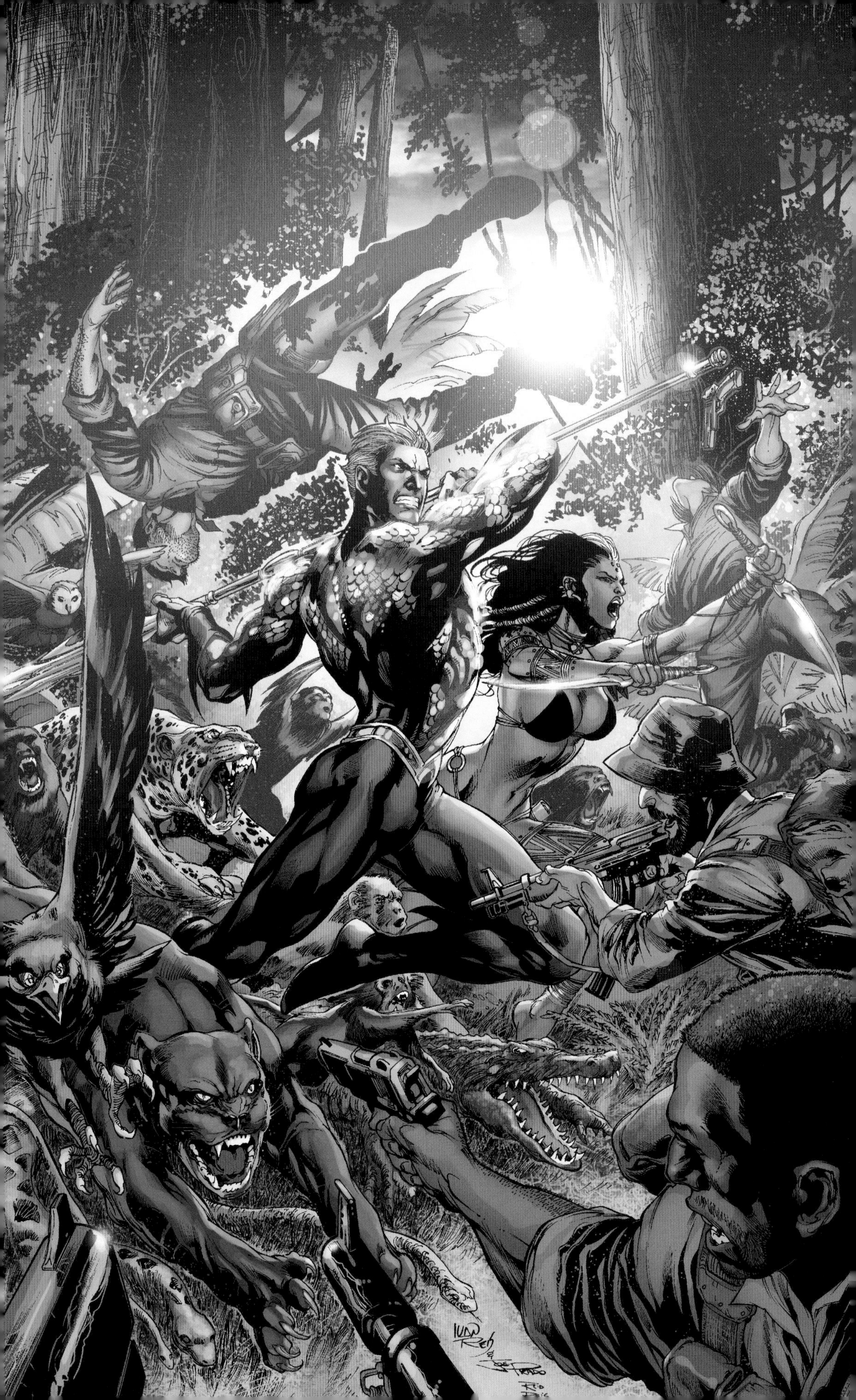

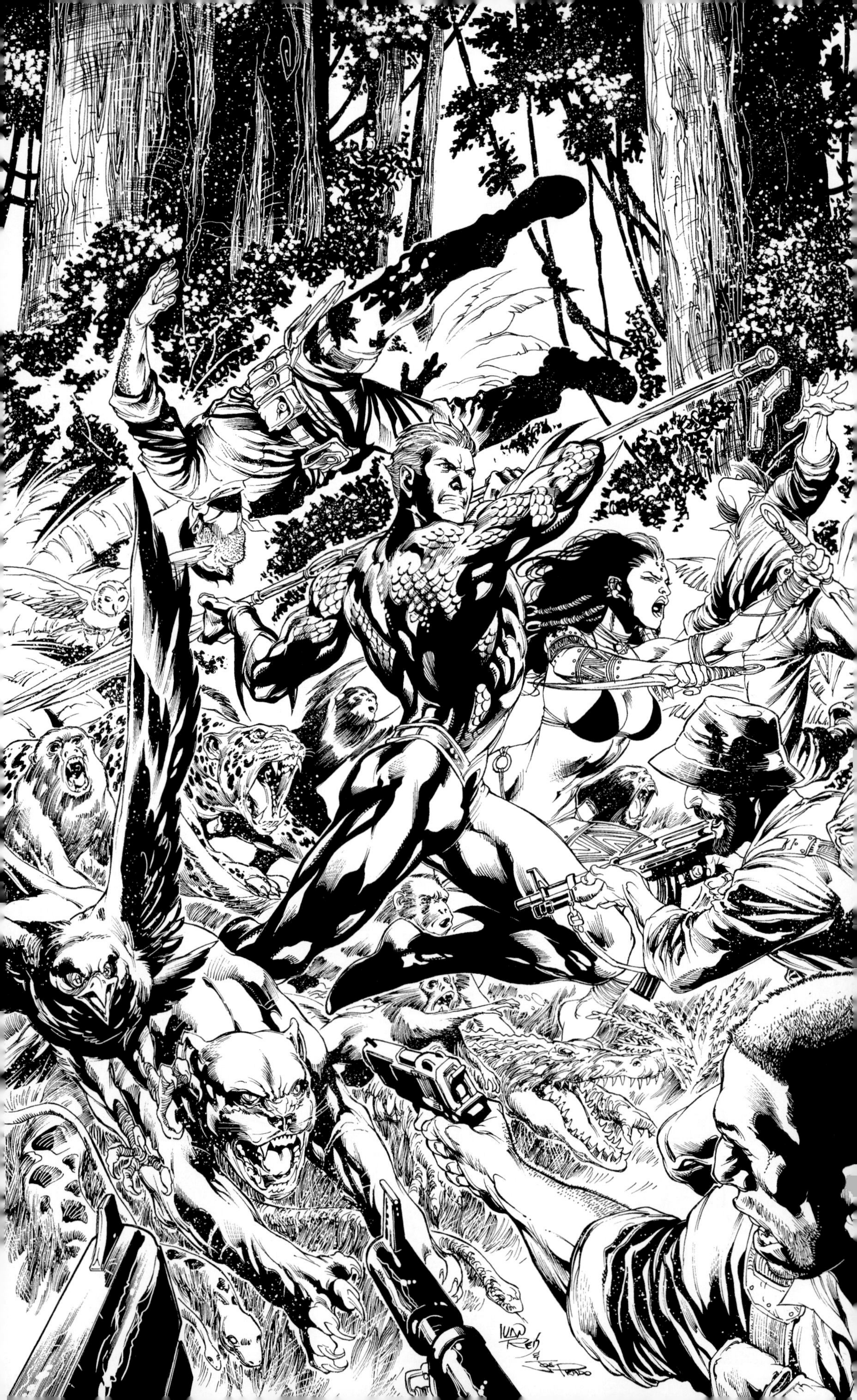

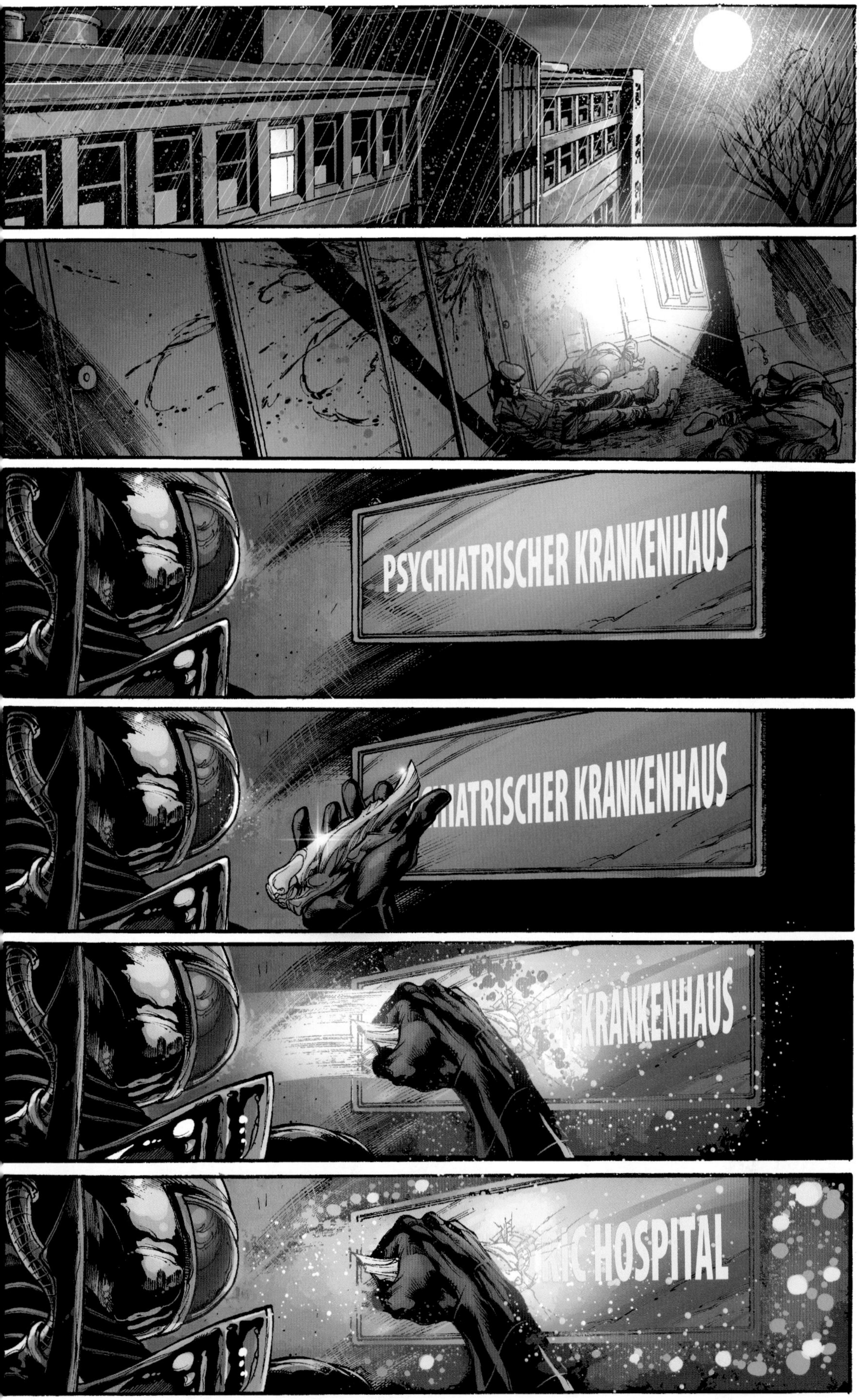

PSYCHIATRISCHER KRANKENHAUS
IATRISCHER KRANKENHAUS
KRANKENHAUS
HOSPITAL

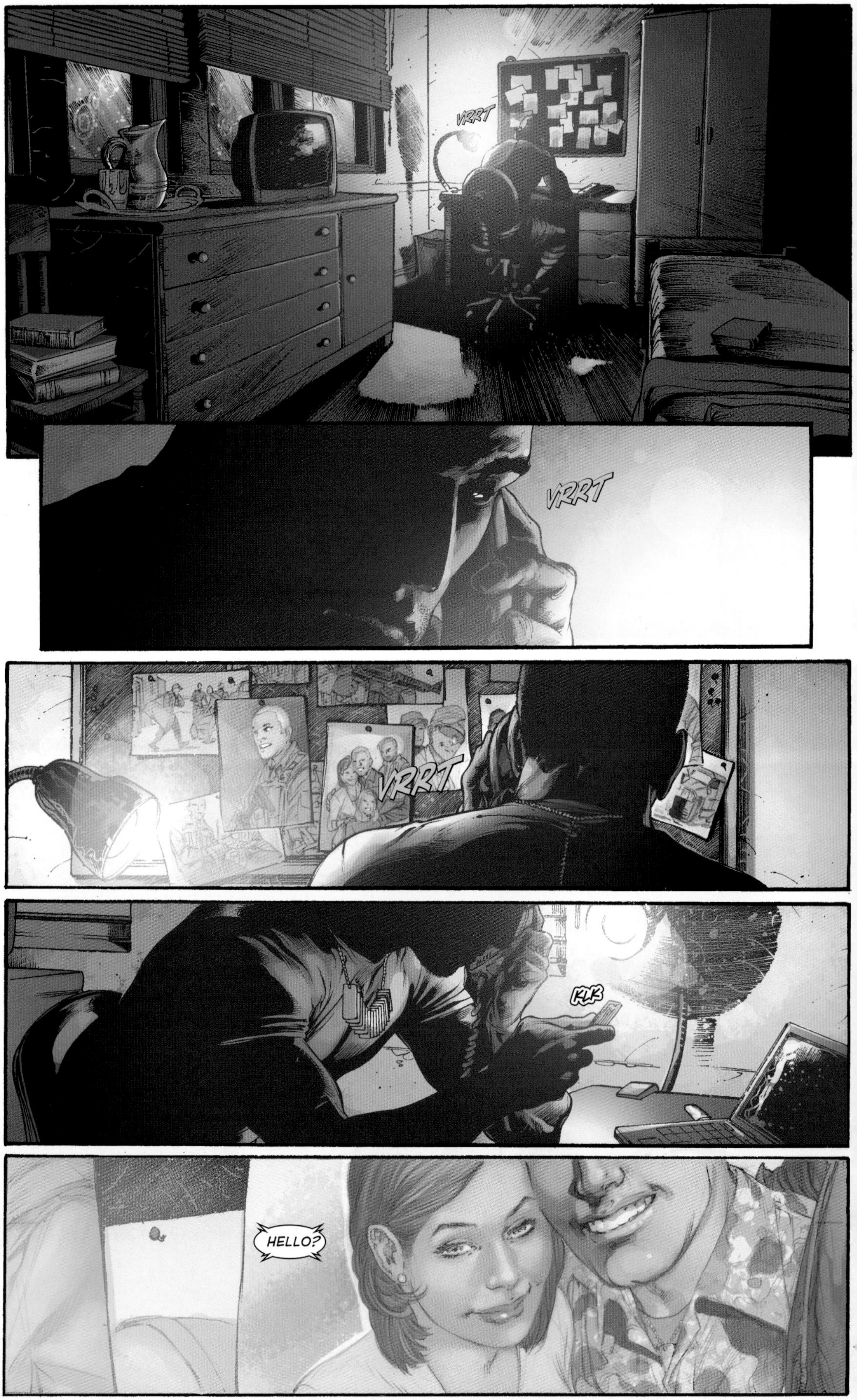
VRRT
VRRT
VRRT
KLIK
HELLO?

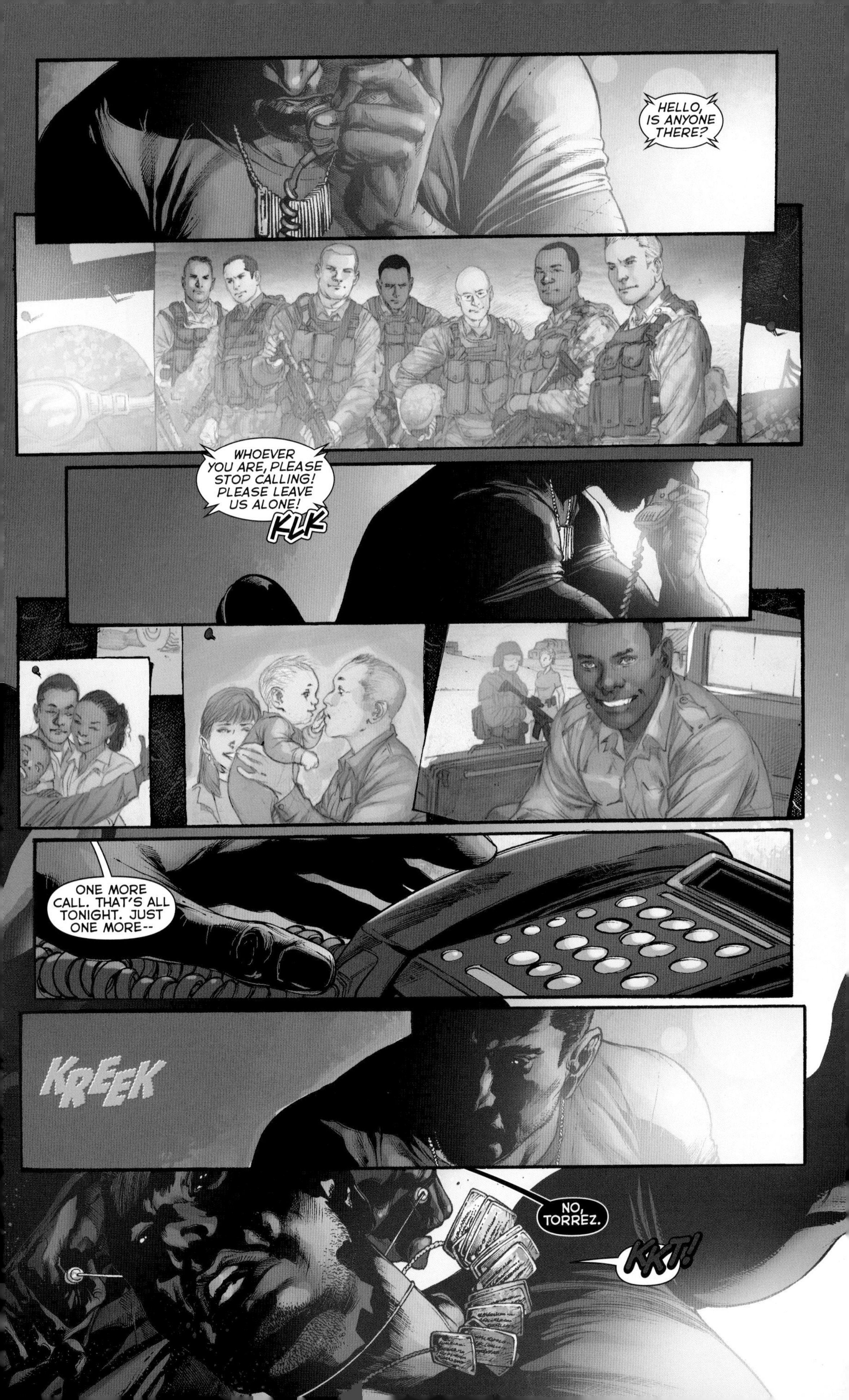
HELLO, IS ANYONE THERE?
WHOEVER YOU ARE, PLEASE STOP CALLING! PLEASE LEAVE US ALONE!
KLIK
ONE MORE CALL. THAT'S ALL TONIGHT. JUST ONE MORE--
KREEK
NO, TORREZ.
KKT!

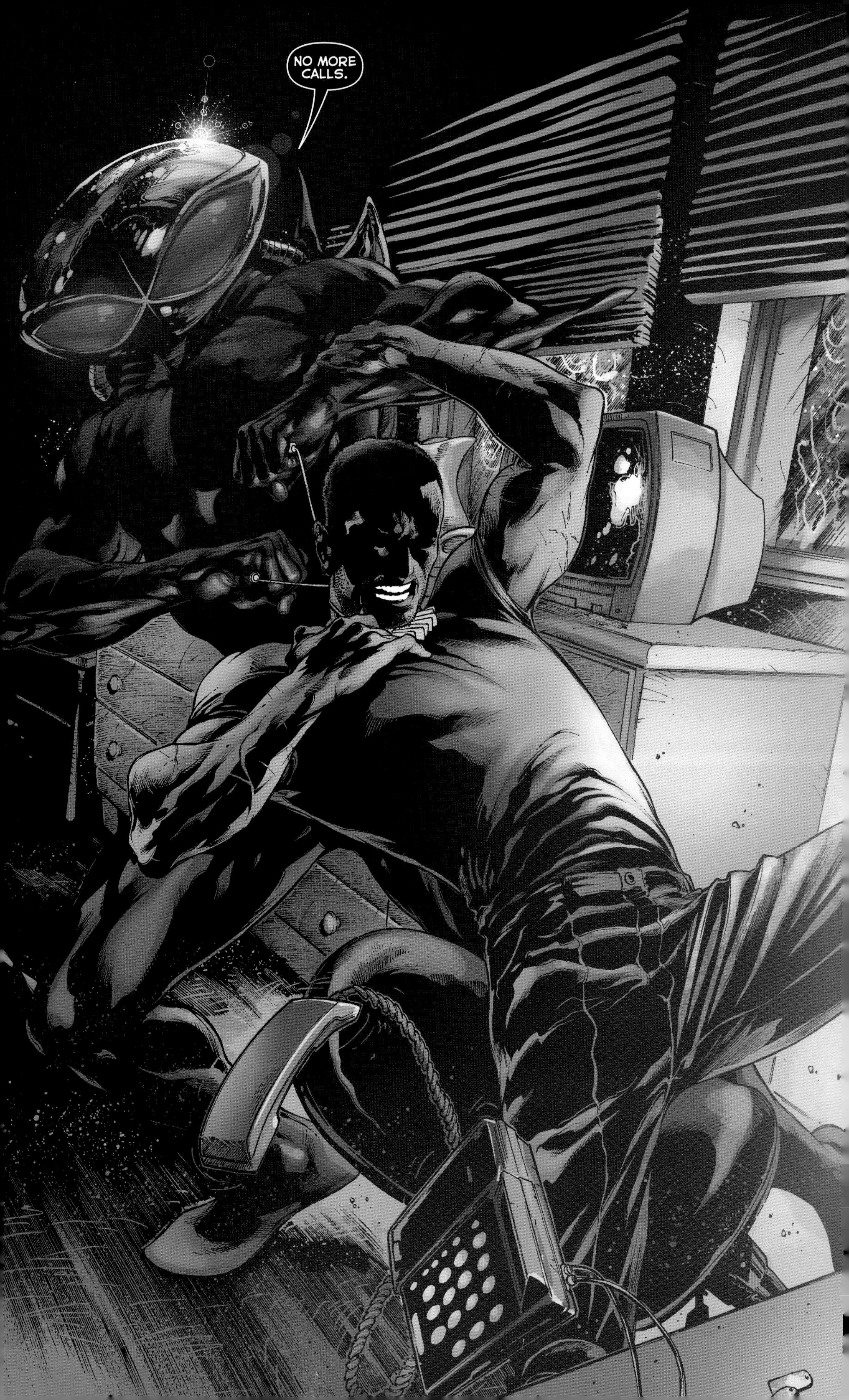
NO MORE CALLS.

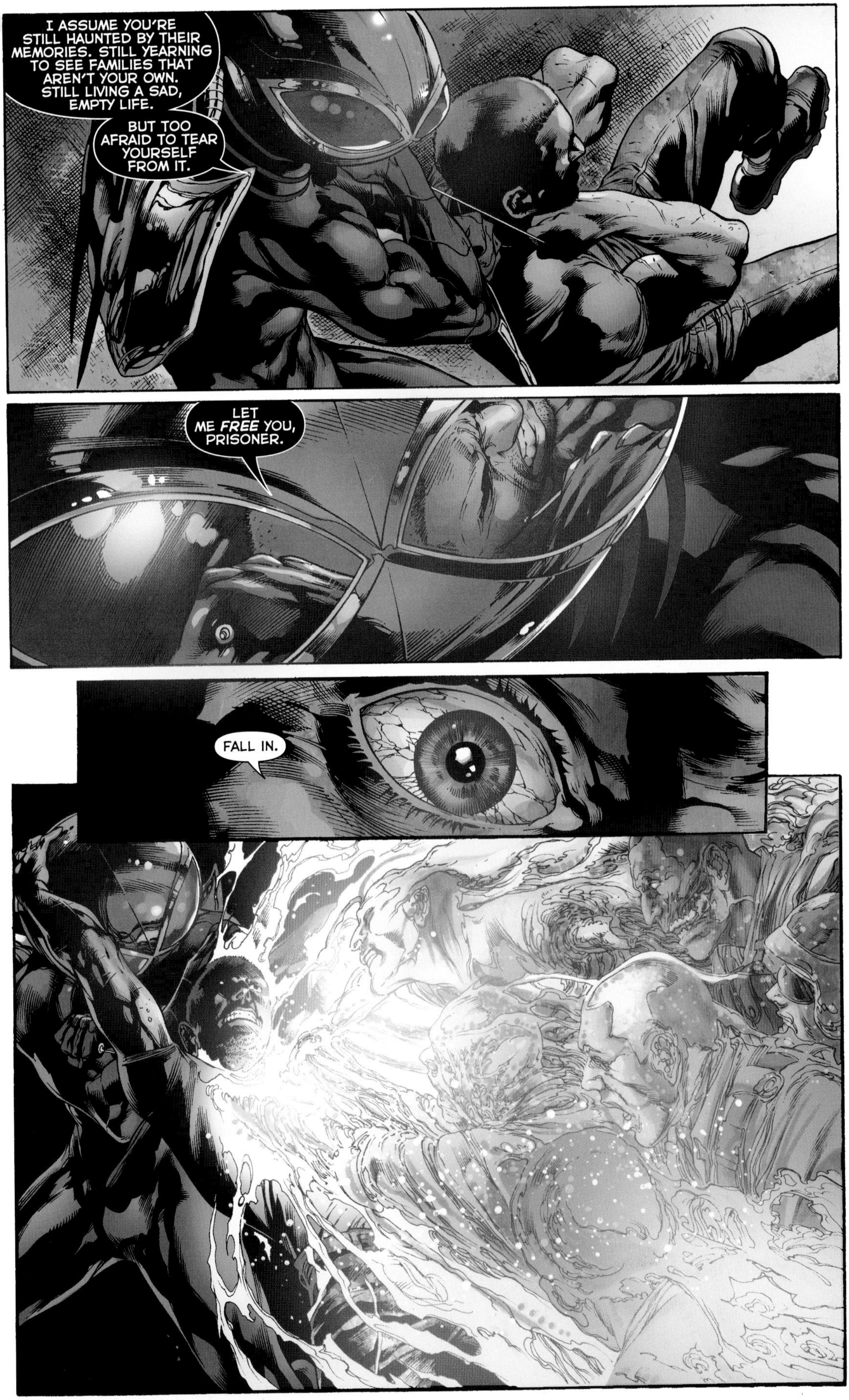
I ASSUME YOU'RE STILL HAUNTED BY THEIR MEMORIES. STILL YEARNING TO SEE FAMILIES THAT AREN'T YOUR OWN. STILL LIVING A SAD, EMPTY LIFE.
BUT TOO AFRAID TO TEAR YOURSELF FROM IT.
LET ME *FREE* YOU, PRISONER.
FALL IN.

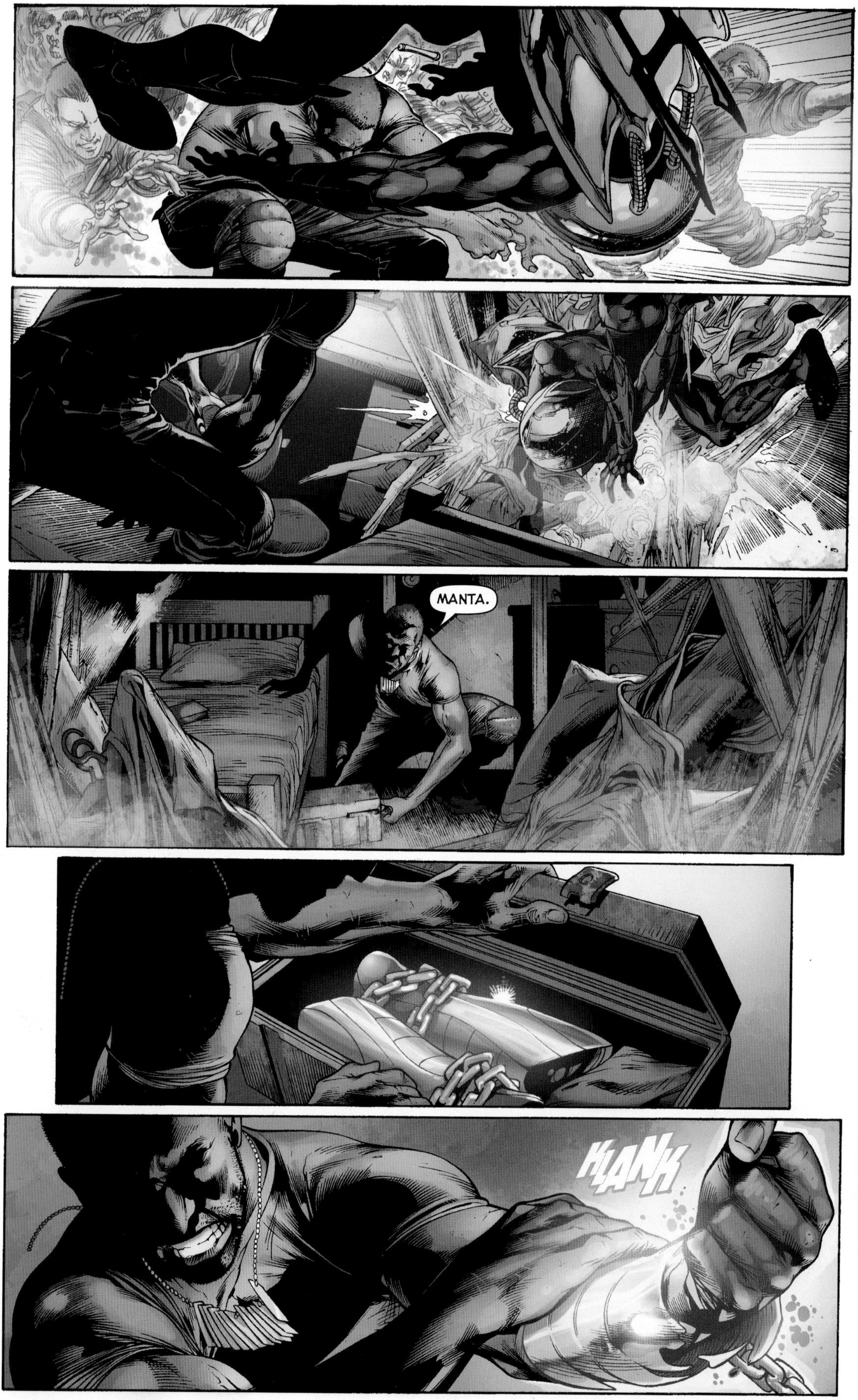
MANTA.
KLANK

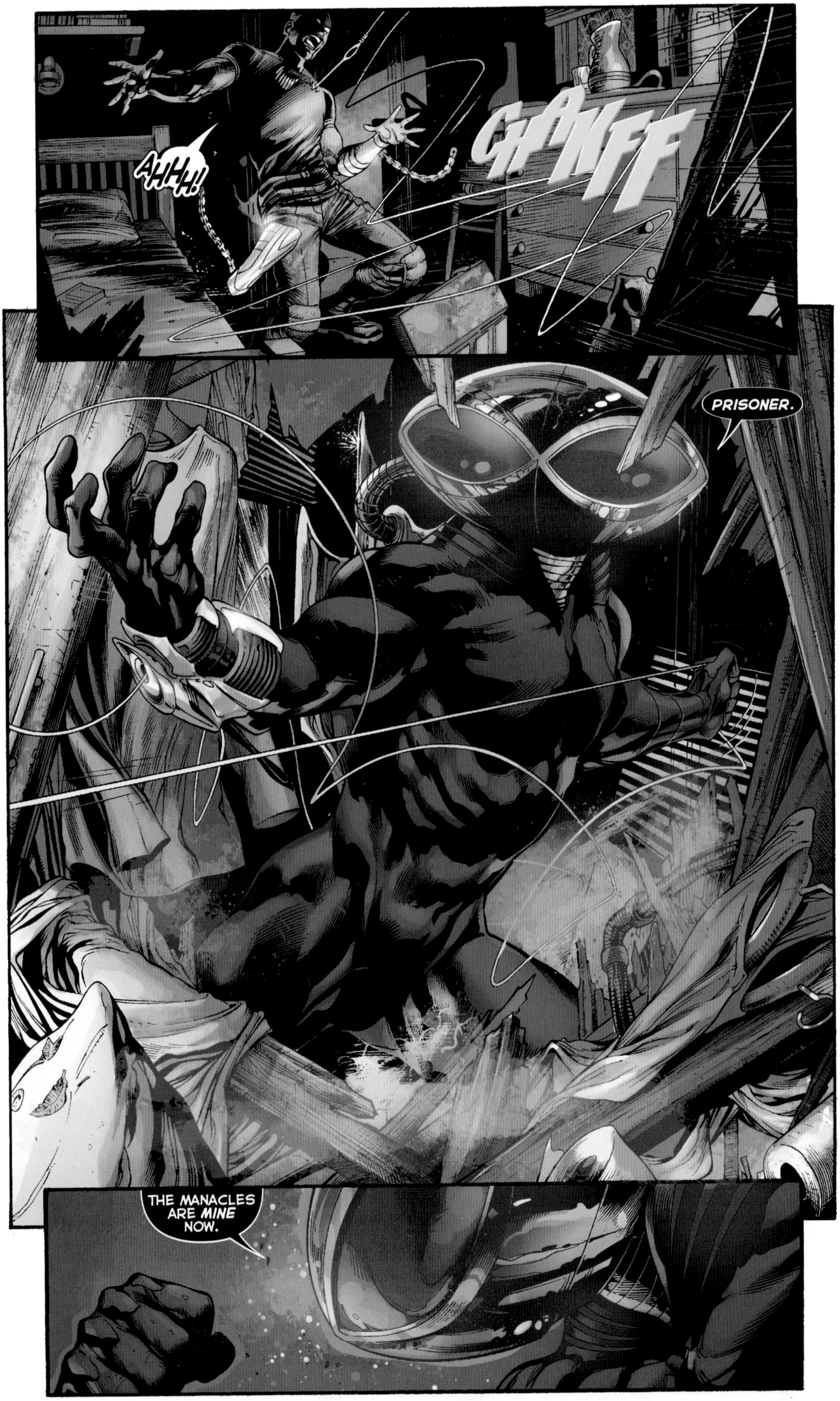
AHHH!
CHANKFF
PRISONER.
THE MANACLES ARE MINE NOW.

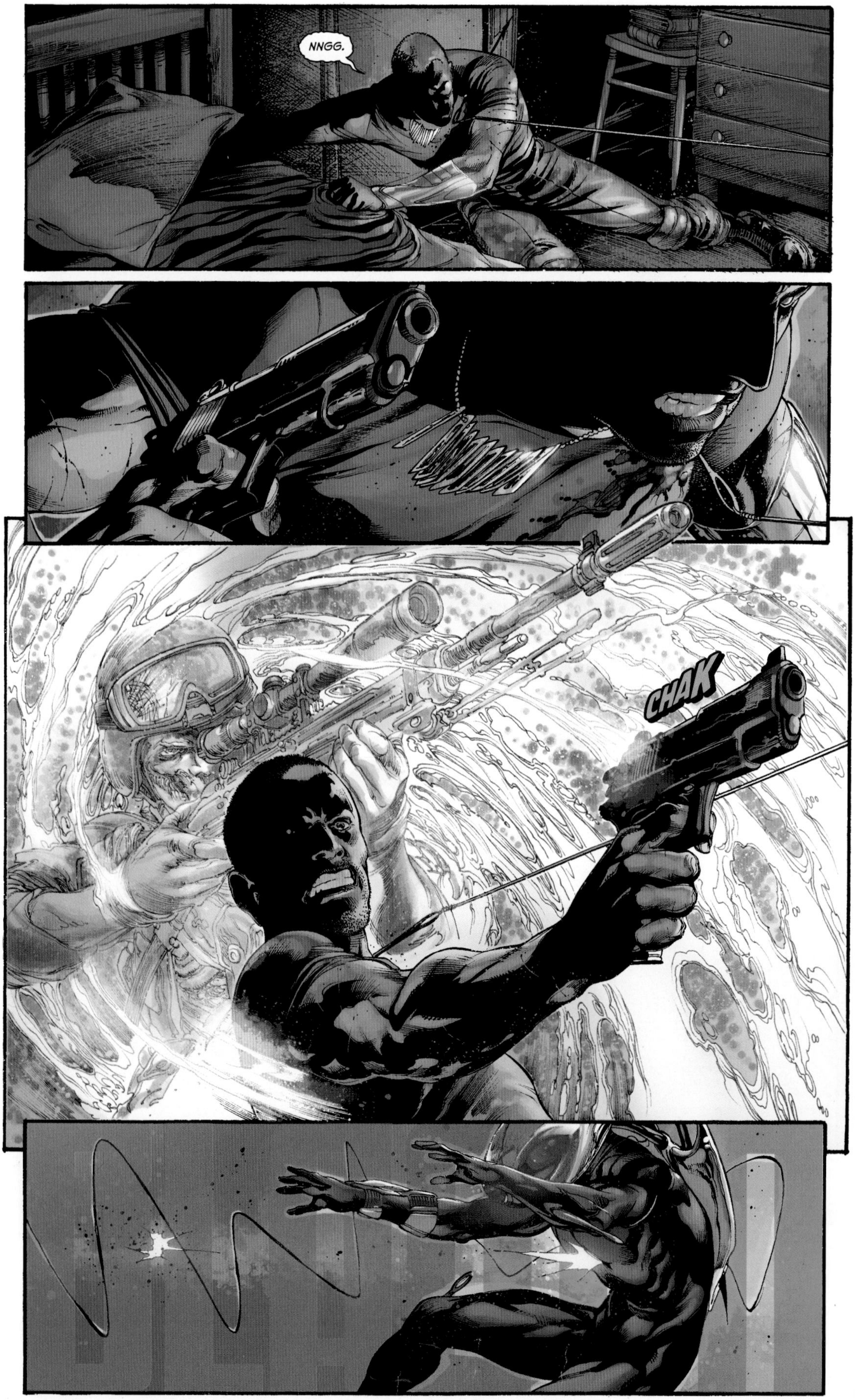
NNGG.
CHAK

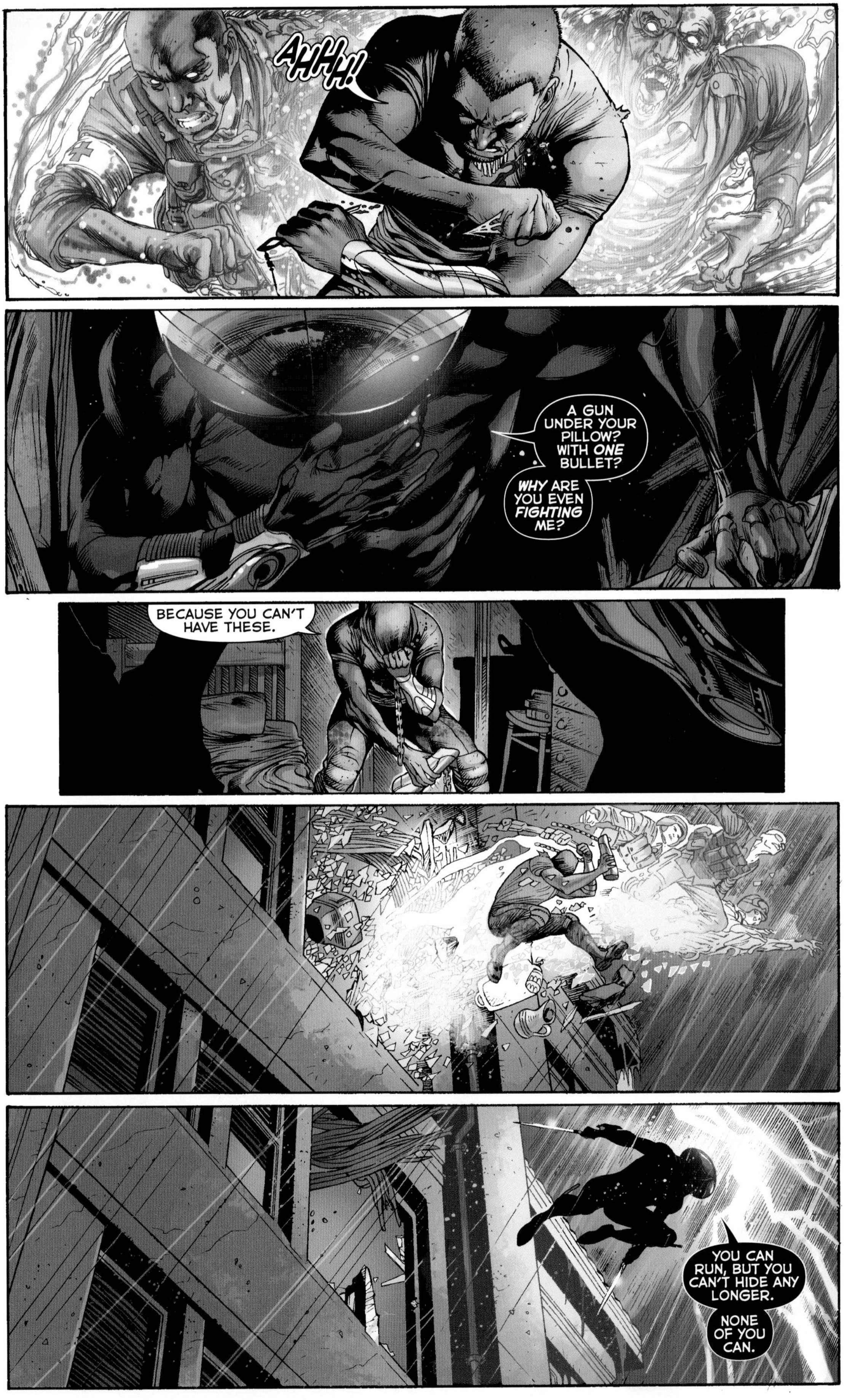
AHHH!
A GUN UNDER YOUR PILLOW? WITH ONE BULLET?
WHY ARE YOU EVEN FIGHTING ME?
BECAUSE YOU CAN'T HAVE THESE.
YOU CAN RUN, BUT YOU CAN'T HIDE ANY LONGER.
NONE OF YOU CAN.

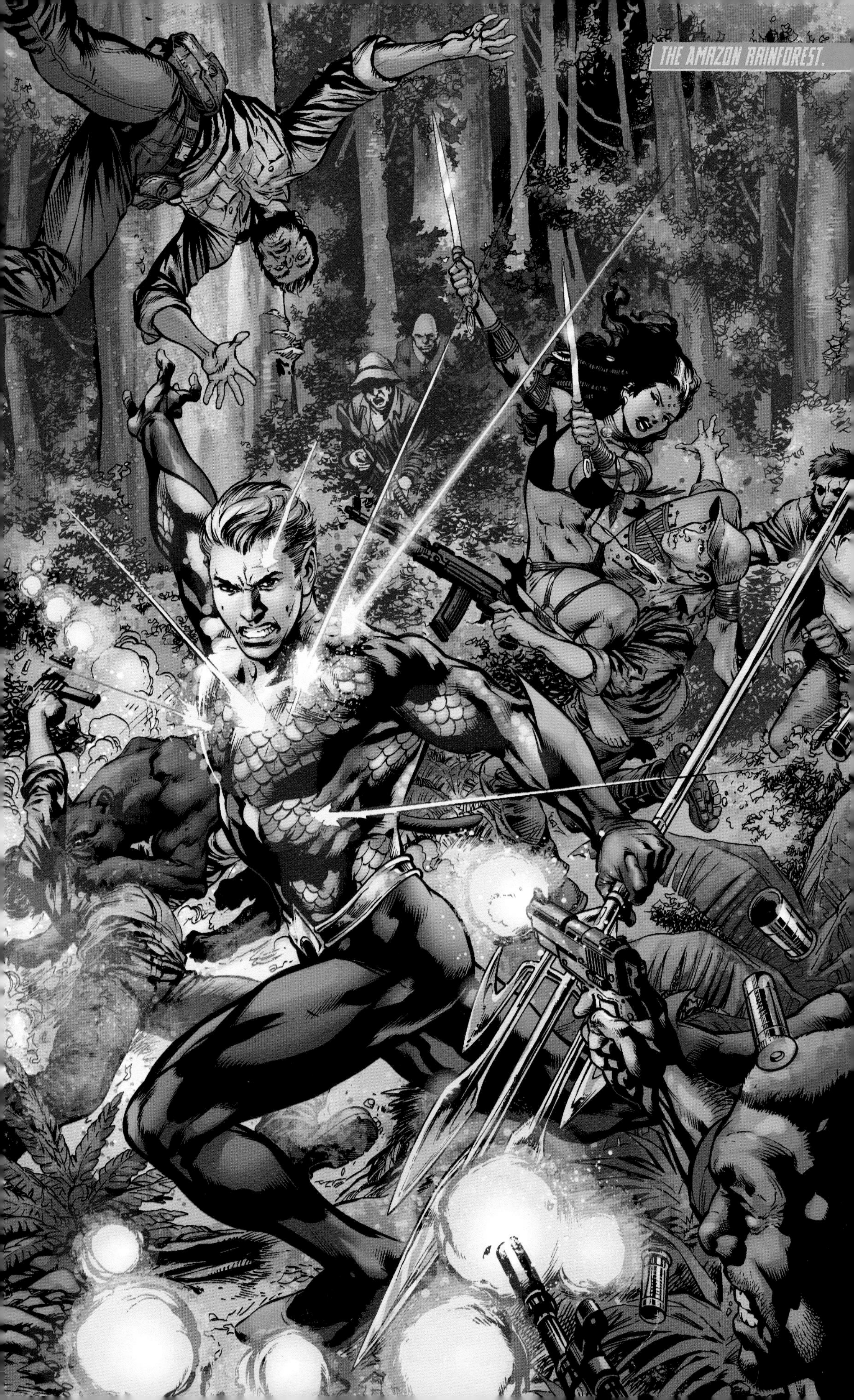
THE AMAZON RAINFOREST.

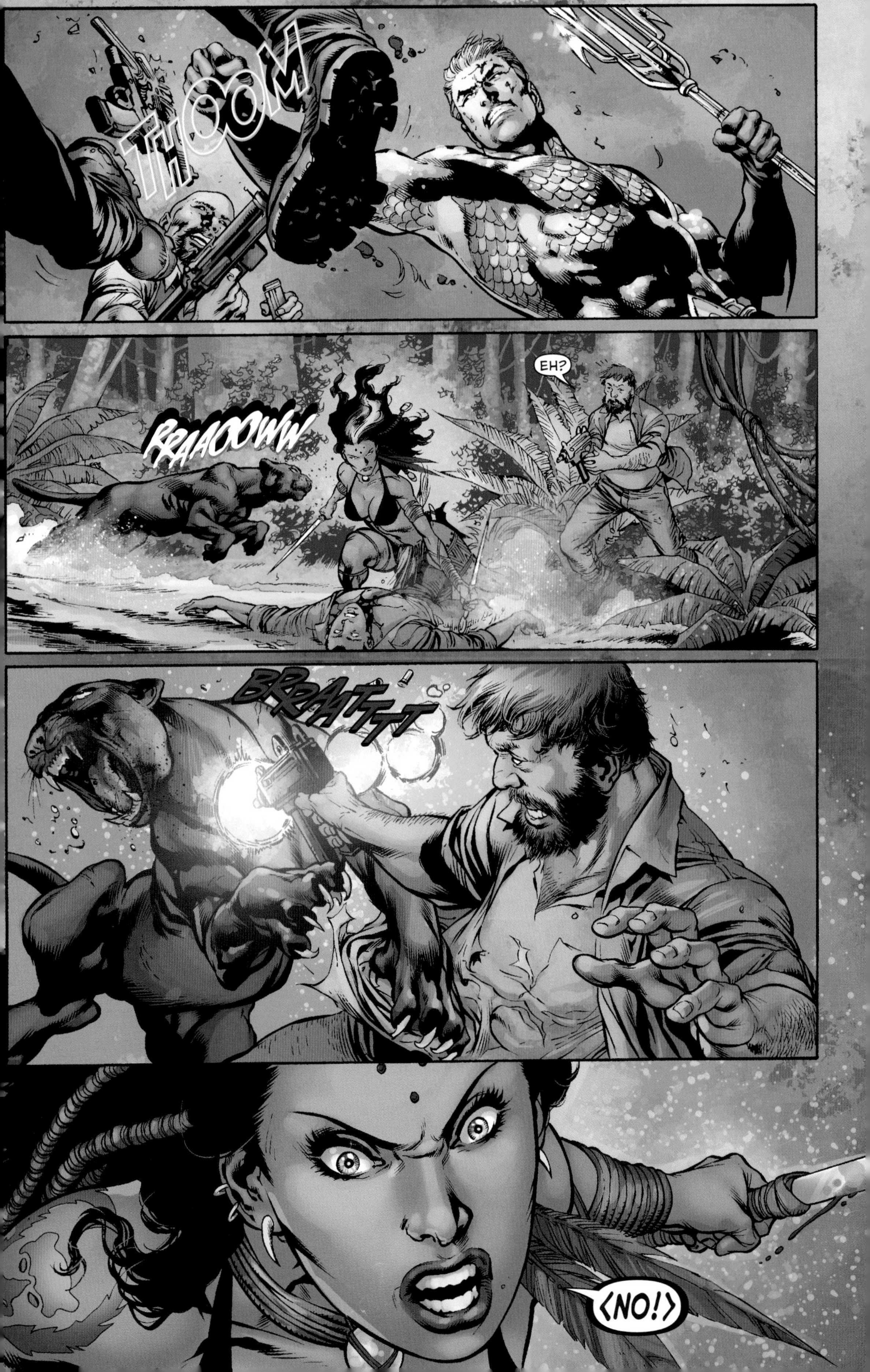
THOOM
EH?
BRAAOOWW
BRRAATTTT
⟨NO!⟩

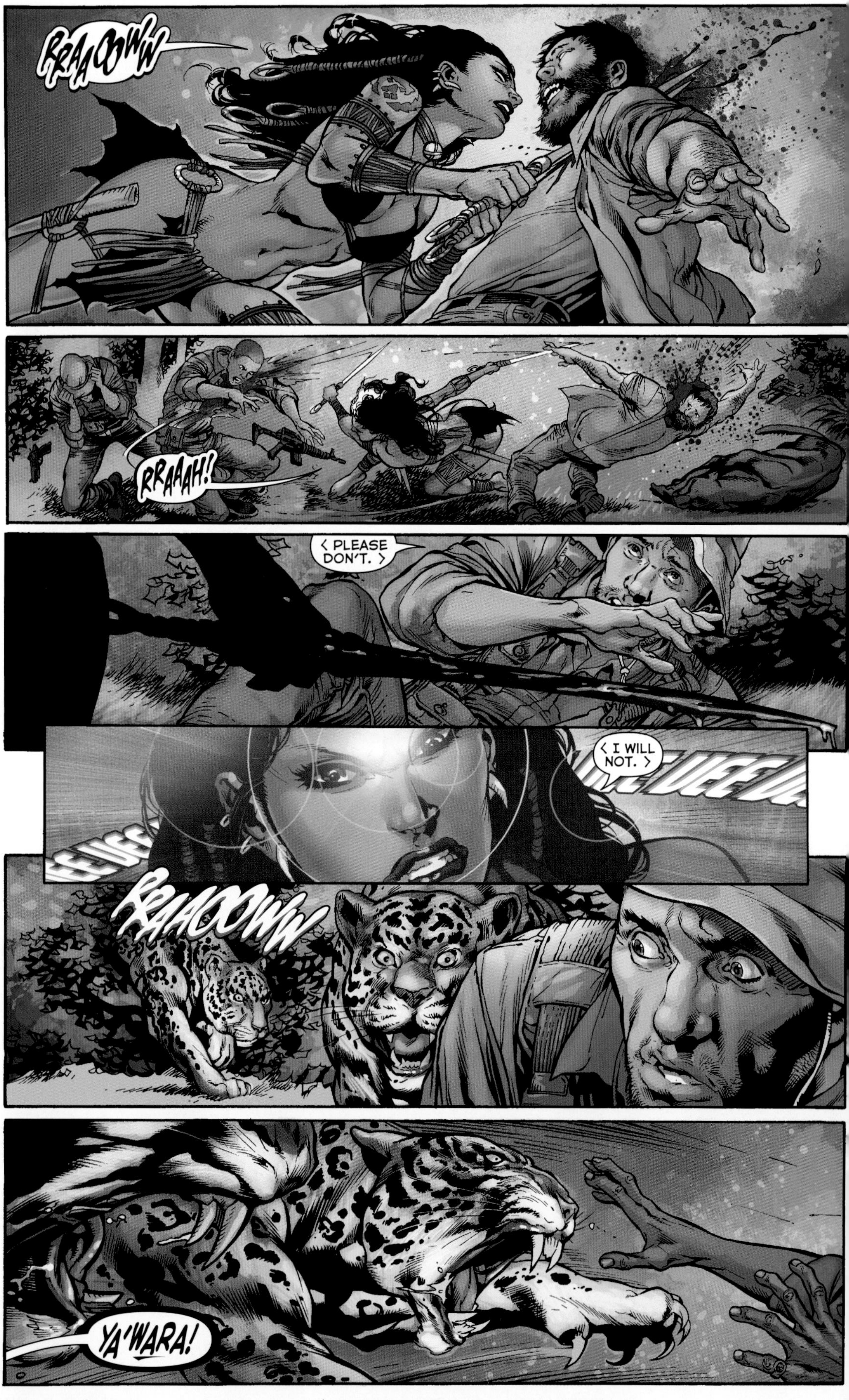
RRAAOOWW
RRAAAH!
< PLEASE DON'T. >
< I WILL NOT. >
RRAAOOWW
YA'WARA!

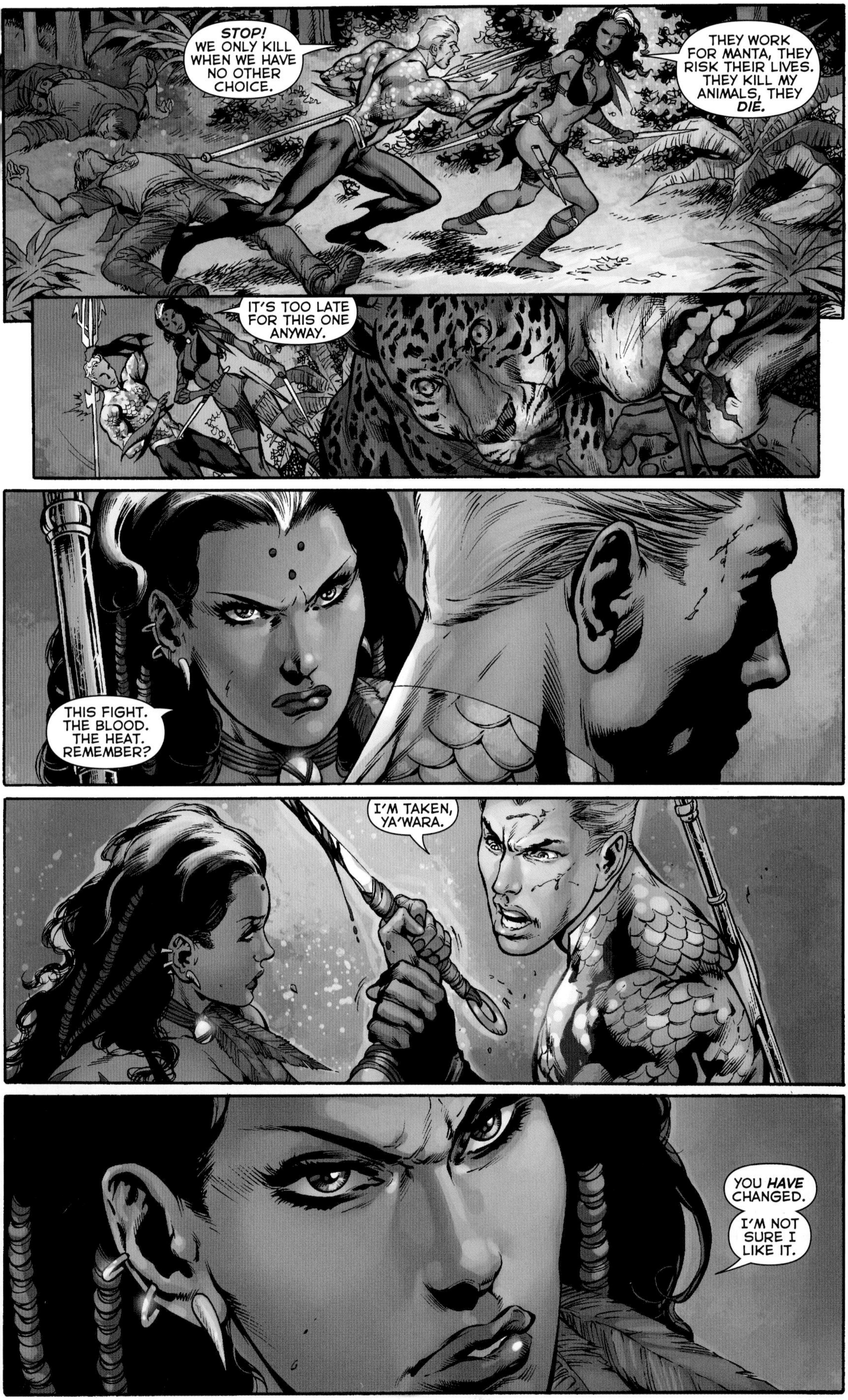
STOP! WE ONLY KILL WHEN WE HAVE NO OTHER CHOICE.
THEY WORK FOR MANTA, THEY RISK THEIR LIVES. THEY KILL MY ANIMALS, THEY DIE.
IT'S TOO LATE FOR THIS ONE ANYWAY.
THIS FIGHT. THE BLOOD. THE HEAT. REMEMBER?
I'M TAKEN, YA'WARA.
YOU HAVE CHANGED.
I'M NOT SURE I LIKE IT.

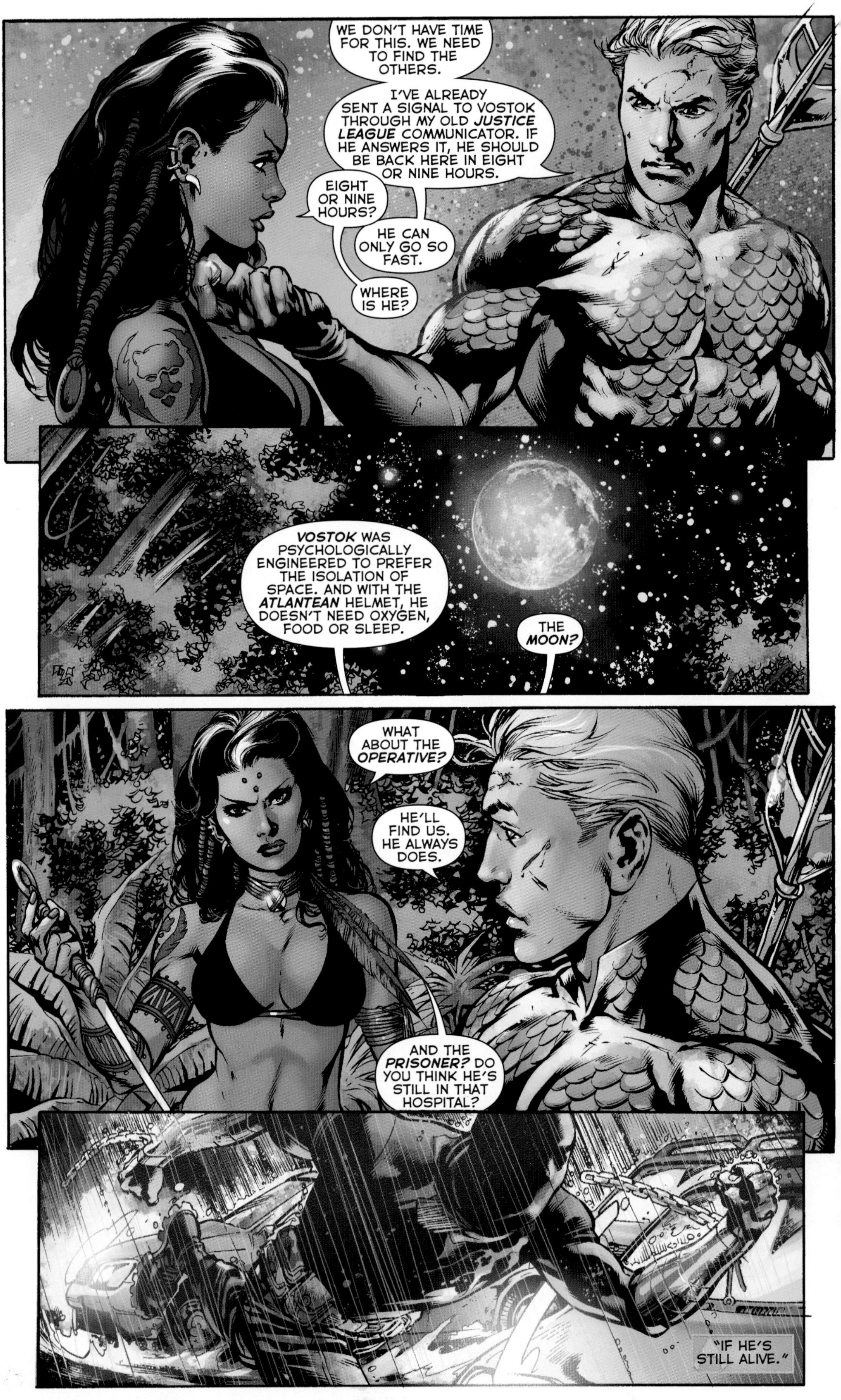

WE DON'T HAVE TIME FOR THIS. WE NEED TO FIND THE OTHERS.
I'VE ALREADY SENT A SIGNAL TO VOSTOK THROUGH MY OLD *JUSTICE LEAGUE* COMMUNICATOR. IF HE ANSWERS IT, HE SHOULD BE BACK HERE IN EIGHT OR NINE HOURS.
EIGHT OR NINE HOURS?
HE CAN ONLY GO SO FAST.
WHERE IS HE?
VOSTOK WAS PSYCHOLOGICALLY ENGINEERED TO PREFER THE ISOLATION OF SPACE. AND WITH THE *ATLANTEAN* HELMET, HE DOESN'T NEED OXYGEN, FOOD OR SLEEP.
THE *MOON?*
WHAT ABOUT THE *OPERATIVE?*
HE'LL FIND US. HE ALWAYS DOES.
AND THE *PRISONER?* DO YOU THINK HE'S STILL IN THAT HOSPITAL?
"IF HE'S STILL ALIVE."

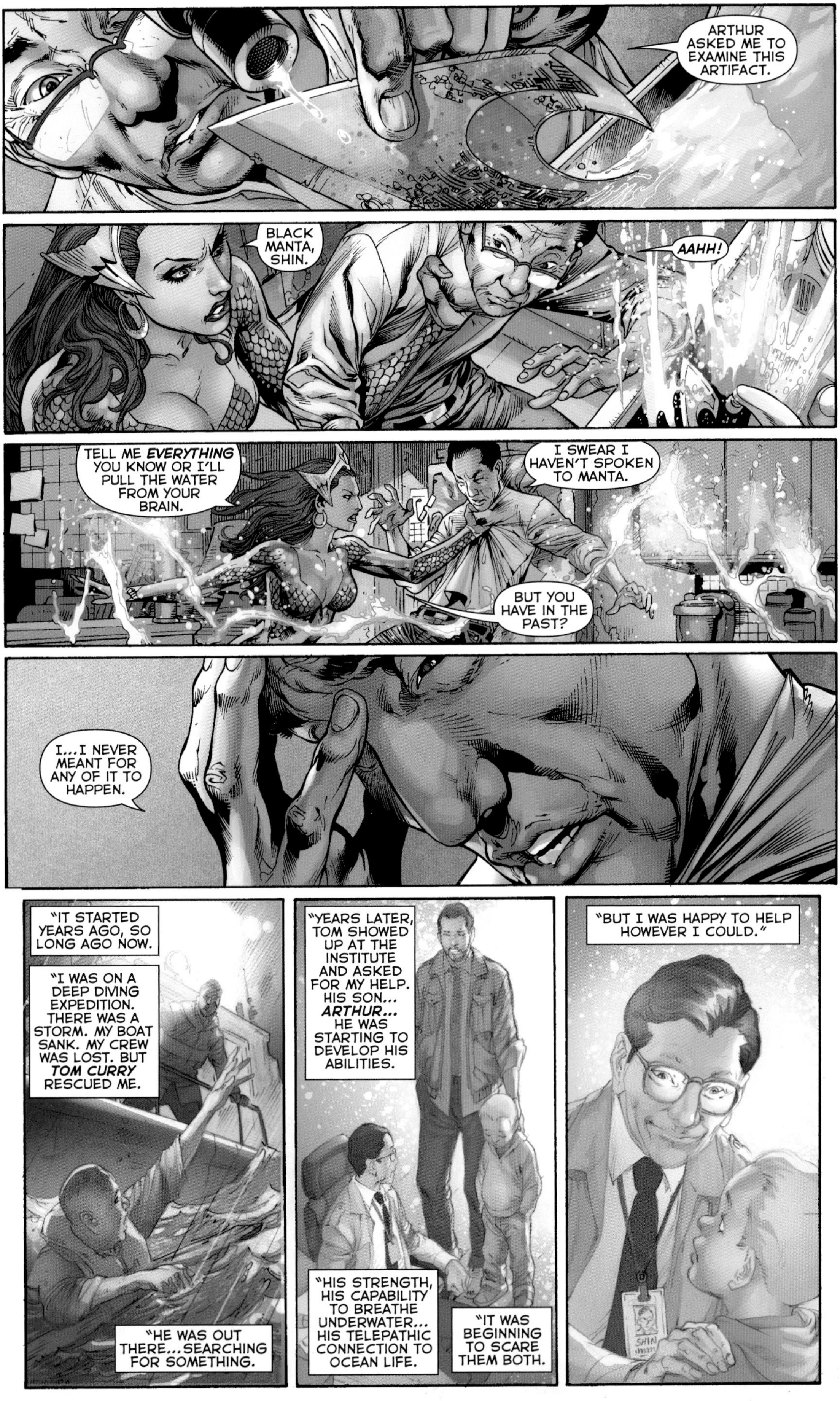
ARTHUR ASKED ME TO EXAMINE THIS ARTIFACT.
BLACK MANTA, SHIN.
AAHH!
TELL ME EVERYTHING YOU KNOW OR I'LL PULL THE WATER FROM YOUR BRAIN.
I SWEAR I HAVEN'T SPOKEN TO MANTA.
BUT YOU HAVE IN THE PAST?
I...I NEVER MEANT FOR ANY OF IT TO HAPPEN.
"IT STARTED YEARS AGO, SO LONG AGO NOW.
"I WAS ON A DEEP DIVING EXPEDITION. THERE WAS A STORM. MY BOAT SANK. MY CREW WAS LOST. BUT TOM CURRY RESCUED ME.
"HE WAS OUT THERE...SEARCHING FOR SOMETHING.
"YEARS LATER, TOM SHOWED UP AT THE INSTITUTE AND ASKED FOR MY HELP. HIS SON... ARTHUR... HE WAS STARTING TO DEVELOP HIS ABILITIES.
"HIS STRENGTH, HIS CAPABILITY TO BREATHE UNDERWATER... HIS TELEPATHIC CONNECTION TO OCEAN LIFE.
"IT WAS BEGINNING TO SCARE THEM BOTH.
"BUT I WAS HAPPY TO HELP HOWEVER I COULD."

AND YOU TAUGHT ARTHUR HOW TO CONTROL HIS ABILITIES?

"I TAUGHT HIM HOW TO LOVE THEM. HIS POWERS ARE A MIRACULOUS *GIFT*.

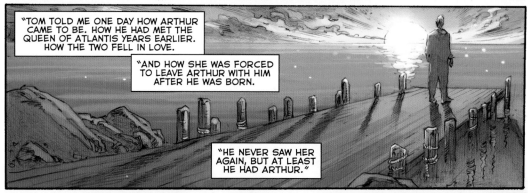

"TOM TOLD ME ONE DAY HOW ARTHUR CAME TO BE. HOW HE HAD MET THE QUEEN OF ATLANTIS YEARS EARLIER. HOW THE TWO FELL IN LOVE.

"AND HOW SHE WAS FORCED TO LEAVE ARTHUR WITH HIM AFTER HE WAS BORN.

"HE NEVER SAW HER AGAIN, BUT AT LEAST HE HAD ARTHUR."

AND THAT BOY WOULD BE THE MOST SIGNIFICANT SCIENTIFIC DISCOVERY OF OUR ERA.

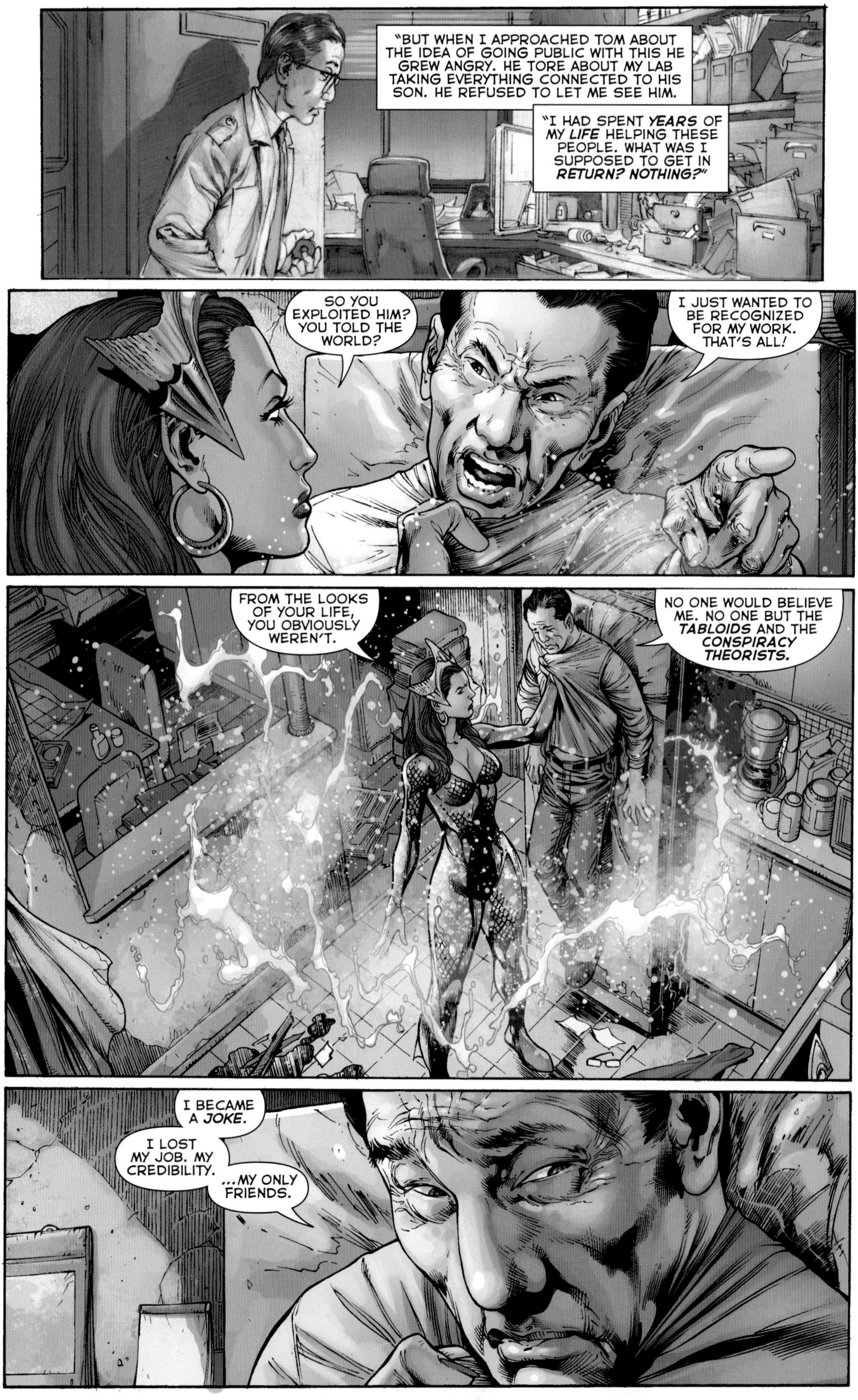
"BUT WHEN I APPROACHED TOM ABOUT THE IDEA OF GOING PUBLIC WITH THIS HE GREW ANGRY. HE TORE ABOUT MY LAB TAKING EVERYTHING CONNECTED TO HIS SON. HE REFUSED TO LET ME SEE HIM.
"I HAD SPENT YEARS OF MY LIFE HELPING THESE PEOPLE. WHAT WAS I SUPPOSED TO GET IN RETURN? NOTHING?"
SO YOU EXPLOITED HIM? YOU TOLD THE WORLD?
I JUST WANTED TO BE RECOGNIZED FOR MY WORK. THAT'S ALL!
FROM THE LOOKS OF YOUR LIFE, YOU OBVIOUSLY WEREN'T.
NO ONE WOULD BELIEVE ME. NO ONE BUT THE TABLOIDS AND THE CONSPIRACY THEORISTS.
I BECAME A JOKE.
I LOST MY JOB. MY CREDIBILITY.
...MY ONLY FRIENDS.

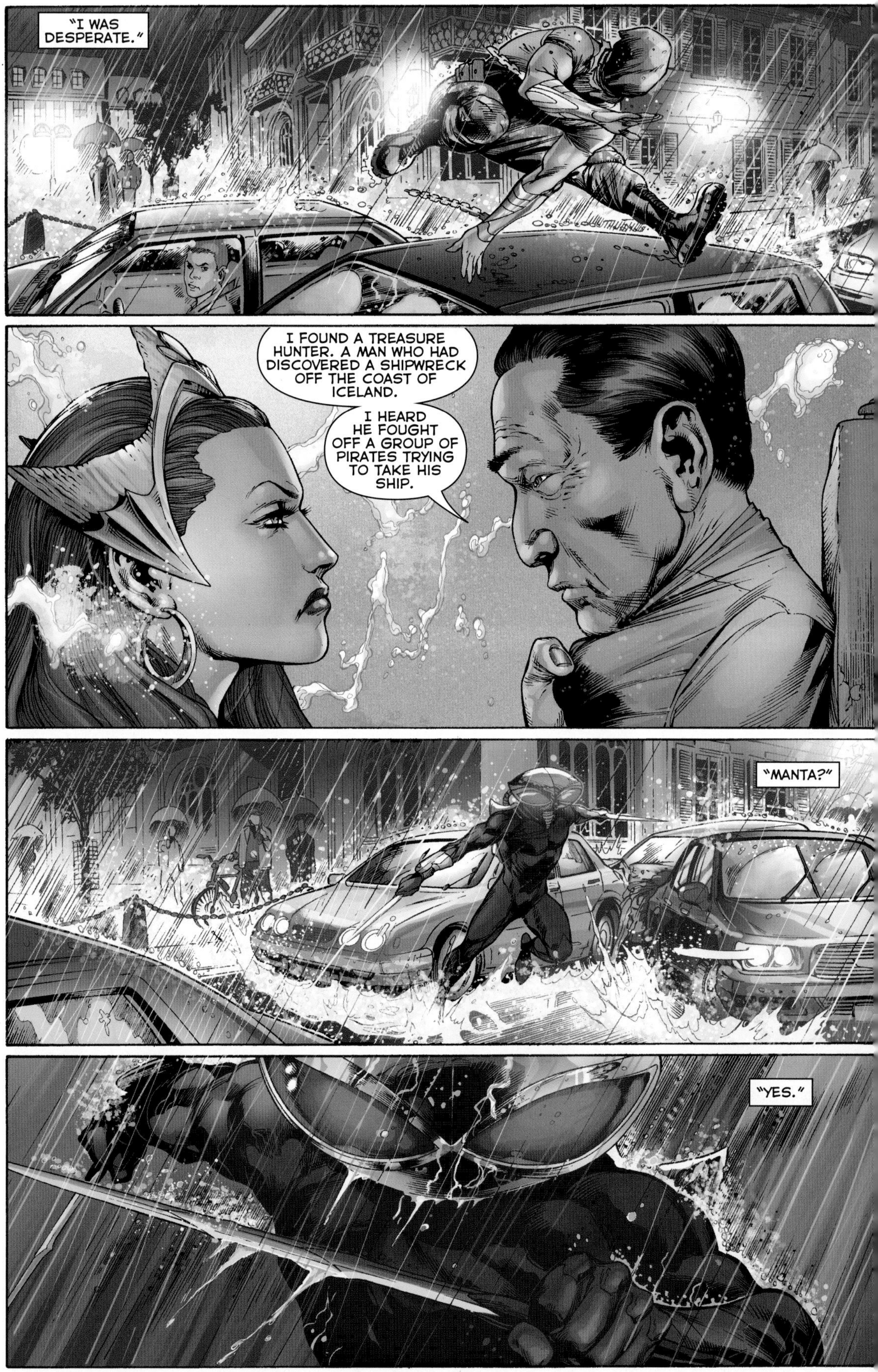
"I WAS DESPERATE."
I FOUND A TREASURE HUNTER. A MAN WHO HAD DISCOVERED A SHIPWRECK OFF THE COAST OF ICELAND.
I HEARD HE FOUGHT OFF A GROUP OF PIRATES TRYING TO TAKE HIS SHIP.
"MANTA?"
"YES."

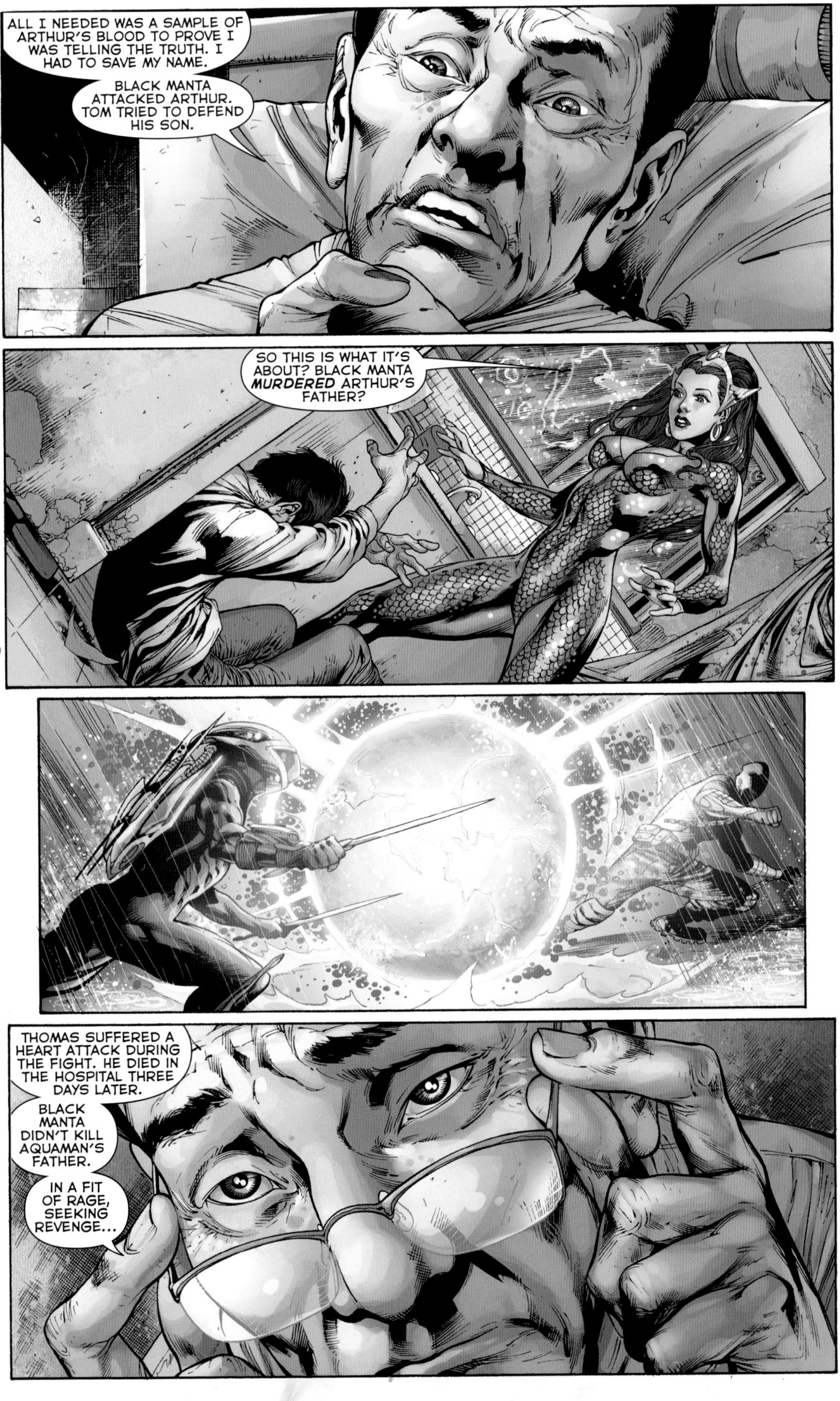
ALL I NEEDED WAS A SAMPLE OF ARTHUR'S BLOOD TO PROVE I WAS TELLING THE TRUTH. I HAD TO SAVE MY NAME.
BLACK MANTA ATTACKED ARTHUR. TOM TRIED TO DEFEND HIS SON.
SO THIS IS WHAT IT'S ABOUT? BLACK MANTA MURDERED ARTHUR'S FATHER?
THOMAS SUFFERED A HEART ATTACK DURING THE FIGHT. HE DIED IN THE HOSPITAL THREE DAYS LATER.
BLACK MANTA DIDN'T KILL AQUAMAN'S FATHER.
IN A FIT OF RAGE, SEEKING REVENGE...

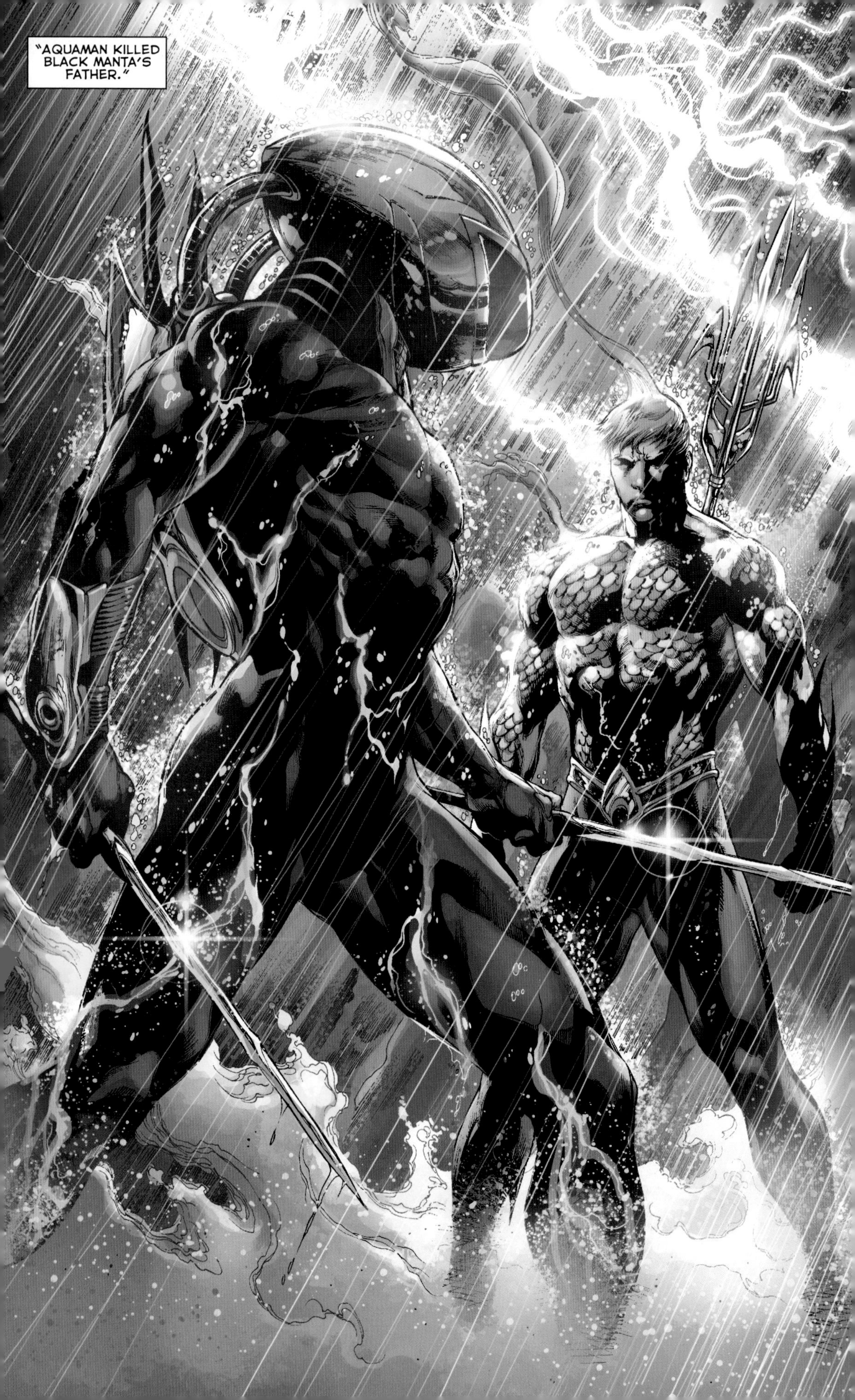
"AQUAMAN KILLED BLACK MANTA'S FATHER."

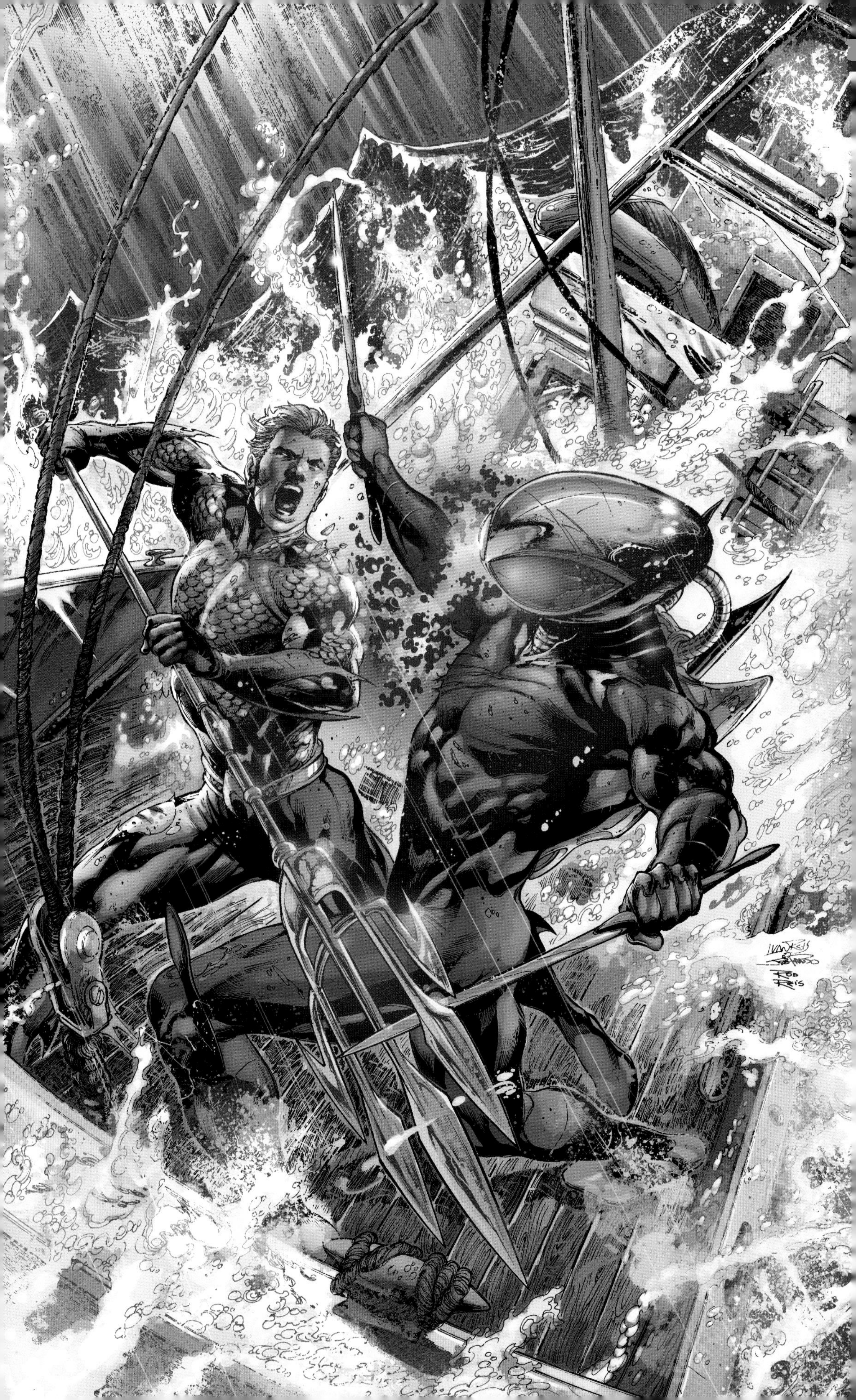
IVAN REIS
ROD REIS

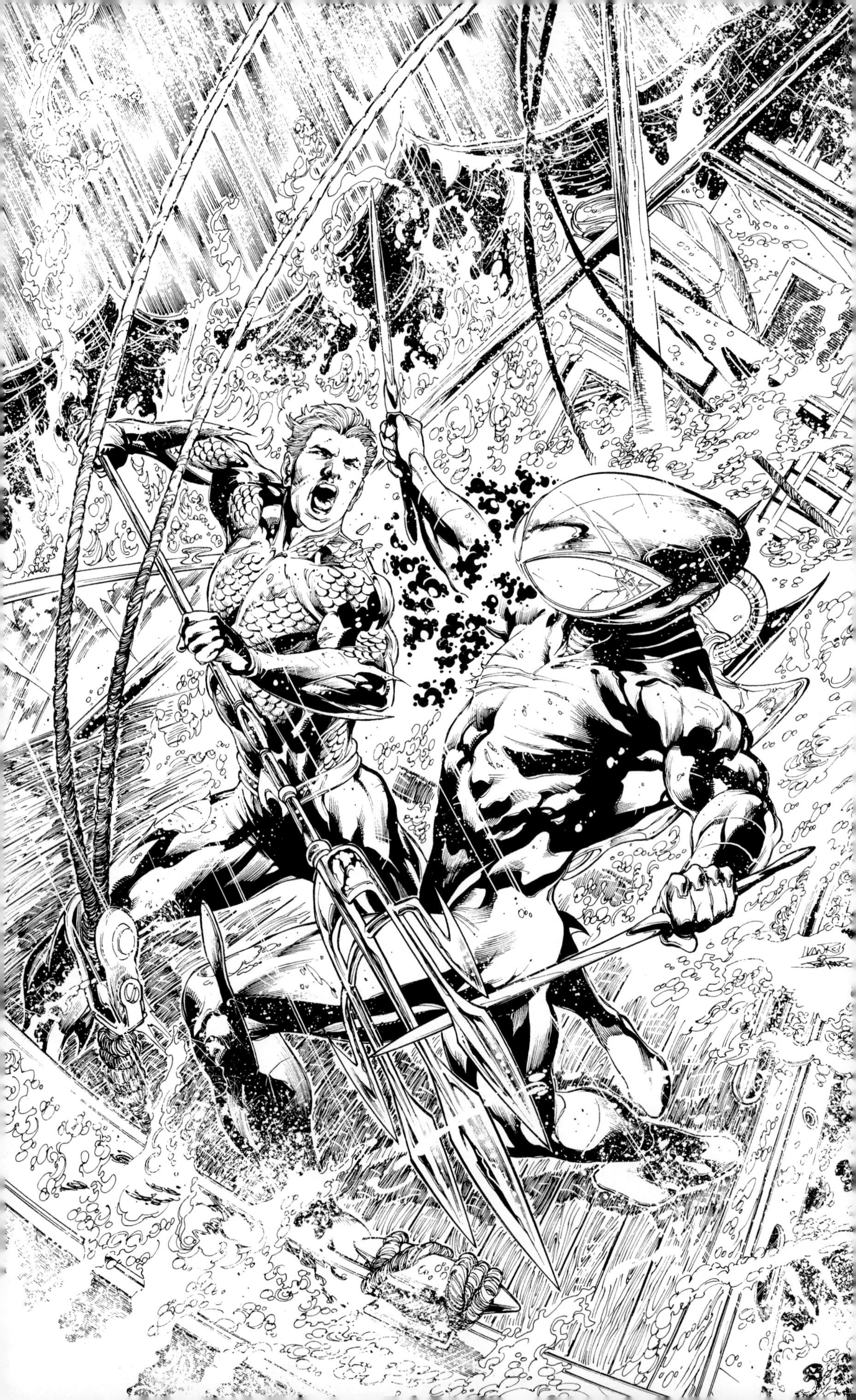

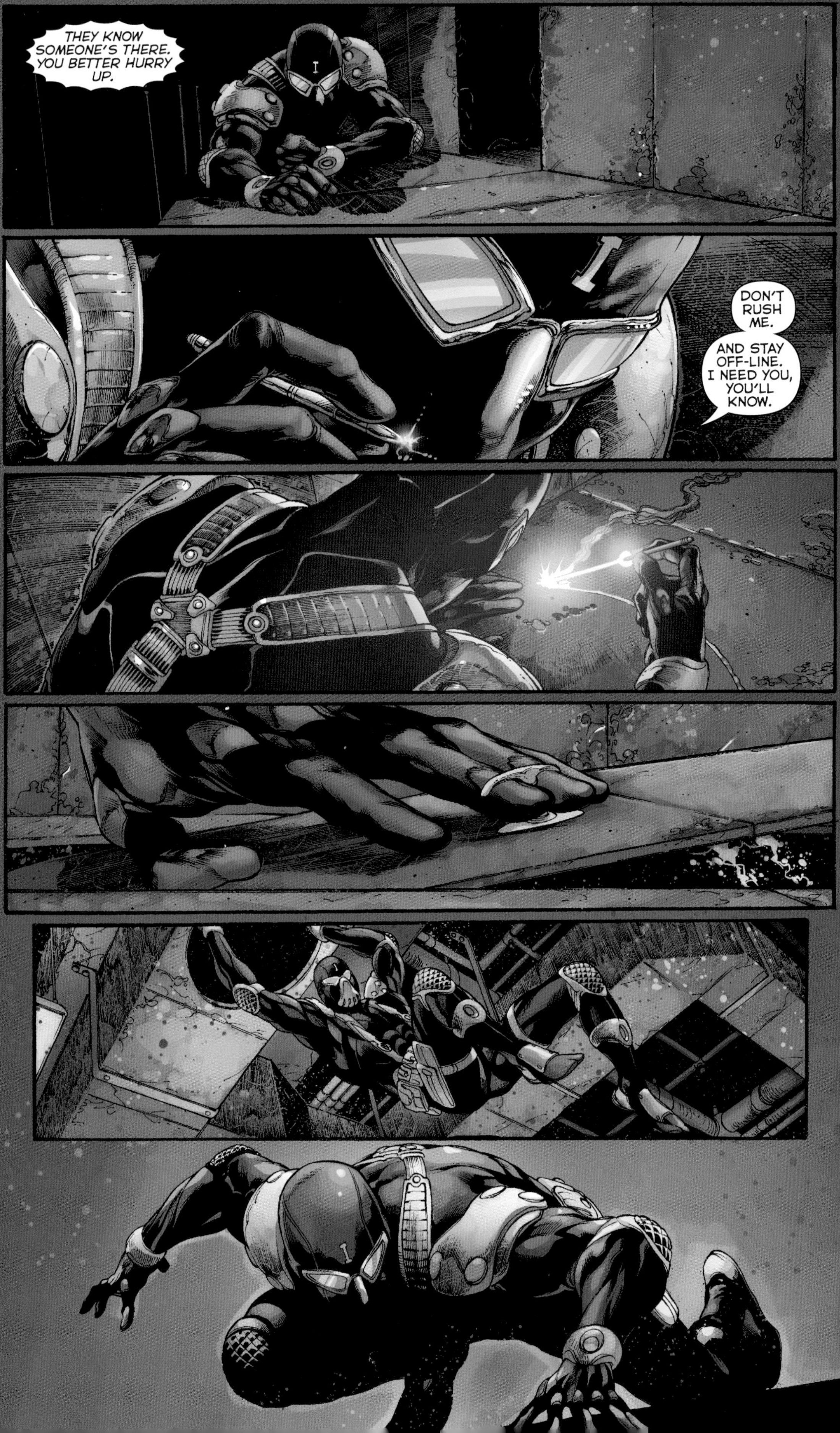
THEY KNOW SOMEONE'S THERE. YOU BETTER HURRY UP.
DON'T RUSH ME.
AND STAY OFF-LINE. I NEED YOU, YOU'LL KNOW.

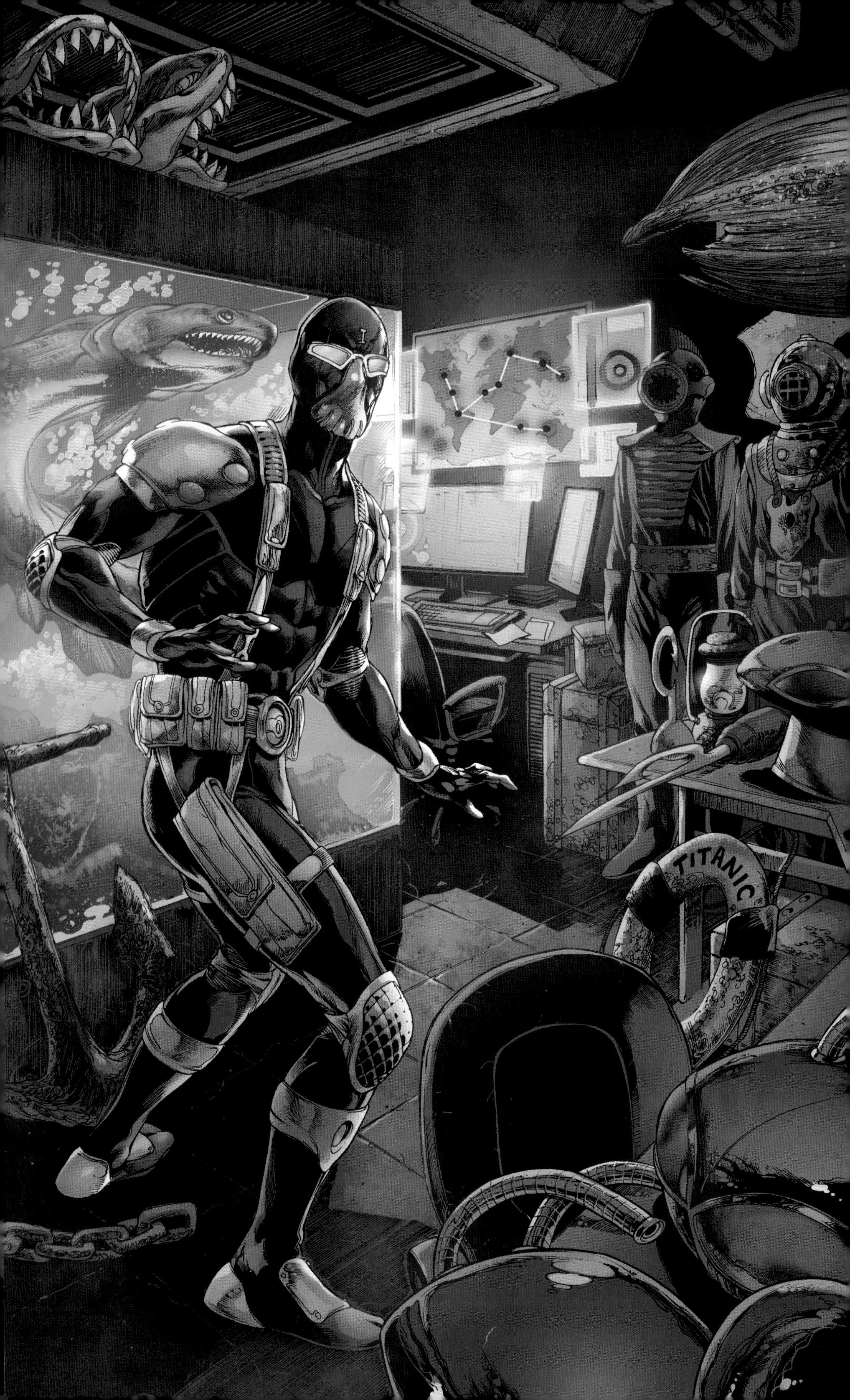
TITANIC

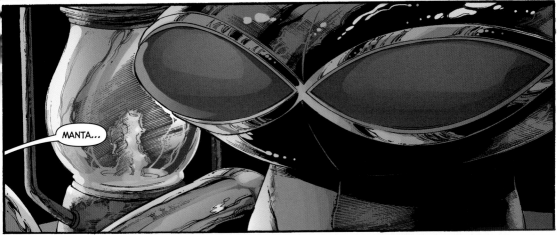

MANTA...

HOW DID YOU FIND US?

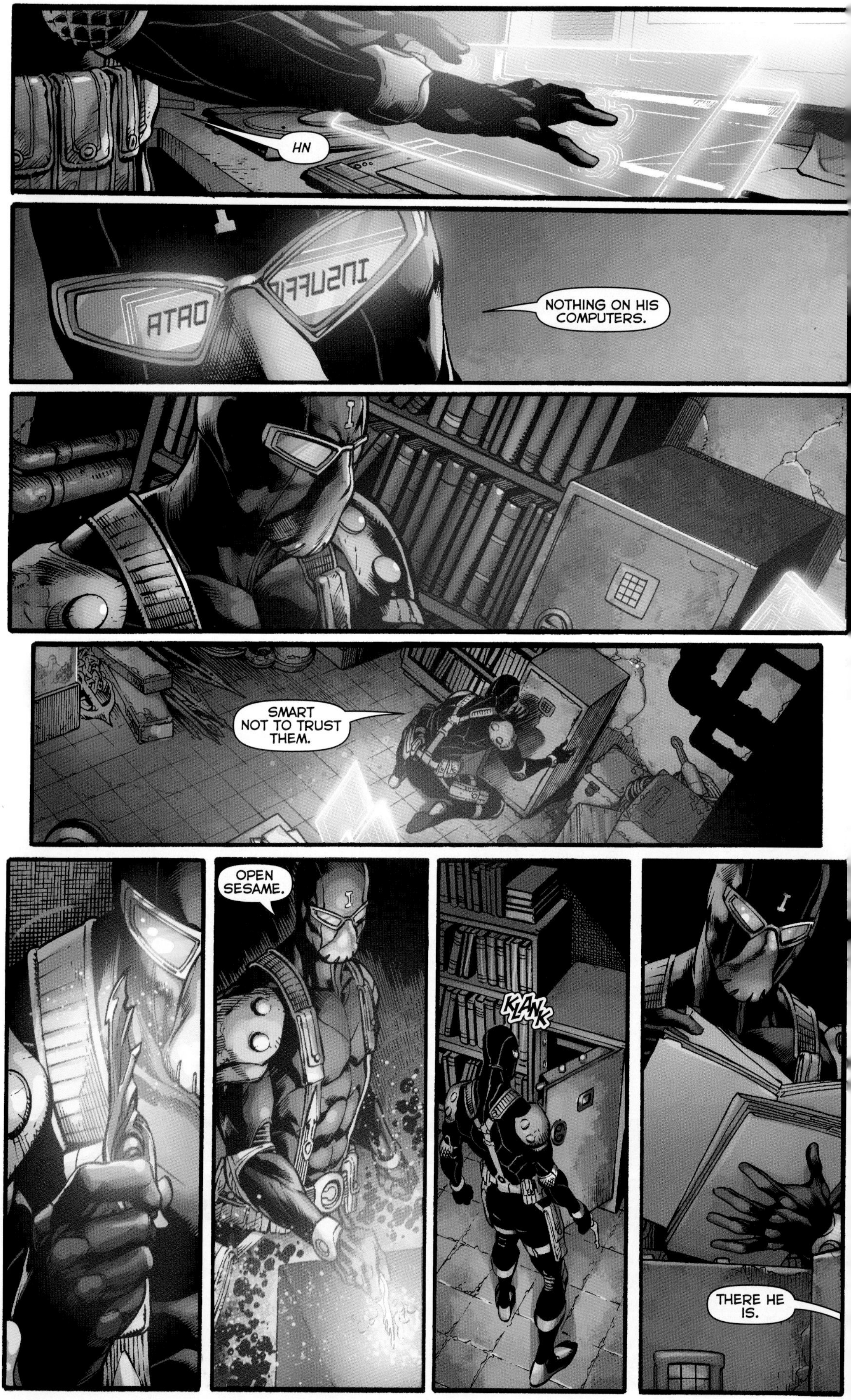
HN
NOTHING ON HIS COMPUTERS.
SMART NOT TO TRUST THEM.
OPEN SESAME.
KLANK
THERE HE IS.

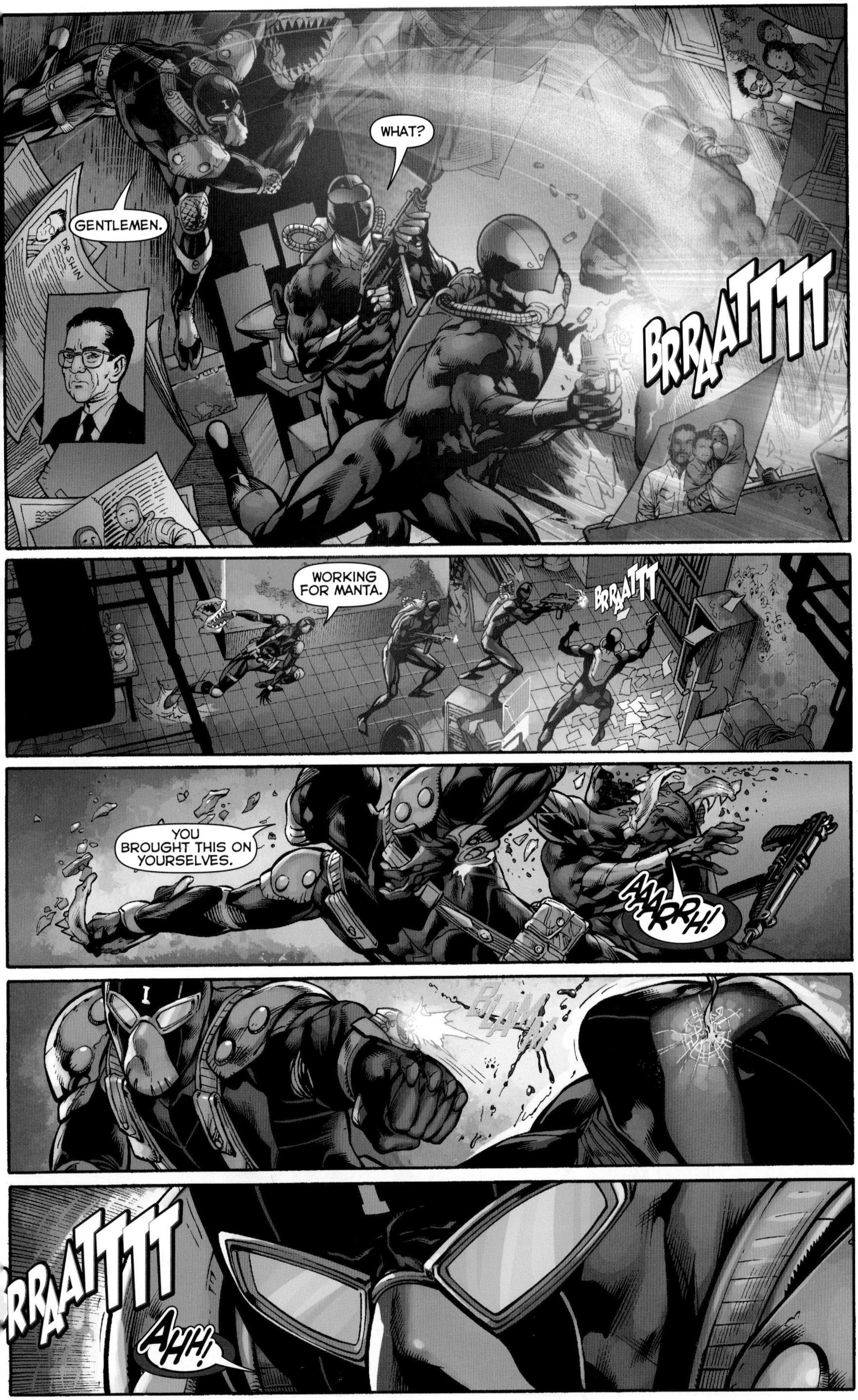
GENTLEMEN.
WHAT?
DR. SHIN
BRRAATTTT
WORKING FOR MANTA.
BRRAATTT
YOU BROUGHT THIS ON YOURSELVES.
AAARRH!
BLAM BLAM
RRAATTTT
AHH!

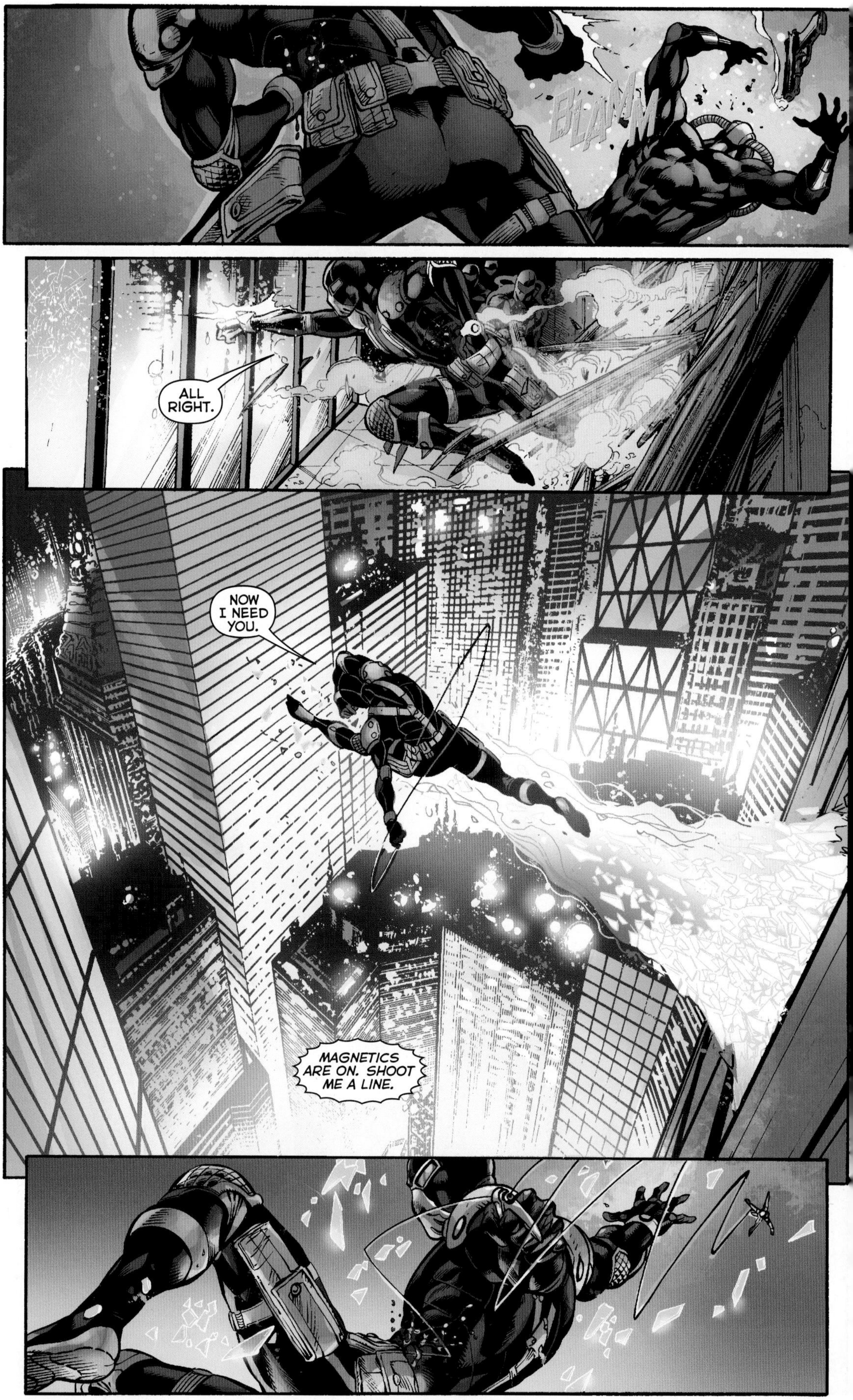
BLAMM
ALL RIGHT.
NOW I NEED YOU.
MAGNETICS ARE ON. SHOOT ME A LINE.

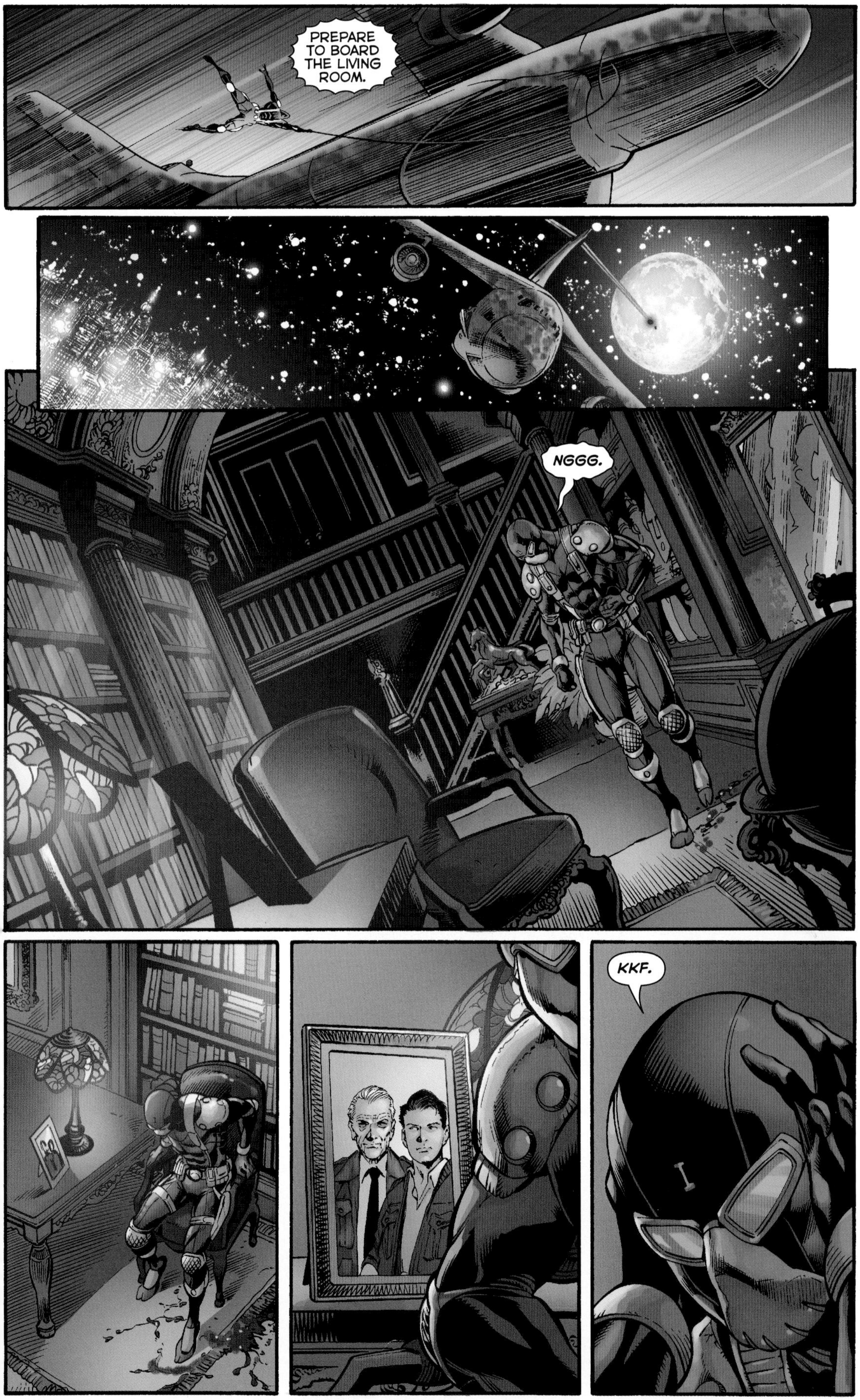
PREPARE TO BOARD THE LIVING ROOM.
NGGG.
KKF.

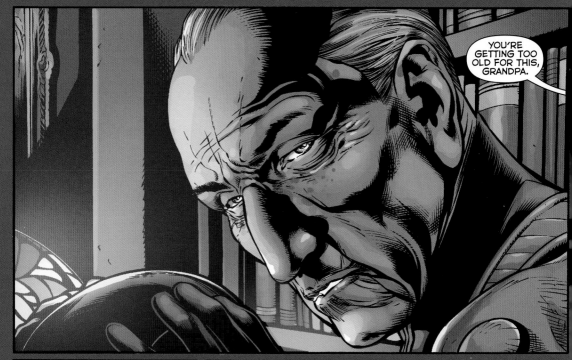

YOU'RE GETTING TOO OLD FOR THIS, GRANDPA.

THAT SUIT ISN'T GOING TO KEEP YOU MOVING FOREVER.

GET BACK TO THE COCKPIT, AARON.

AUTOPILOT'S ON. THE PLANE'S OKAY FOR THE MOMENT.

SO AM I.

WHEN IS THE *OPERATIVE* GOING TO RETIRE? WHEN ARE YOU GOING TO *QUIT* TRYING TO SAVE THE WORLD?

WHEN I THINK SOMEONE ELSE CAN DO IT.

NOW LOCK IN THE BOOKCASES AND SET THE LIVING ROOM FOR HYPERSONIC SPEED.

"WE NEED TO GET TO AQUAMAN."

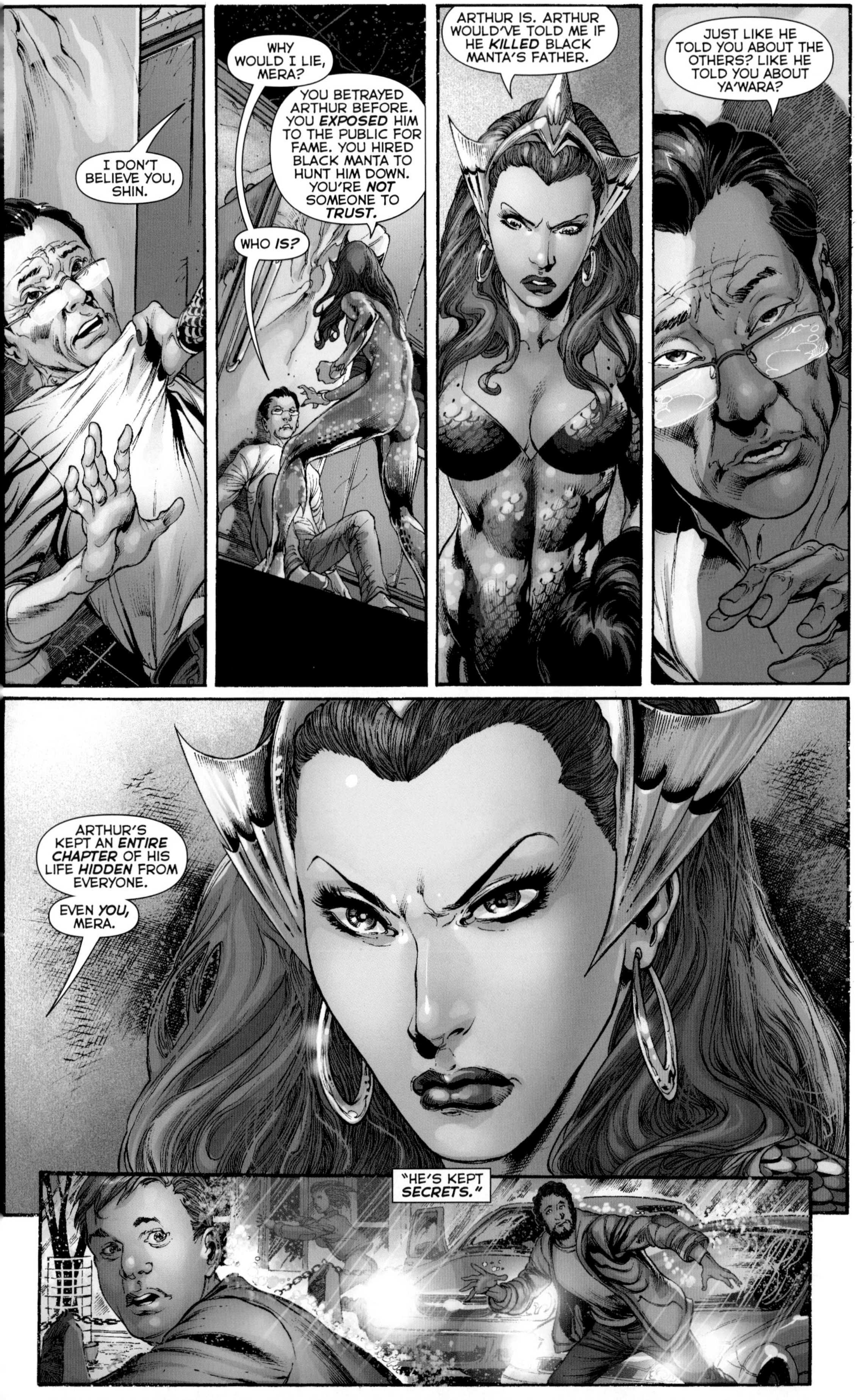
I DON'T BELIEVE YOU, SHIN.
WHY WOULD I LIE, MERA?
YOU BETRAYED ARTHUR BEFORE. YOU EXPOSED HIM TO THE PUBLIC FOR FAME. YOU HIRED BLACK MANTA TO HUNT HIM DOWN. YOU'RE NOT SOMEONE TO TRUST.
WHO IS?
ARTHUR IS. ARTHUR WOULD'VE TOLD ME IF HE KILLED BLACK MANTA'S FATHER.
JUST LIKE HE TOLD YOU ABOUT THE OTHERS? LIKE HE TOLD YOU ABOUT YA'WARA?
ARTHUR'S KEPT AN ENTIRE CHAPTER OF HIS LIFE HIDDEN FROM EVERYONE.
EVEN YOU, MERA.
"HE'S KEPT SECRETS."

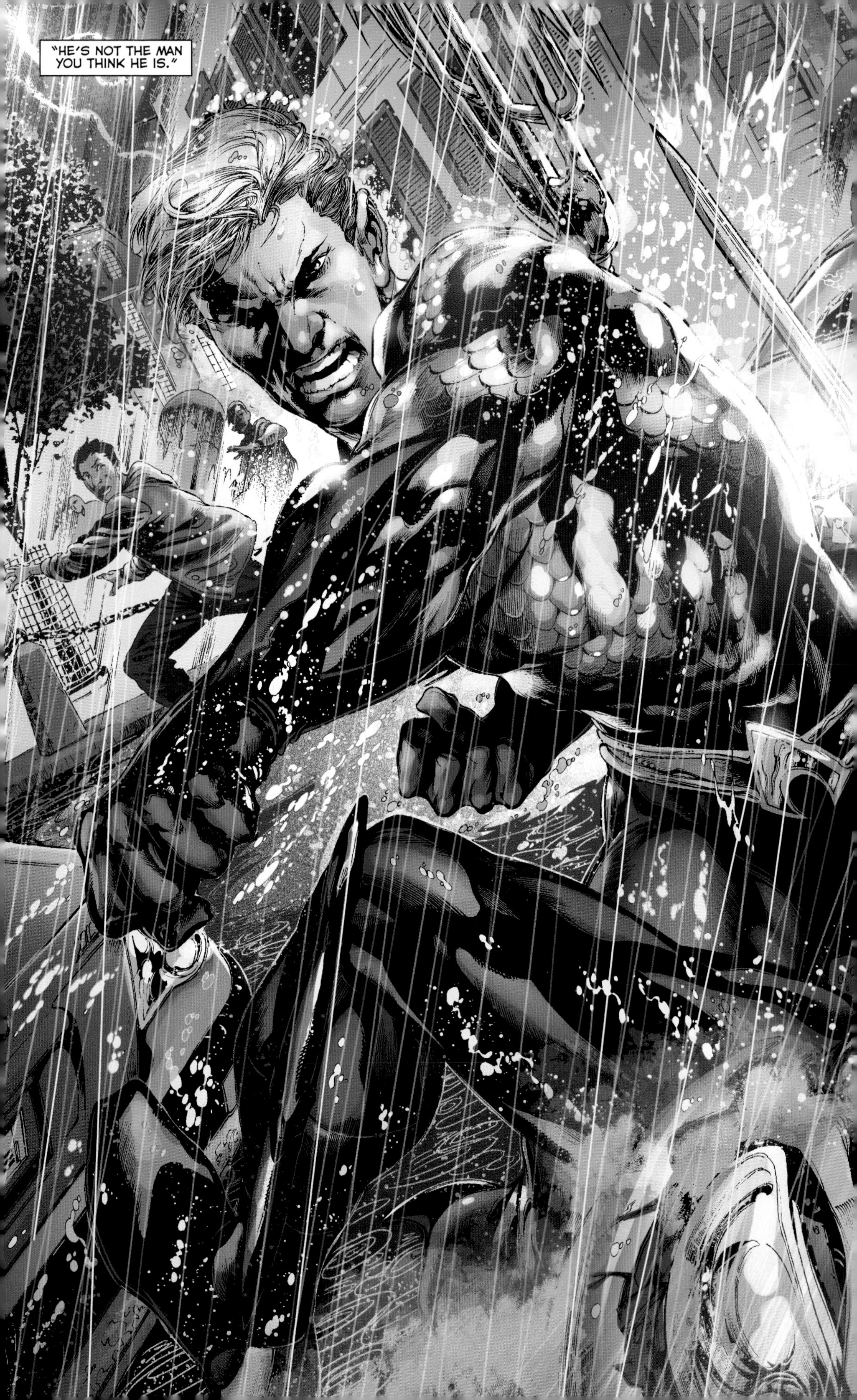
"HE'S NOT THE MAN YOU THINK HE IS."

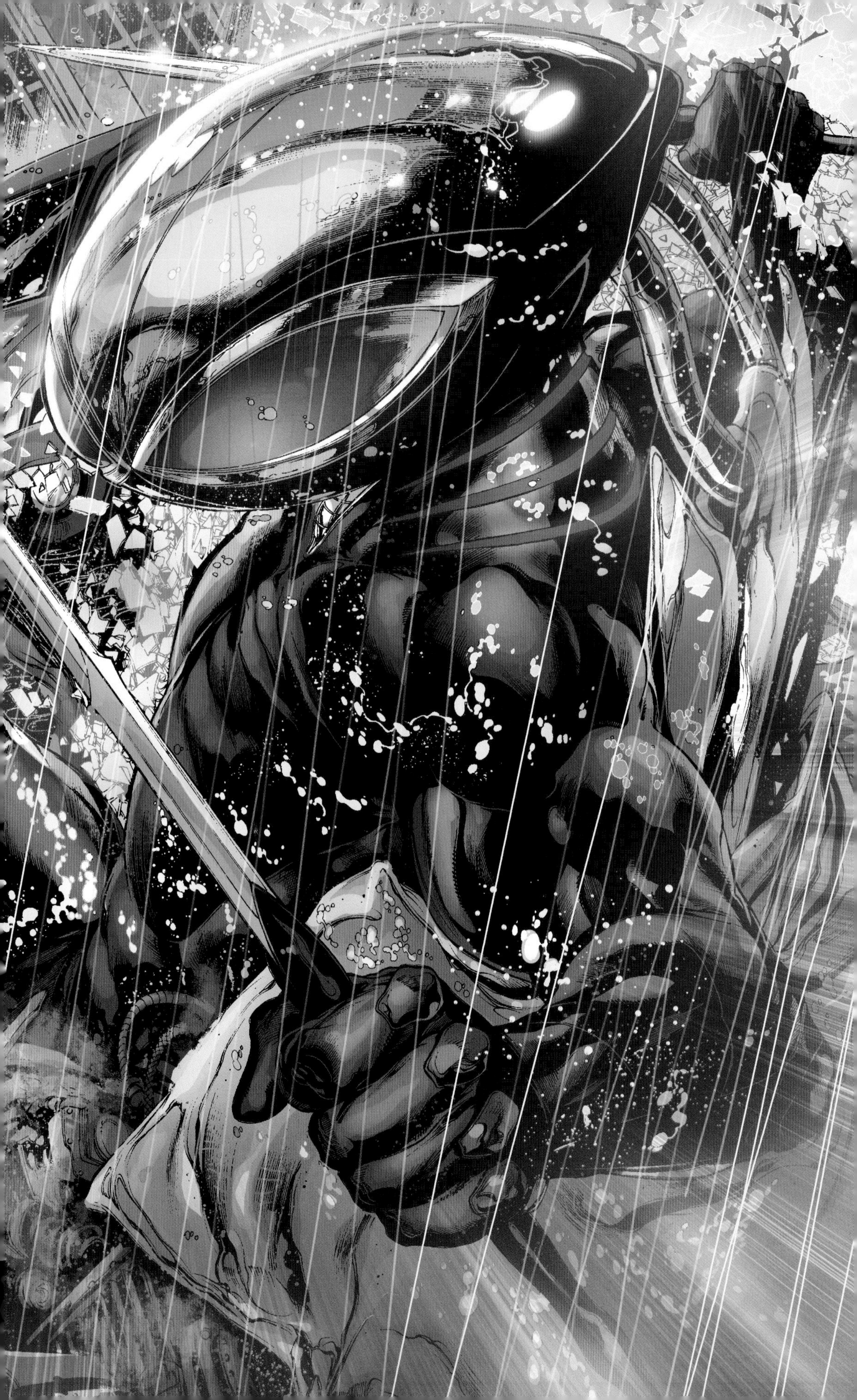

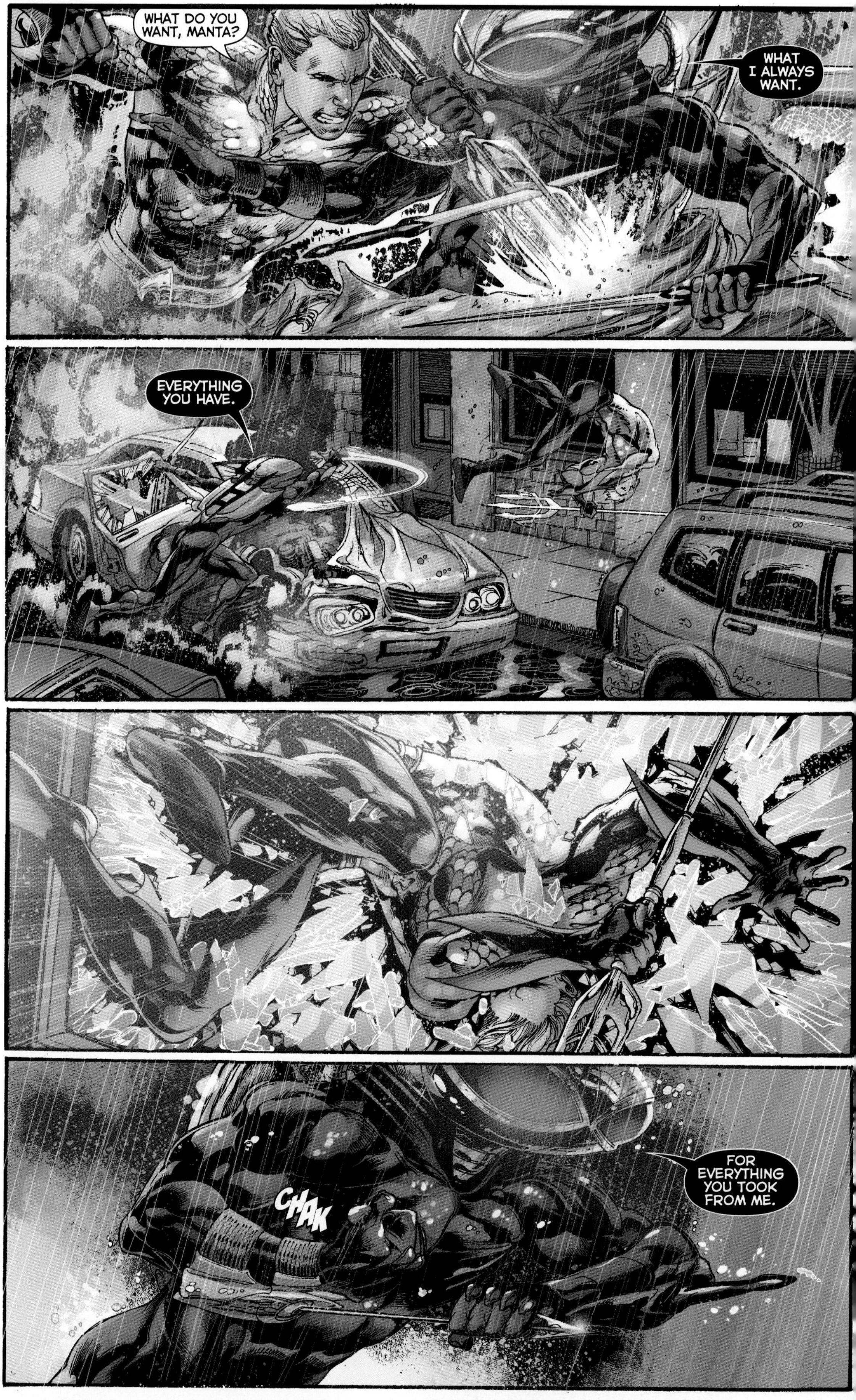
WHAT DO YOU WANT, MANTA?
WHAT I ALWAYS WANT.
EVERYTHING YOU HAVE.
CHAK
FOR EVERYTHING YOU TOOK FROM ME.

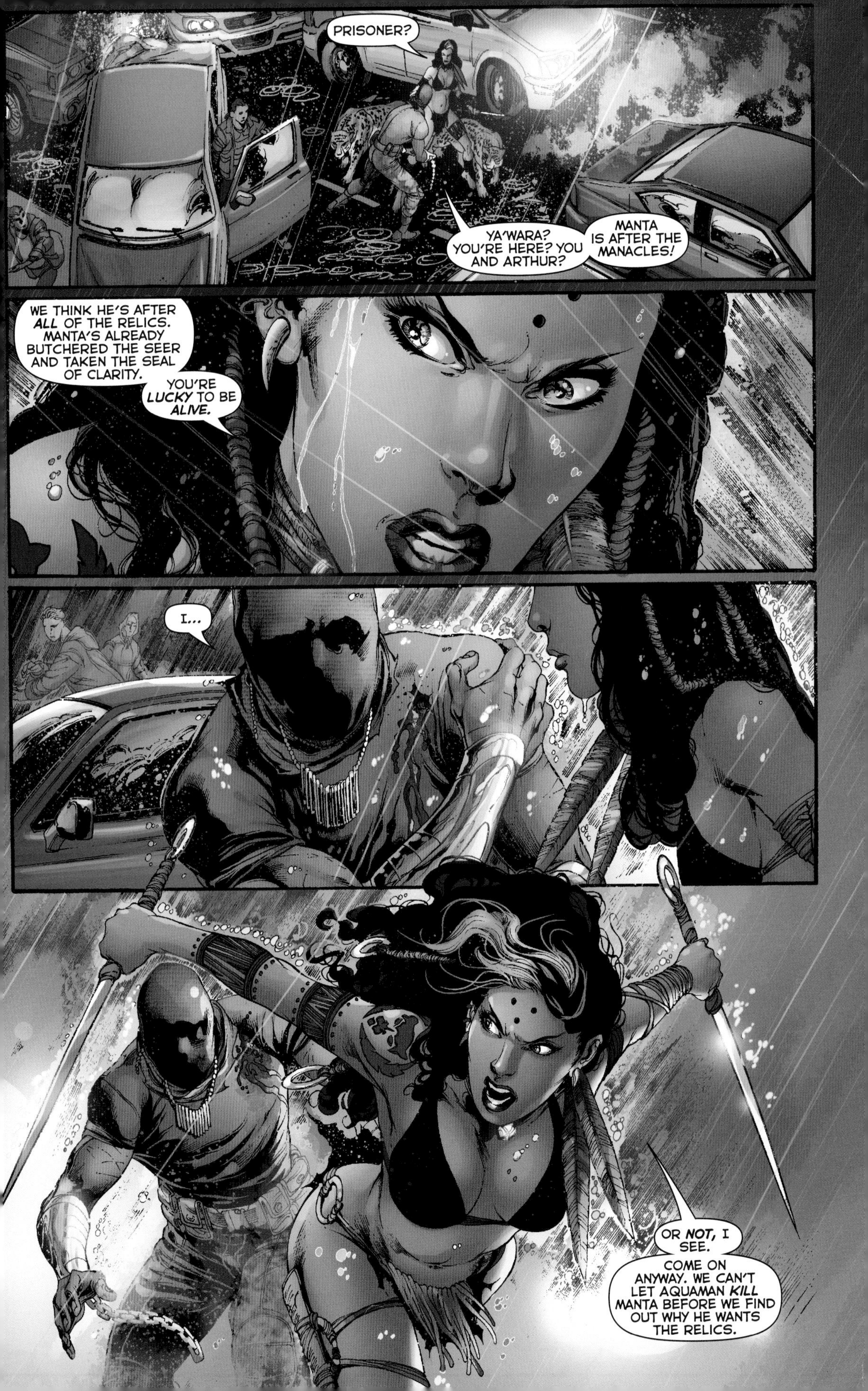
PRISONER?
YA'WARA? YOU'RE HERE? YOU AND ARTHUR?
MANTA IS AFTER THE MANACLES!
WE THINK HE'S AFTER *ALL* OF THE RELICS. MANTA'S ALREADY BUTCHERED THE SEER AND TAKEN THE SEAL OF CLARITY.
YOU'RE *LUCKY* TO BE *ALIVE.*
I...
OR *NOT*, I SEE.
COME ON ANYWAY. WE CAN'T LET AQUAMAN *KILL* MANTA BEFORE WE FIND OUT WHY HE WANTS THE RELICS.

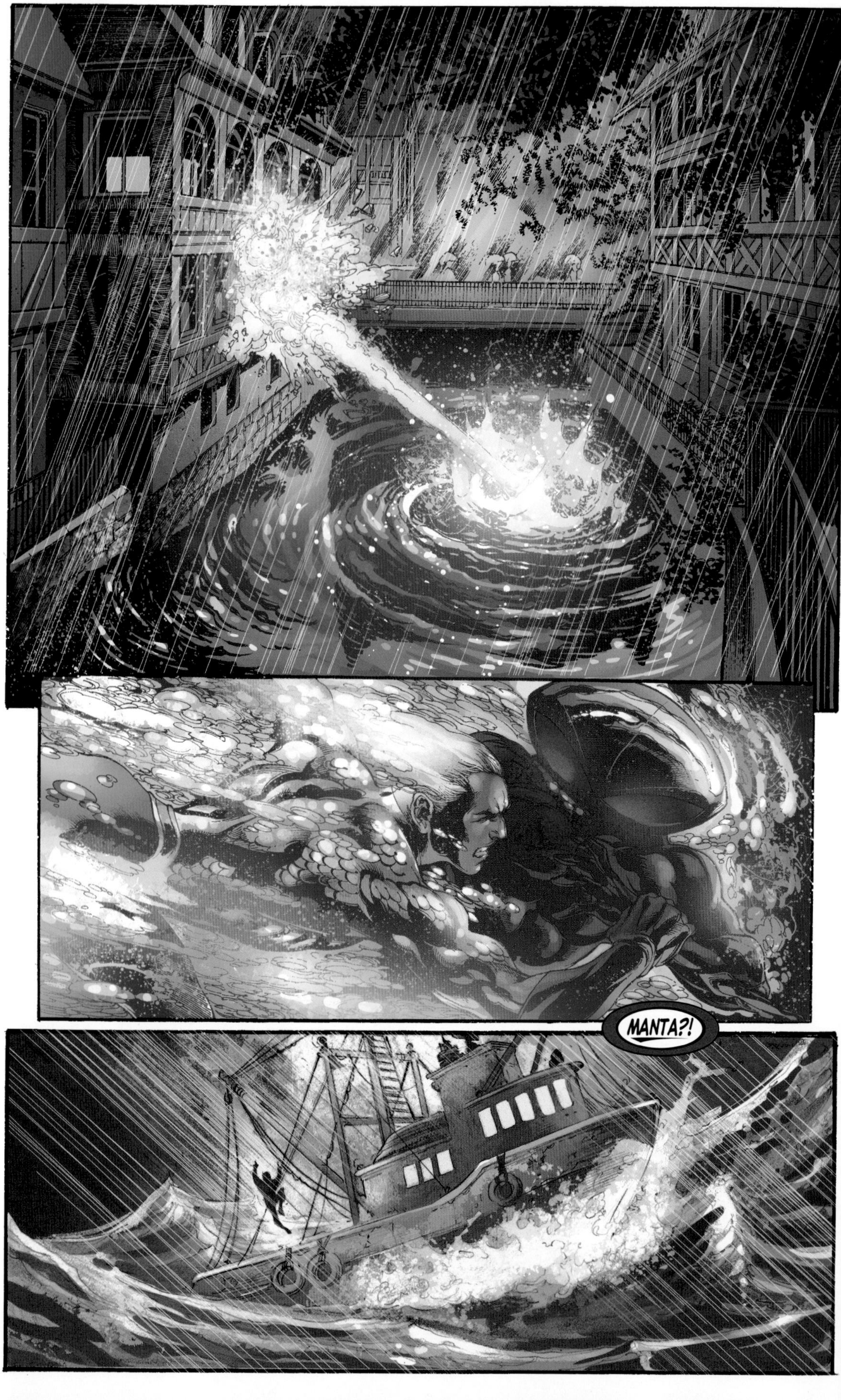
MANTA?!

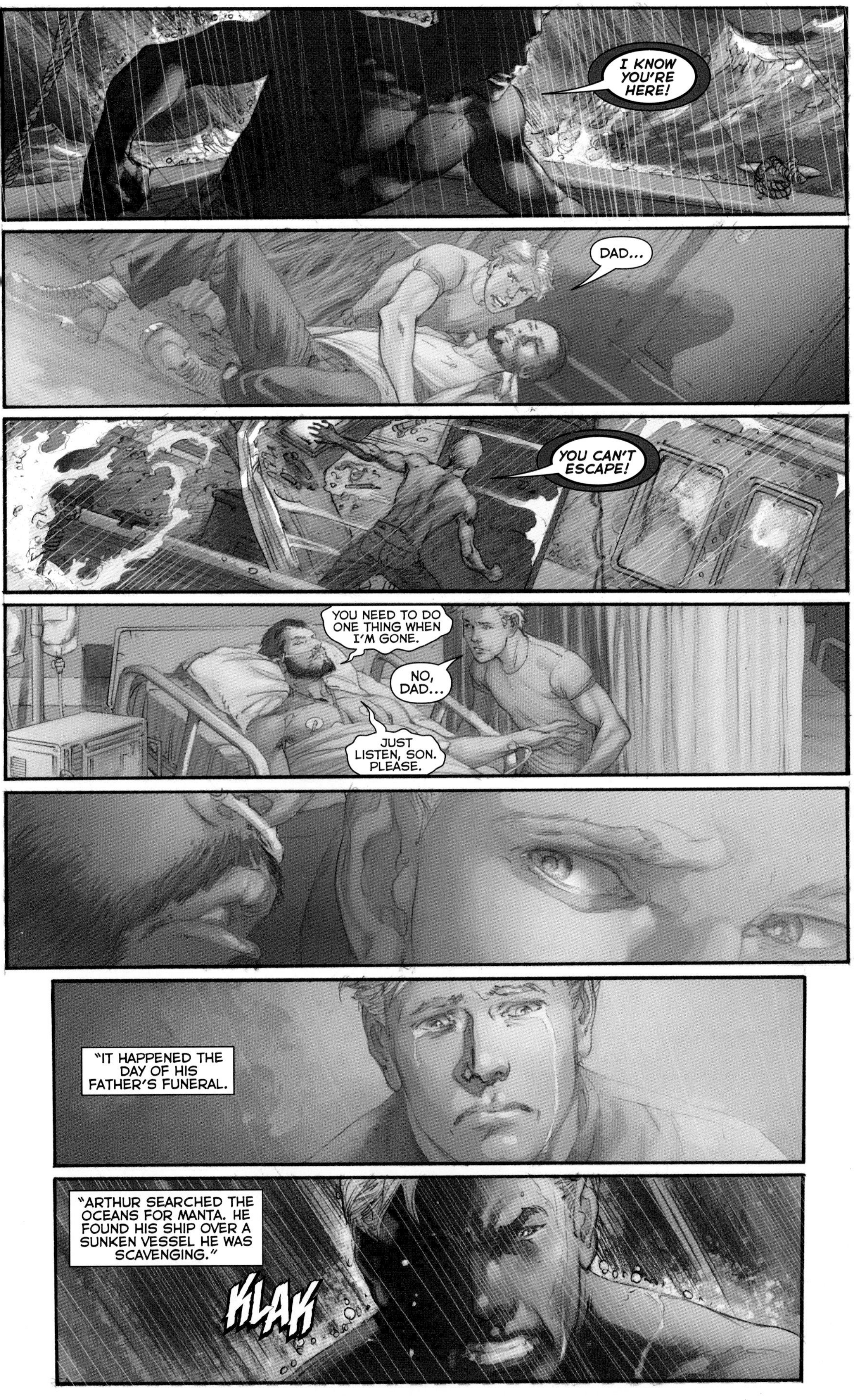
I KNOW YOU'RE HERE!
DAD...
YOU CAN'T ESCAPE!
YOU NEED TO DO ONE THING WHEN I'M GONE.
NO, DAD...
JUST LISTEN, SON. PLEASE.
"IT HAPPENED THE DAY OF HIS FATHER'S FUNERAL.
"ARTHUR SEARCHED THE OCEANS FOR MANTA. HE FOUND HIS SHIP OVER A SUNKEN VESSEL HE WAS SCAVENGING."
KLAK

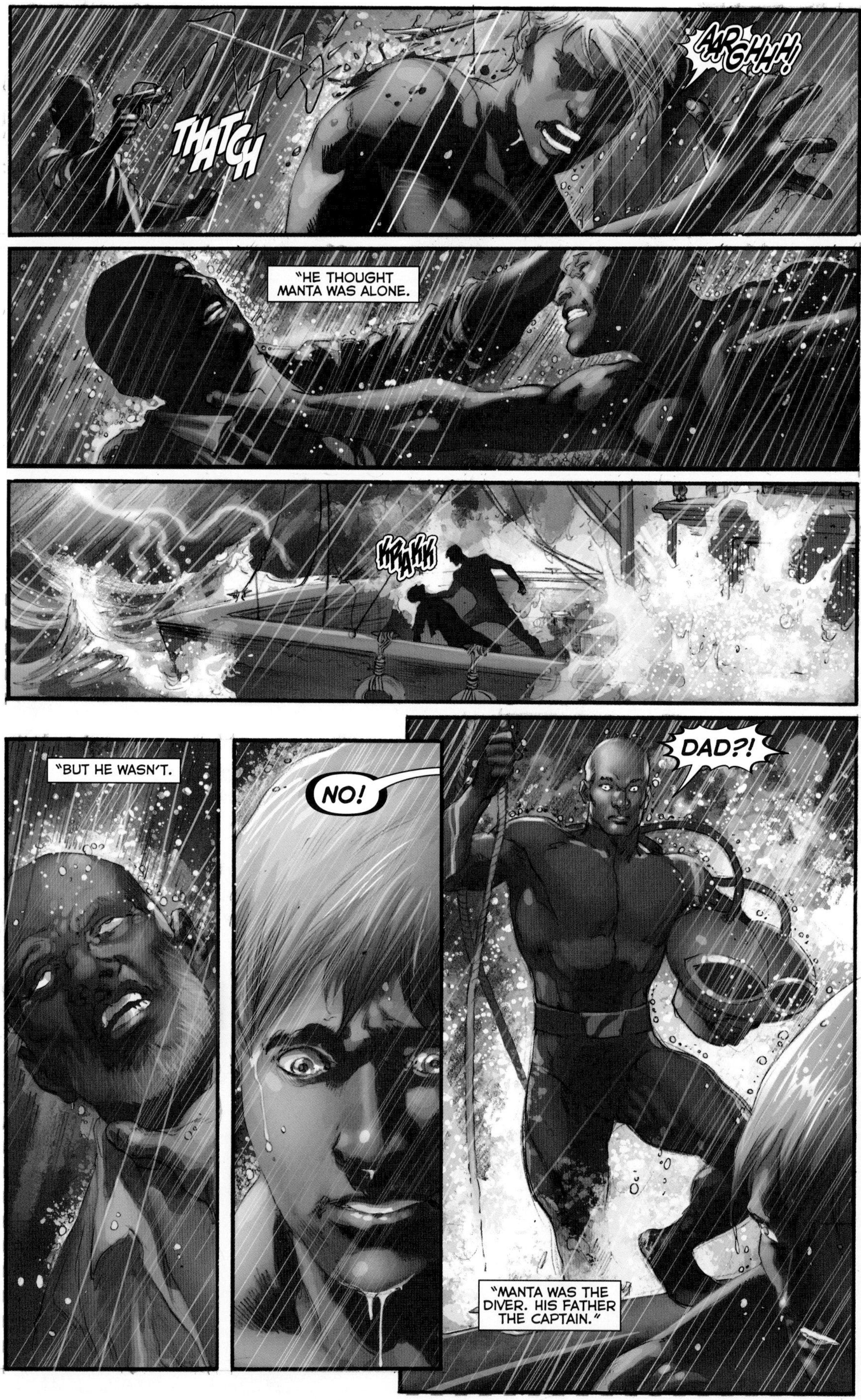
AARGHHH!
THATCH
"HE THOUGHT MANTA WAS ALONE.
KRAKK
"BUT HE WASN'T.
NO!
DAD?!
"MANTA WAS THE DIVER. HIS FATHER THE CAPTAIN."

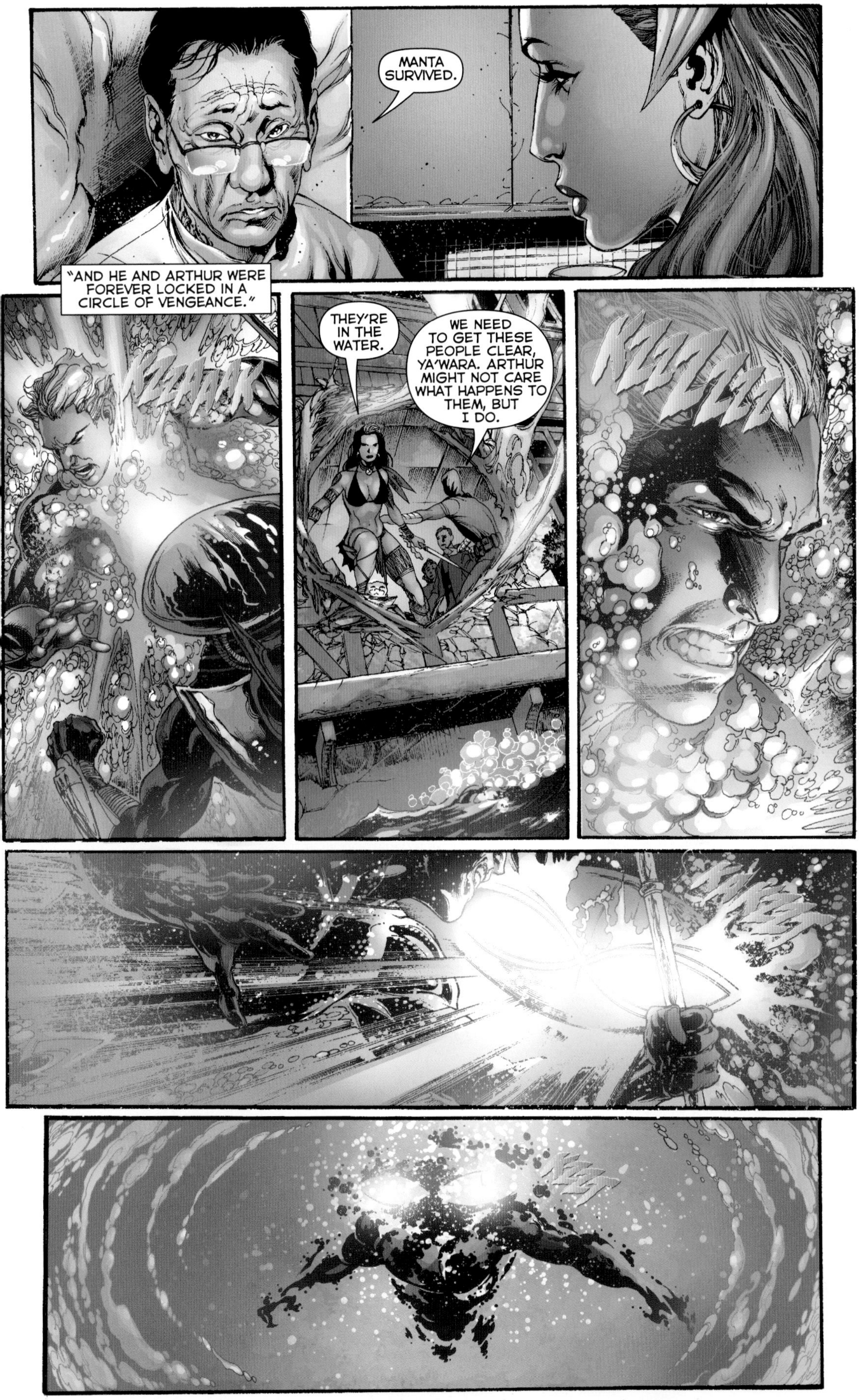
MANTA SURVIVED.
"AND HE AND ARTHUR WERE FOREVER LOCKED IN A CIRCLE OF VENGEANCE."
THEY'RE IN THE WATER.
WE NEED TO GET THESE PEOPLE CLEAR, YA'WARA. ARTHUR MIGHT NOT CARE WHAT HAPPENS TO THEM, BUT I DO.

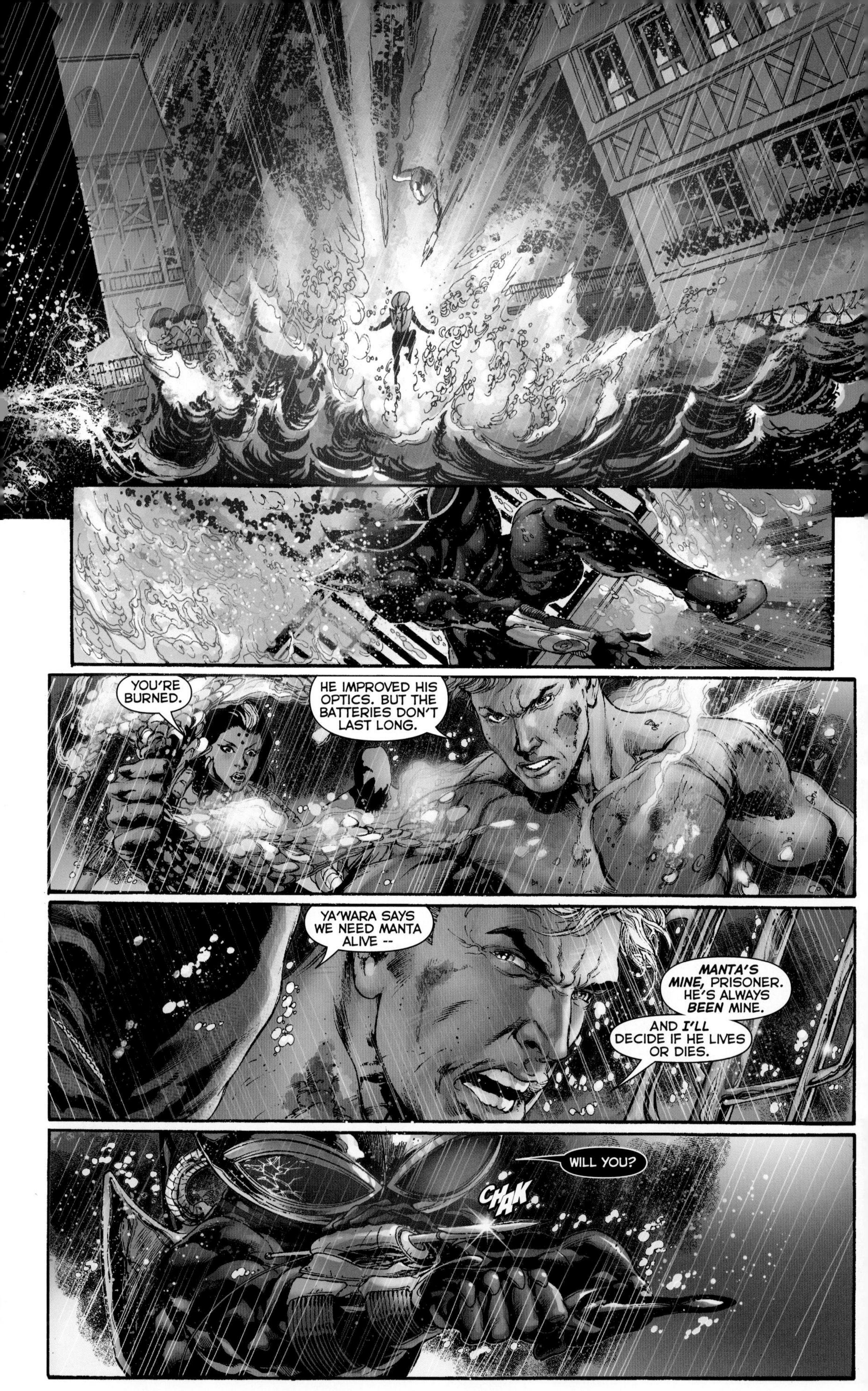
YOU'RE BURNED.
HE IMPROVED HIS OPTICS. BUT THE BATTERIES DON'T LAST LONG.
YA'WARA SAYS WE NEED MANTA ALIVE --
MANTA'S MINE, PRISONER. HE'S ALWAYS BEEN MINE.
AND I'LL DECIDE IF HE LIVES OR DIES.
WILL YOU?
CHAK

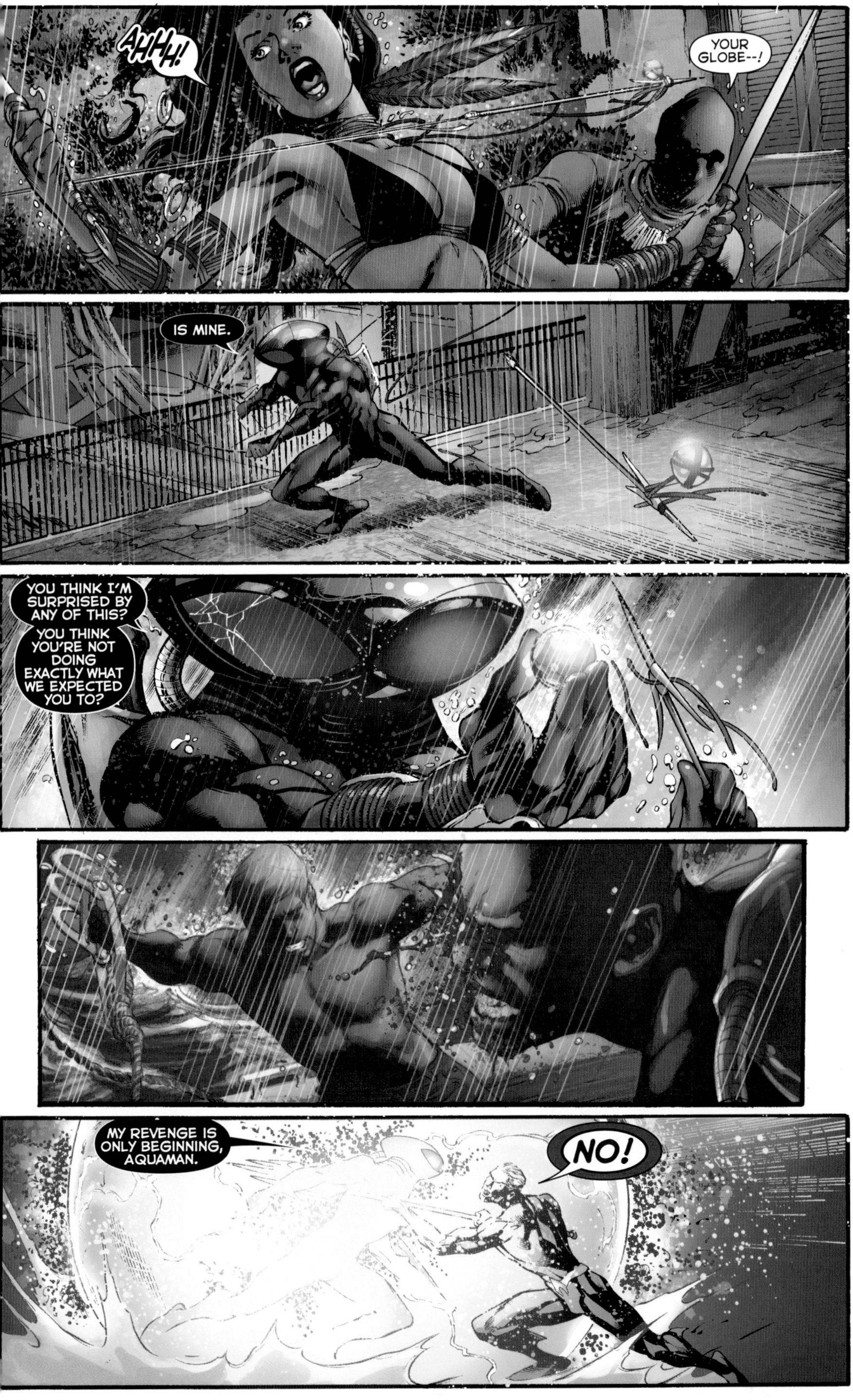
AHHH!
YOUR GLOBE--!
IS MINE.
YOU THINK I'M SURPRISED BY ANY OF THIS?
YOU THINK YOU'RE NOT DOING EXACTLY WHAT WE EXPECTED YOU TO?
MY REVENGE IS ONLY BEGINNING, AQUAMAN.
NO!

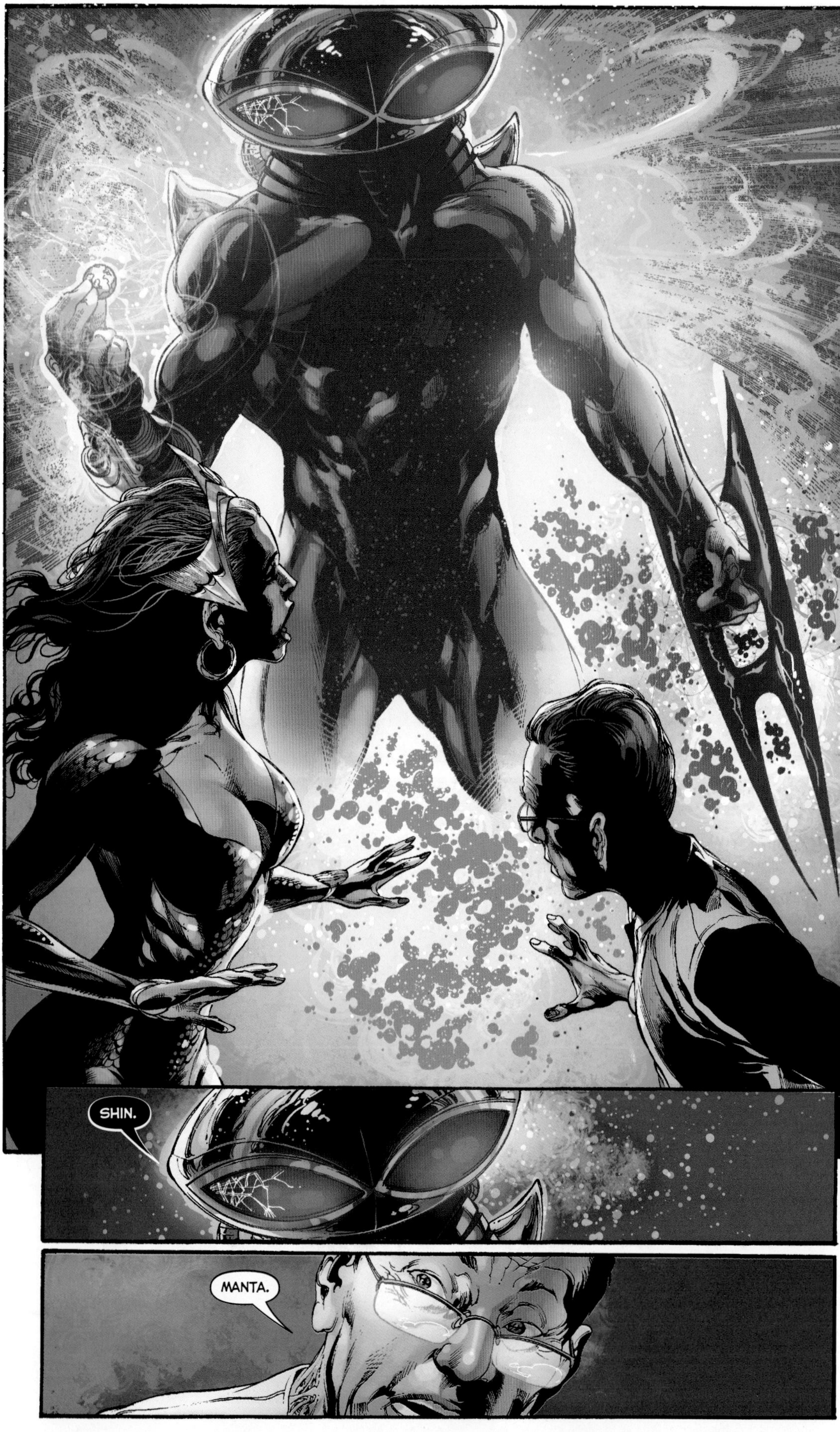
SHIN.
MANTA.

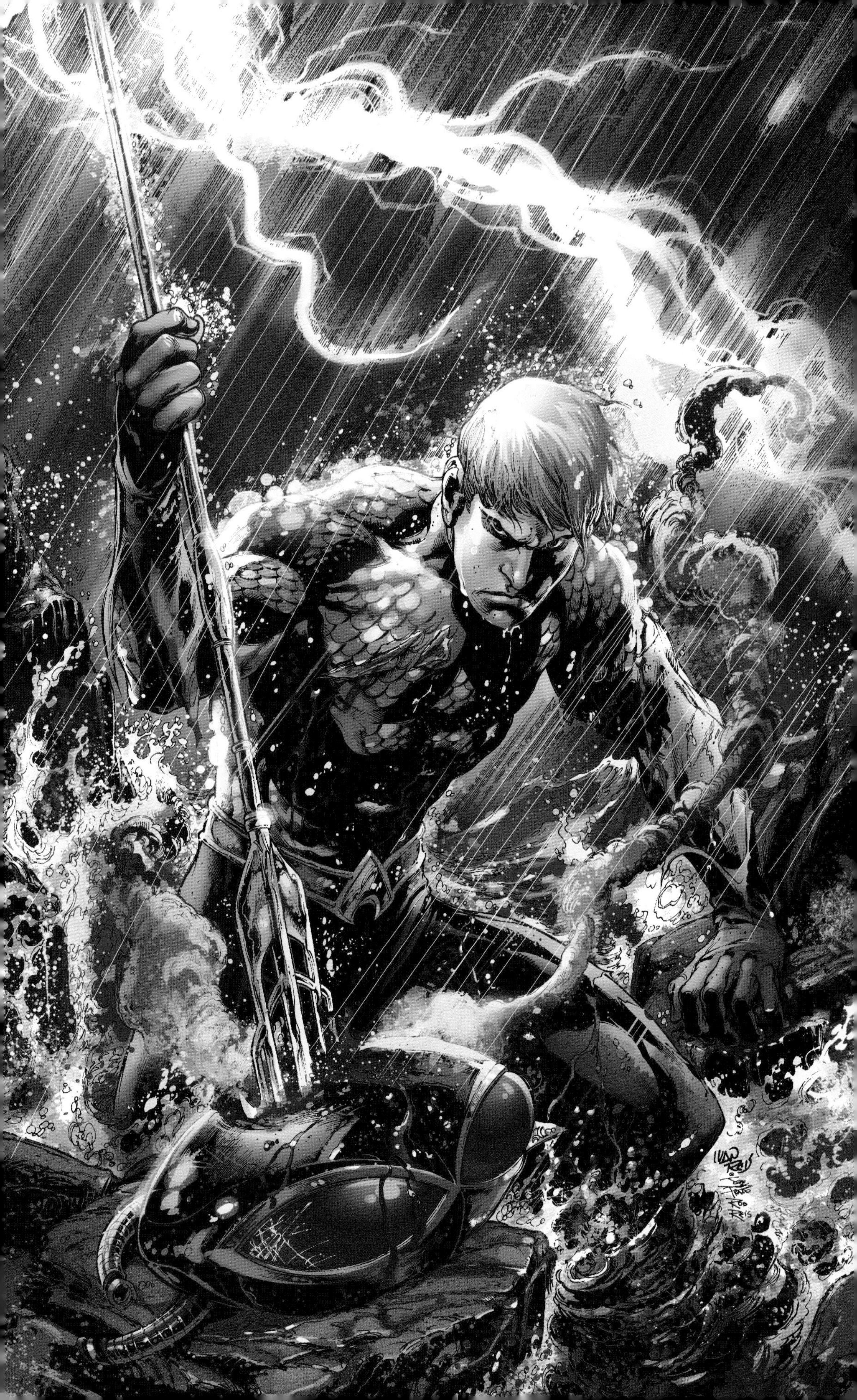

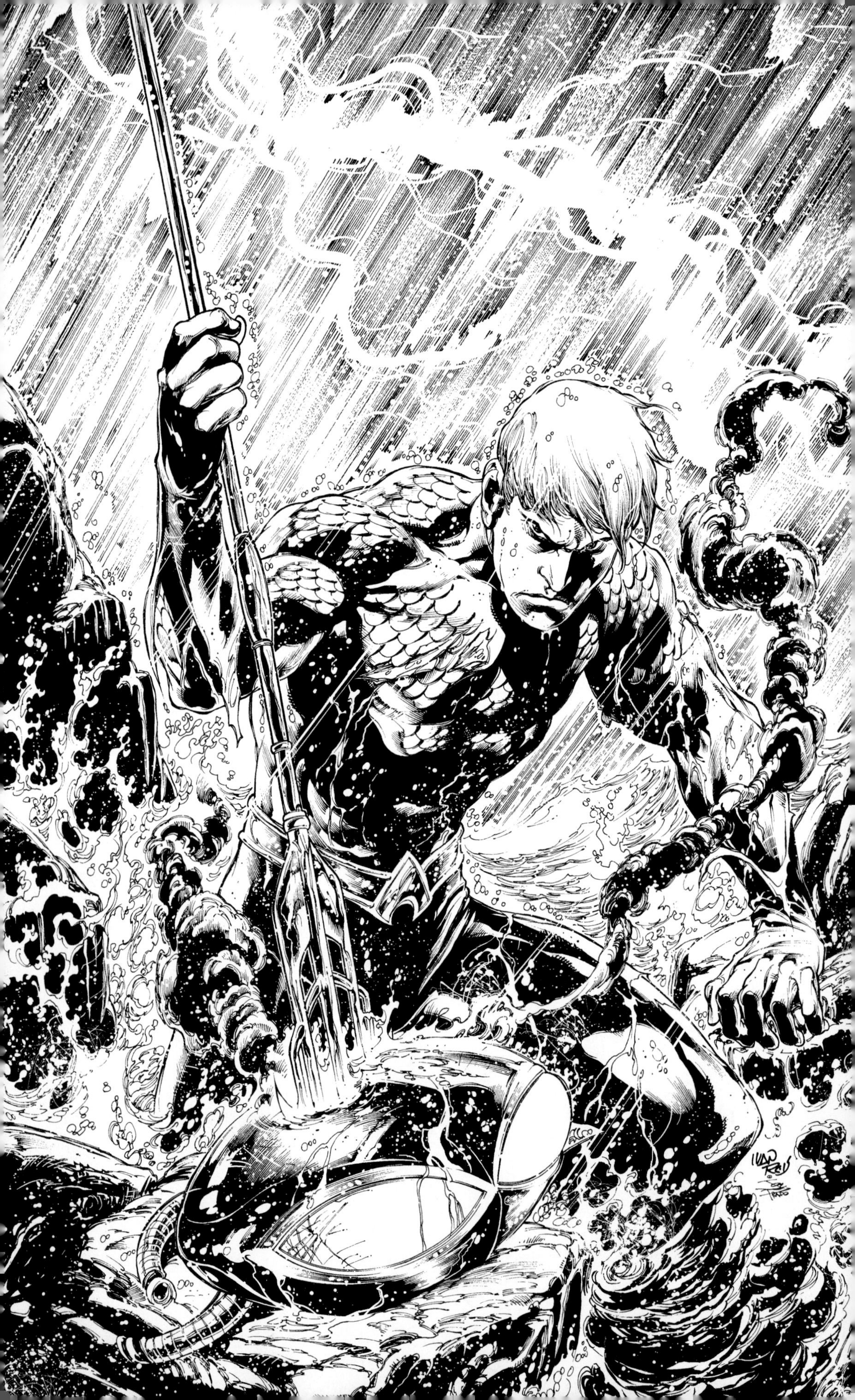

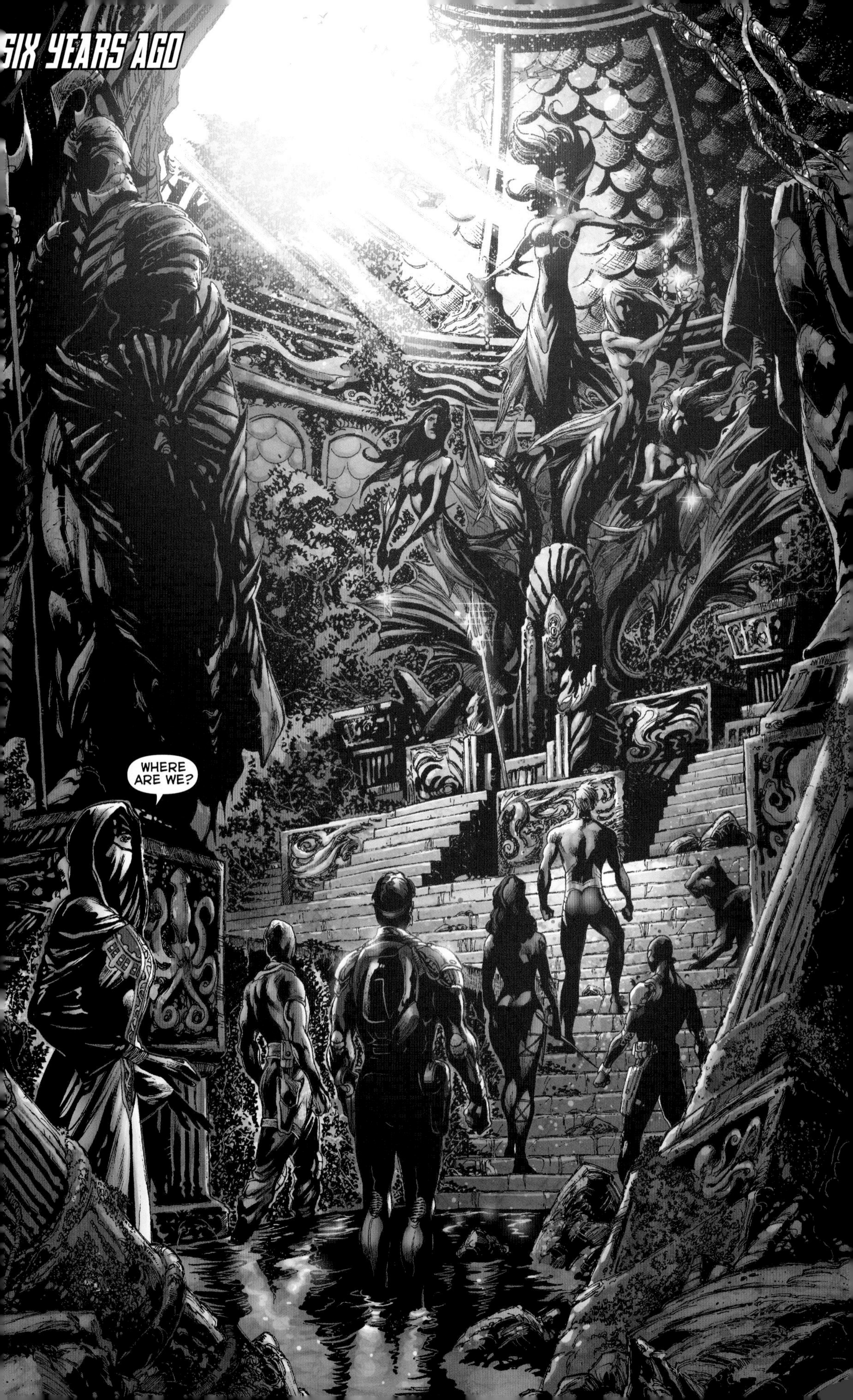
SIX YEARS AGO
WHERE ARE WE?

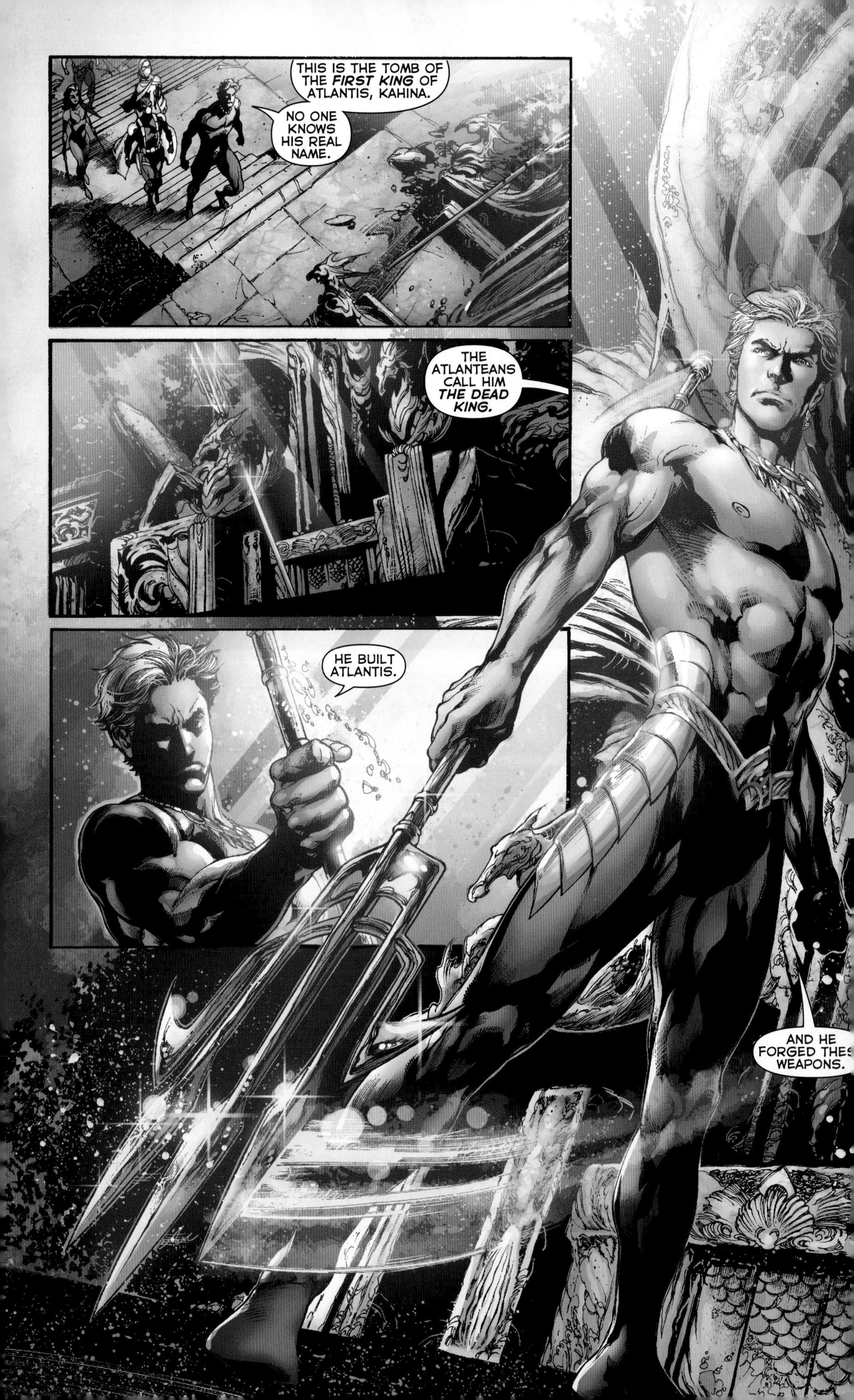
THIS IS THE TOMB OF THE *FIRST KING* OF ATLANTIS, KAHINA.
NO ONE KNOWS HIS REAL NAME.
THE ATLANTEANS CALL HIM ***THE DEAD KING.***
HE BUILT ATLANTIS.
AND HE FORGED THES WEAPONS.

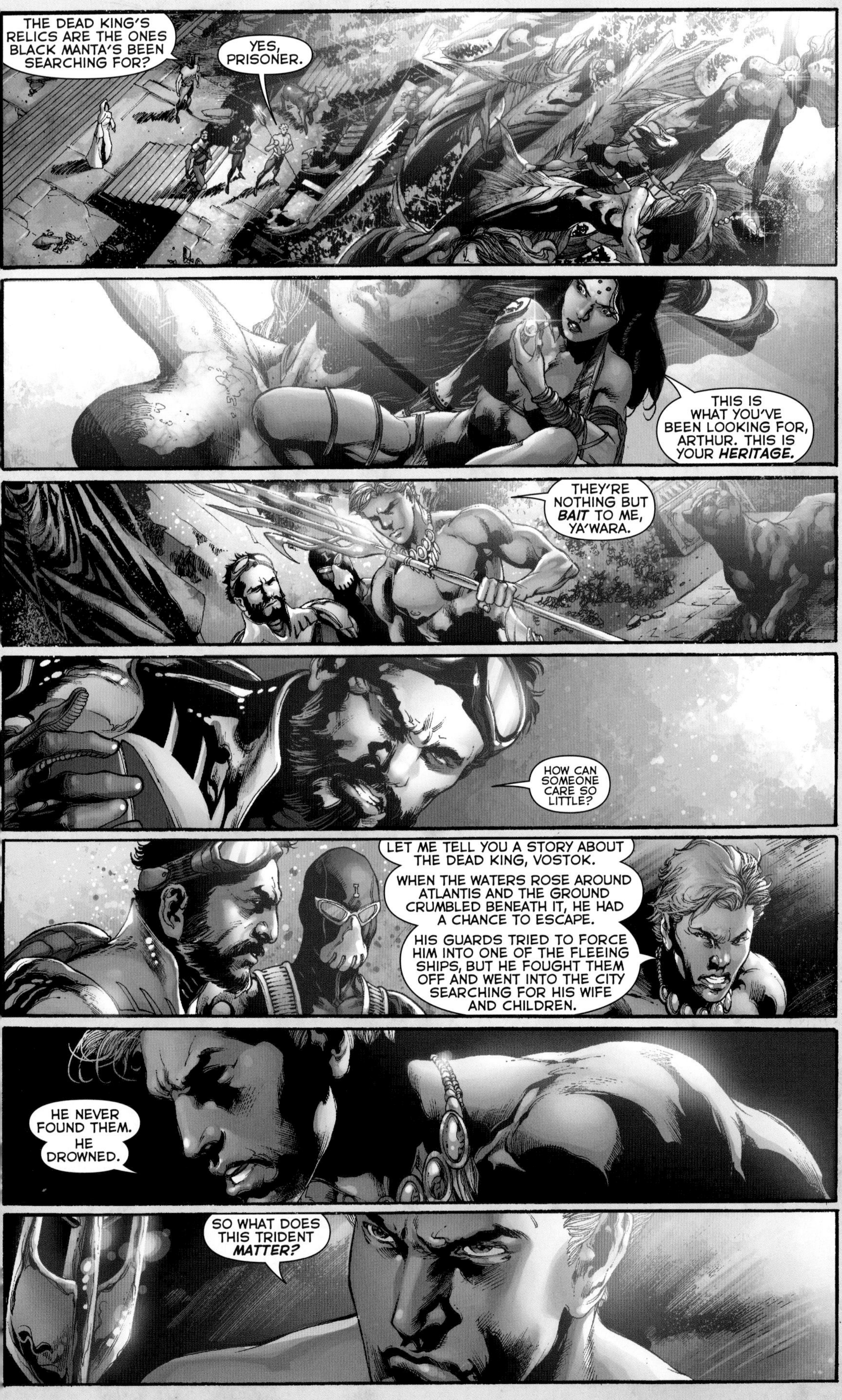
THE DEAD KING'S RELICS ARE THE ONES BLACK MANTA'S BEEN SEARCHING FOR?
YES, PRISONER.
THIS IS WHAT YOU'VE BEEN LOOKING FOR, ARTHUR. THIS IS YOUR *HERITAGE.*
THEY'RE NOTHING BUT *BAIT* TO ME, YA'WARA.
HOW CAN SOMEONE CARE SO LITTLE?
LET ME TELL YOU A STORY ABOUT THE DEAD KING, VOSTOK.
WHEN THE WATERS ROSE AROUND ATLANTIS AND THE GROUND CRUMBLED BENEATH IT, HE HAD A CHANCE TO ESCAPE.
HIS GUARDS TRIED TO FORCE HIM INTO ONE OF THE FLEEING SHIPS, BUT HE FOUGHT THEM OFF AND WENT INTO THE CITY SEARCHING FOR HIS WIFE AND CHILDREN.
HE NEVER FOUND THEM. HE DROWNED.
SO WHAT DOES THIS TRIDENT *MATTER?*

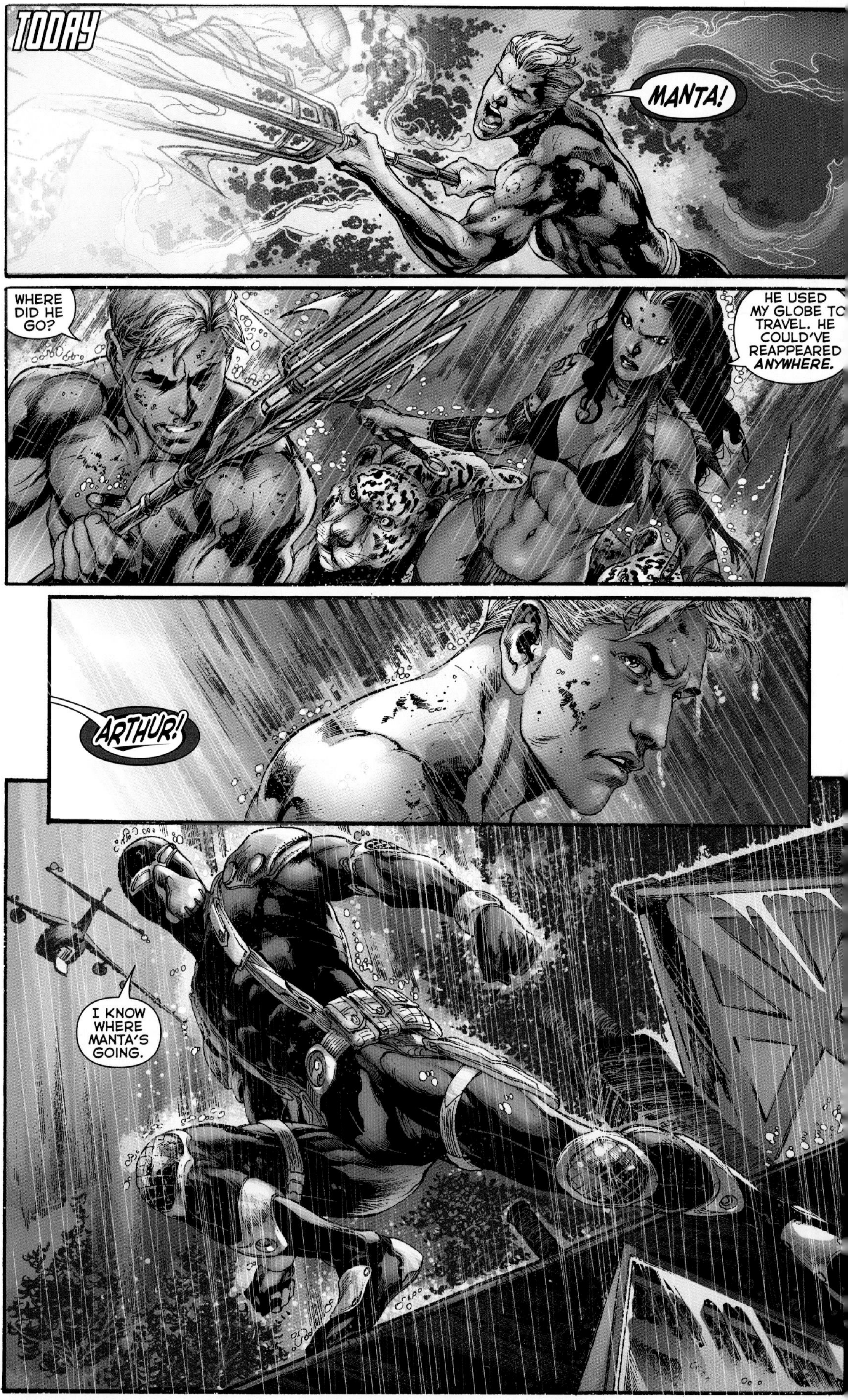
TODAY
MANTA!
WHERE DID HE GO?
HE USED MY GLOBE TO TRAVEL. HE COULD'VE REAPPEARED *ANYWHERE*.
ARTHUR!
I KNOW WHERE MANTA'S GOING.

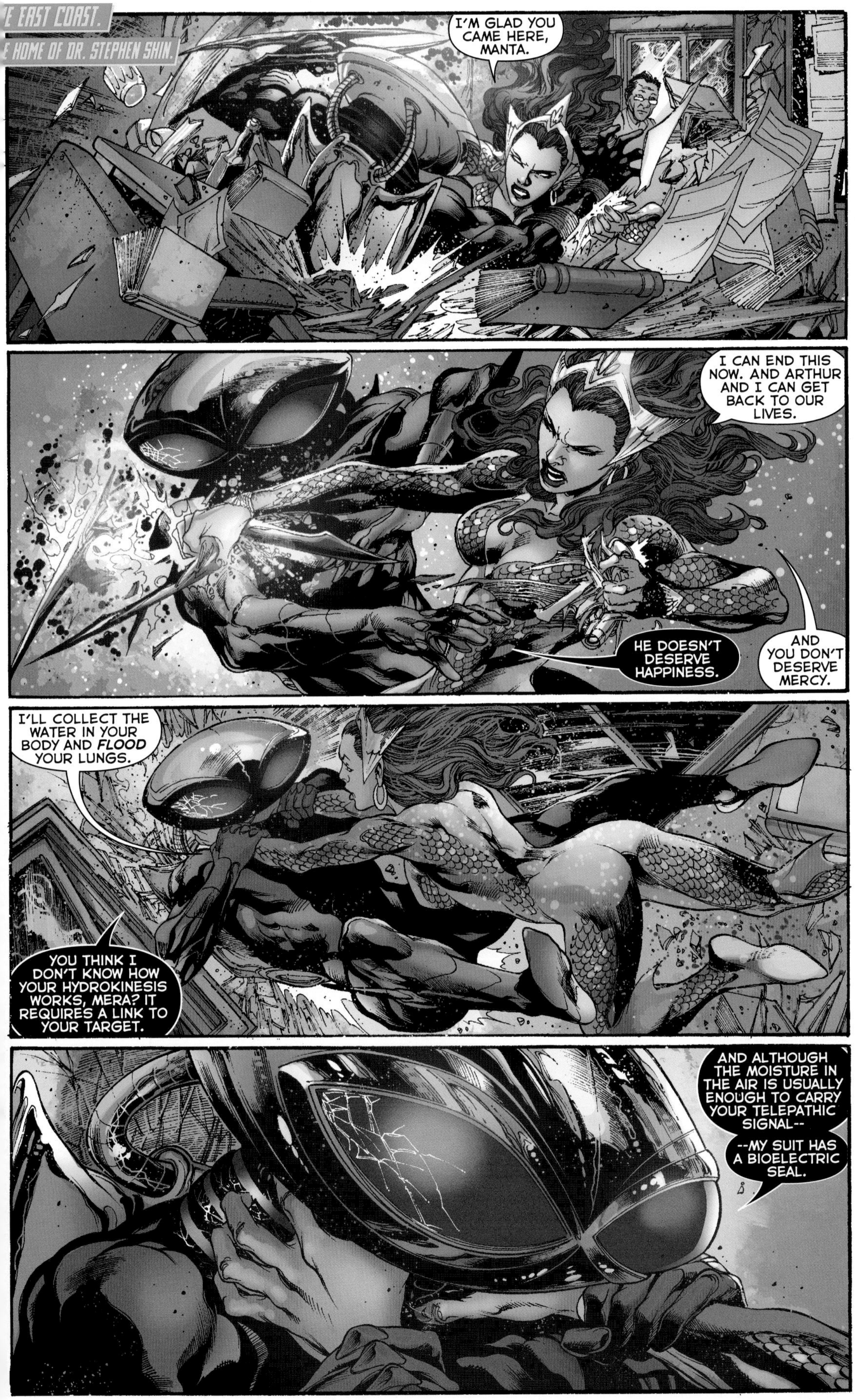

E EAST COAST.
E HOME OF DR. STEPHEN SHIN.
I'M GLAD YOU CAME HERE, MANTA.
I CAN END THIS NOW. AND ARTHUR AND I CAN GET BACK TO OUR LIVES.
HE DOESN'T DESERVE HAPPINESS.
AND YOU DON'T DESERVE MERCY.
I'LL COLLECT THE WATER IN YOUR BODY AND *FLOOD* YOUR LUNGS.
YOU THINK I DON'T KNOW HOW YOUR HYDROKINESIS WORKS, MERA? IT REQUIRES A LINK TO YOUR TARGET.
AND ALTHOUGH THE MOISTURE IN THE AIR IS USUALLY ENOUGH TO CARRY YOUR TELEPATHIC SIGNAL--
--MY SUIT HAS A BIOELECTRIC SEAL.

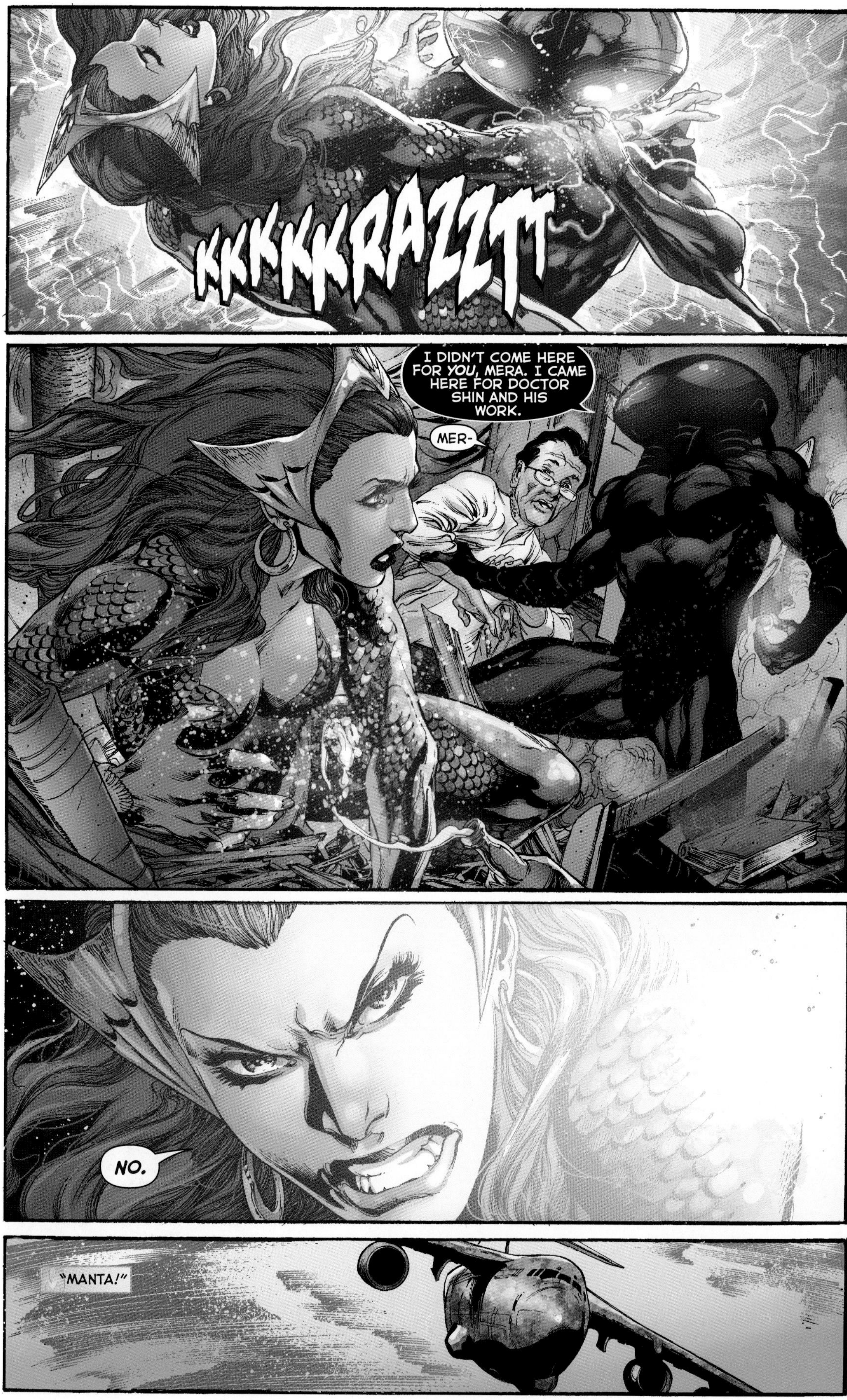
KKKKKRAZZTT
I DIDN'T COME HERE FOR *YOU*, MERA. I CAME HERE FOR DOCTOR SHIN AND HIS WORK.
MER-
NO.
"MANTA!"

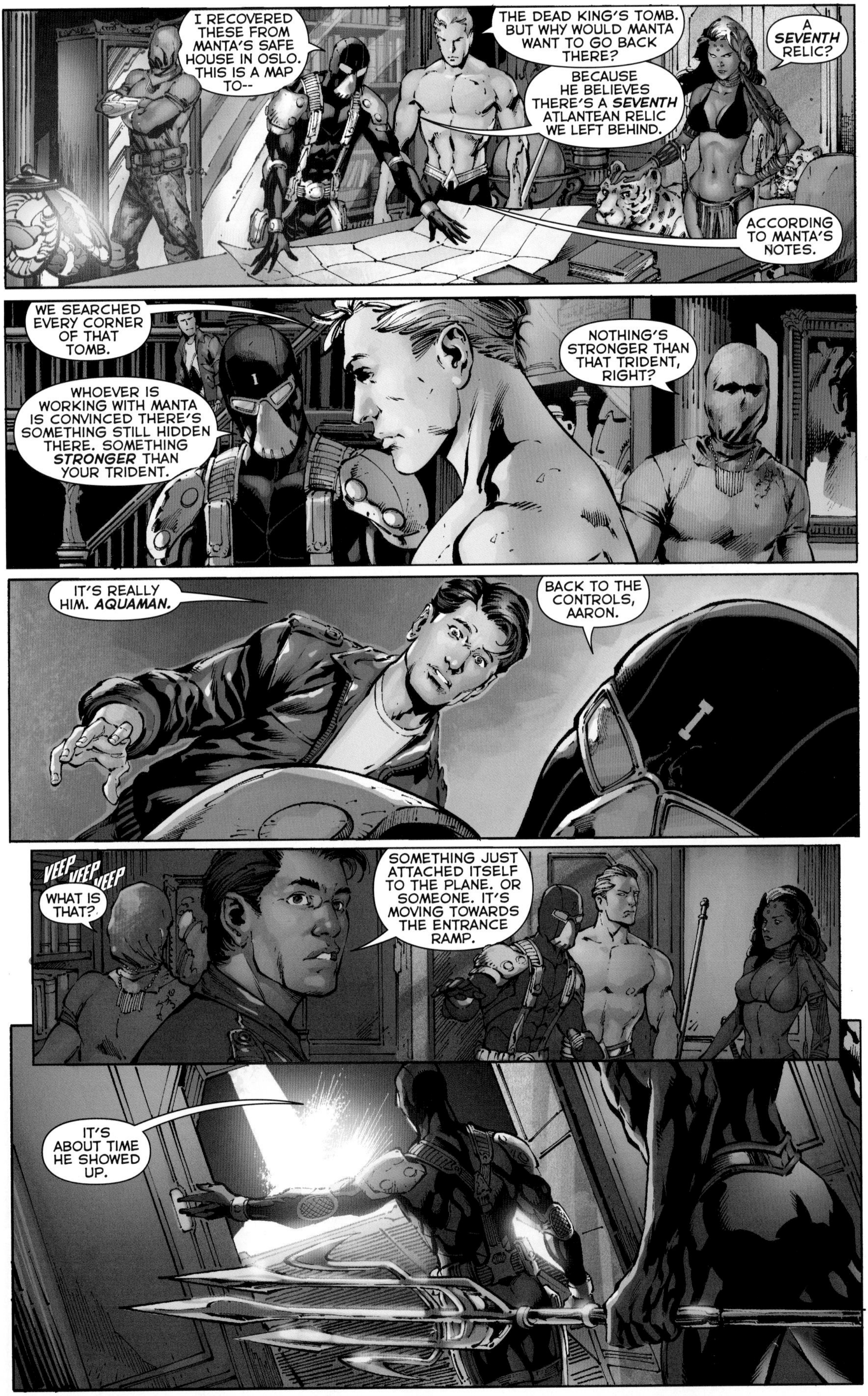
I RECOVERED THESE FROM MANTA'S SAFE HOUSE IN OSLO. THIS IS A MAP TO--
THE DEAD KING'S TOMB. BUT WHY WOULD MANTA WANT TO GO BACK THERE?
BECAUSE HE BELIEVES THERE'S A SEVENTH ATLANTEAN RELIC WE LEFT BEHIND.
A SEVENTH RELIC?
ACCORDING TO MANTA'S NOTES.
WE SEARCHED EVERY CORNER OF THAT TOMB.
WHOEVER IS WORKING WITH MANTA IS CONVINCED THERE'S SOMETHING STILL HIDDEN THERE. SOMETHING STRONGER THAN YOUR TRIDENT.
NOTHING'S STRONGER THAN THAT TRIDENT, RIGHT?
IT'S REALLY HIM. AQUAMAN.
BACK TO THE CONTROLS, AARON.
VEEP VEEP VEEP
WHAT IS THAT?
SOMETHING JUST ATTACHED ITSELF TO THE PLANE. OR SOMEONE. IT'S MOVING TOWARDS THE ENTRANCE RAMP.
IT'S ABOUT TIME HE SHOWED UP.

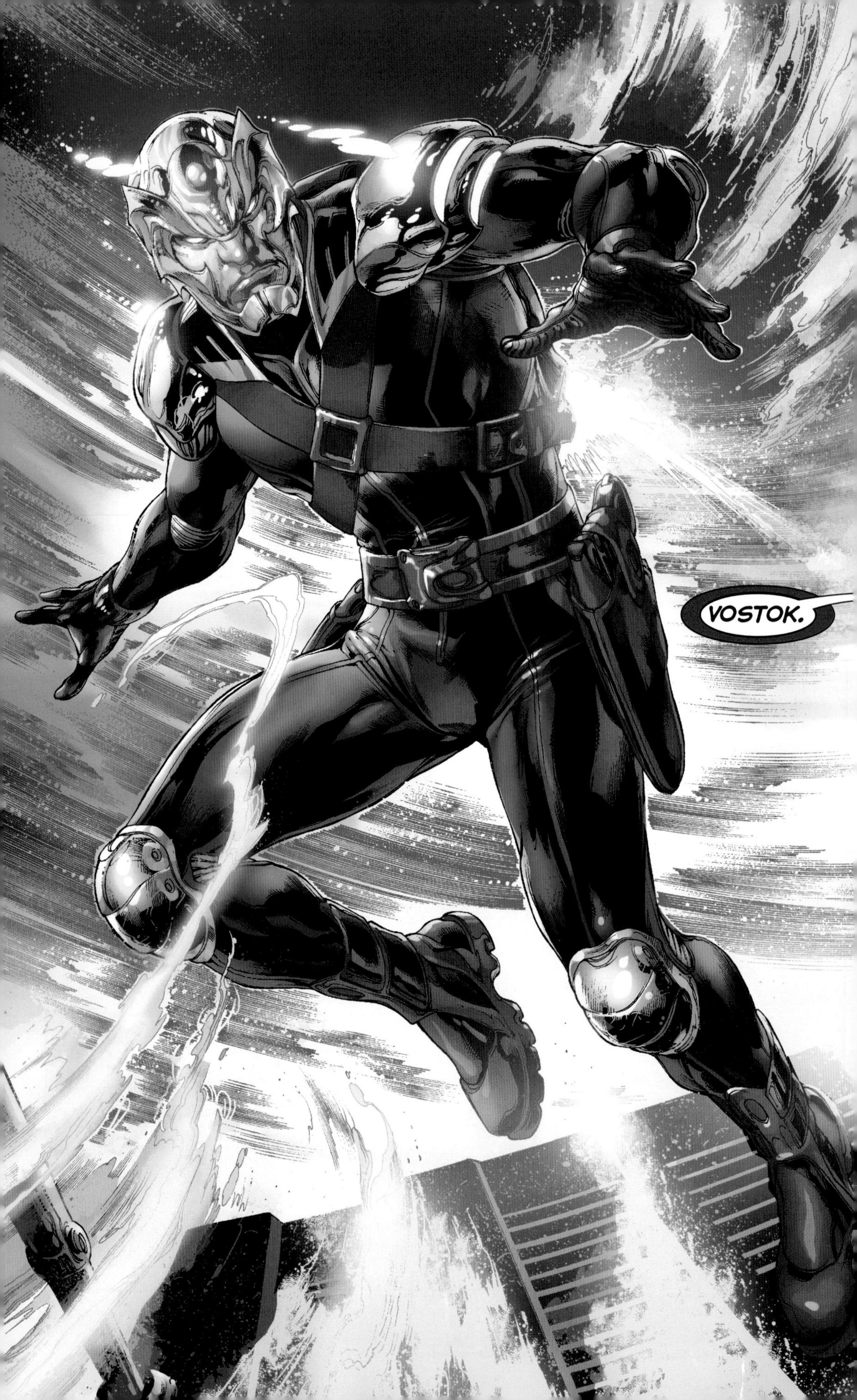
VOSTOK.

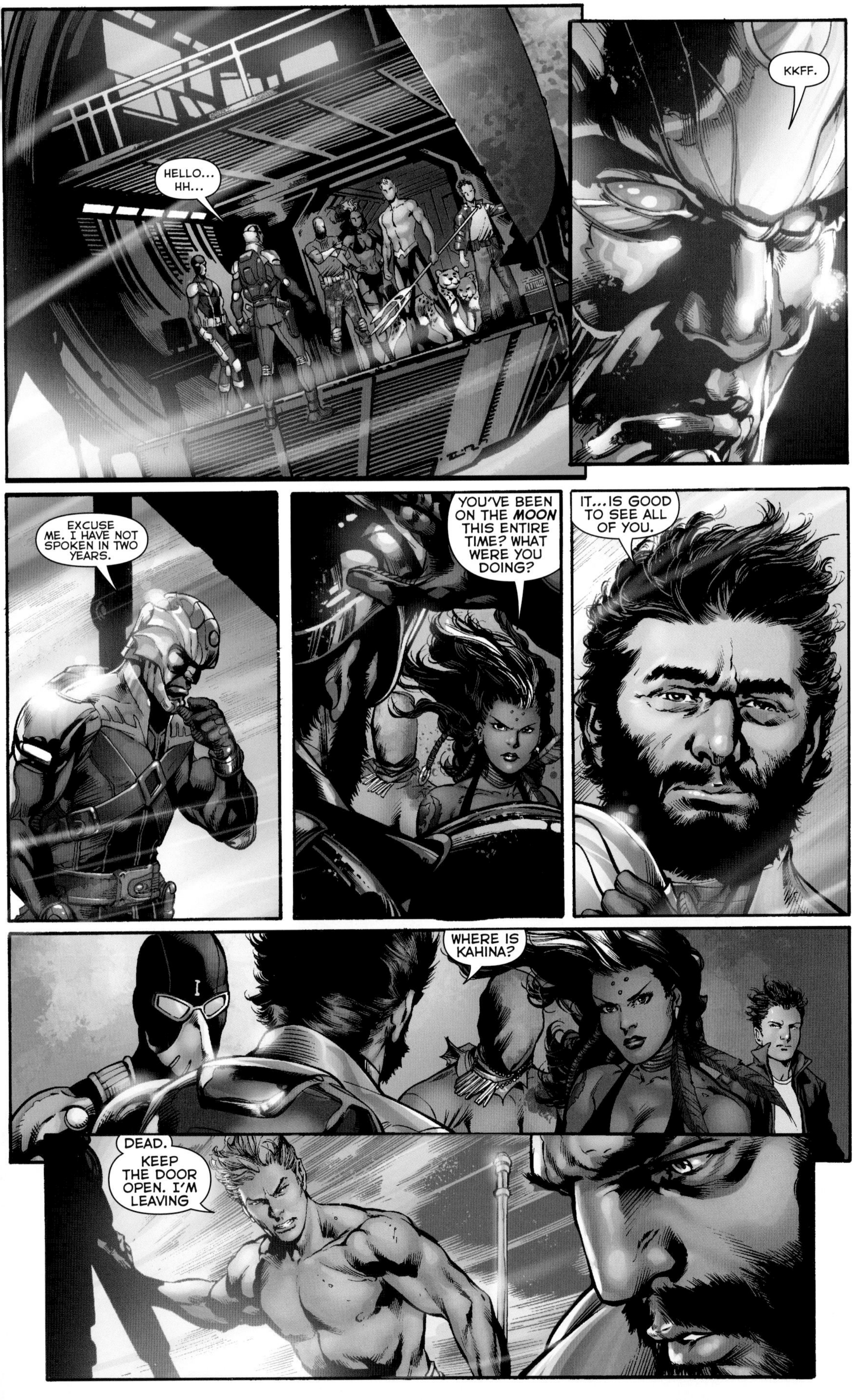
HELLO... HH...
KKFF.
EXCUSE ME. I HAVE NOT SPOKEN IN TWO YEARS.
YOU'VE BEEN ON THE ***MOON*** THIS ENTIRE TIME? WHAT WERE YOU DOING?
IT...IS GOOD TO SEE ALL OF YOU.
WHERE IS KAHINA?
DEAD.
KEEP THE DOOR OPEN. I'M LEAVING

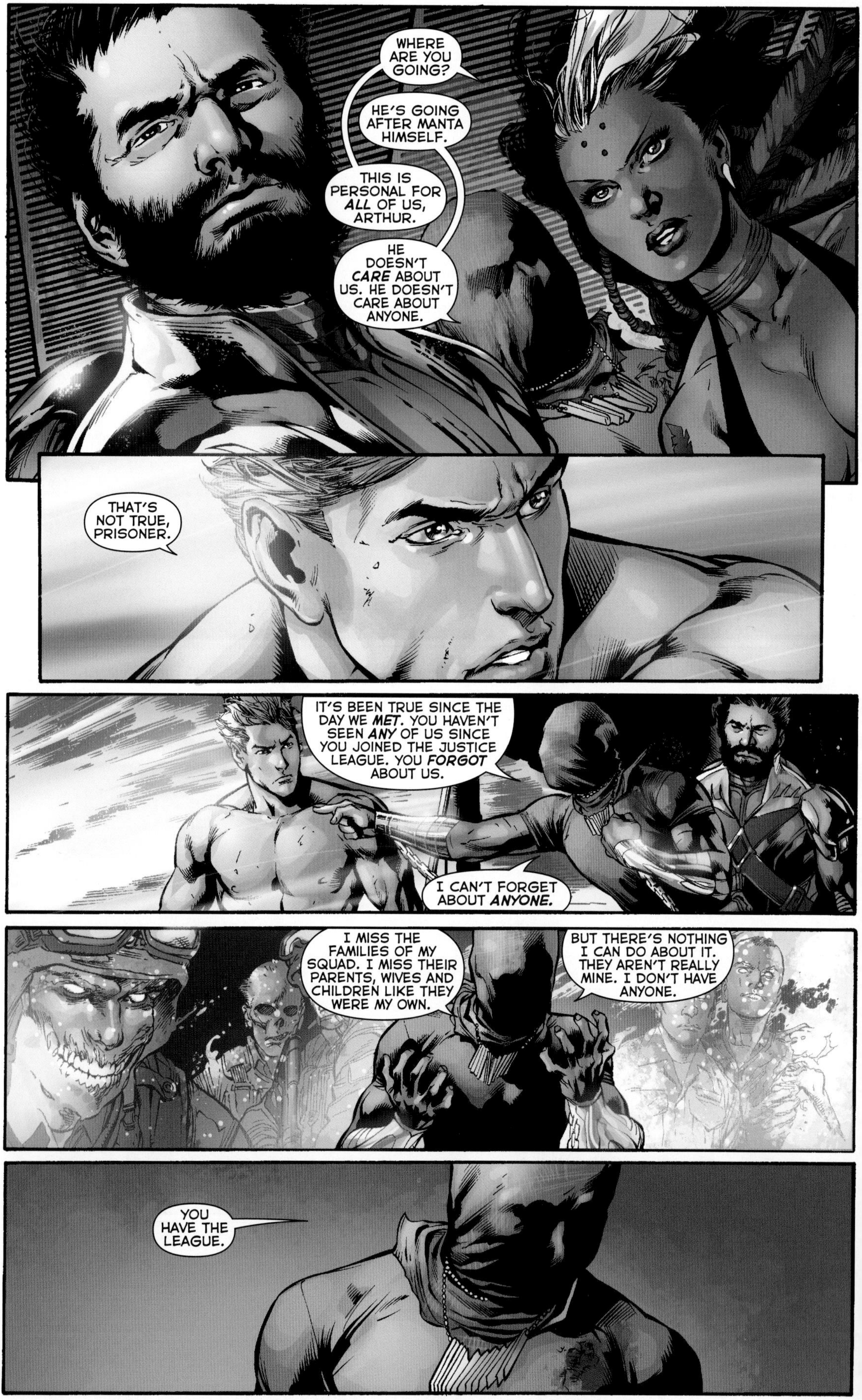
WHERE ARE YOU GOING?
HE'S GOING AFTER MANTA HIMSELF.
THIS IS PERSONAL FOR ALL OF US, ARTHUR.
HE DOESN'T CARE ABOUT US. HE DOESN'T CARE ABOUT ANYONE.
THAT'S NOT TRUE, PRISONER.
IT'S BEEN TRUE SINCE THE DAY WE MET. YOU HAVEN'T SEEN ANY OF US SINCE YOU JOINED THE JUSTICE LEAGUE. YOU FORGOT ABOUT US.
I CAN'T FORGET ABOUT ANYONE.
I MISS THE FAMILIES OF MY SQUAD. I MISS THEIR PARENTS, WIVES AND CHILDREN LIKE THEY WERE MY OWN.
BUT THERE'S NOTHING I CAN DO ABOUT IT. THEY AREN'T REALLY MINE. I DON'T HAVE ANYONE.
YOU HAVE THE LEAGUE.

DON'T PUT THE LEAGUE ON A *PEDESTAL* LIKE EVERYONE ELSE, PRISONER. WE CAN DO THINGS THEY CAN'T.

I ALREADY HAVE THE CHINA ARMED FORCES SCOURING THE OCEAN FOR MANTA, READY TO ENGAGE IF THEY FIND HIM.

SAME WITH THE U.S. NAVY AND THE PACIFIC FLEET.

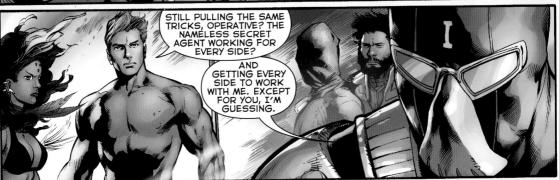

STILL PULLING THE SAME TRICKS, OPERATIVE? THE NAMELESS SECRET AGENT WORKING FOR EVERY SIDE?

AND GETTING EVERY SIDE TO WORK WITH ME. EXCEPT FOR YOU, I'M GUESSING.

MAYBE YOU HAVEN'T CHANGED AFTER ALL. WE HUNT MANTA TOGETHER, ARTHUR. HE CAME AFTER ALL OF US.

AND THAT'S *MY* FAULT, YA'WARA. *I* KILLED HIS FATHER. *I'M* HIS REAL TARGET.

I'M GOING TO *PROTECT* YOU.

I'M GOING ALONE BECAUSE I *DO* CARE.

ARTHUR.

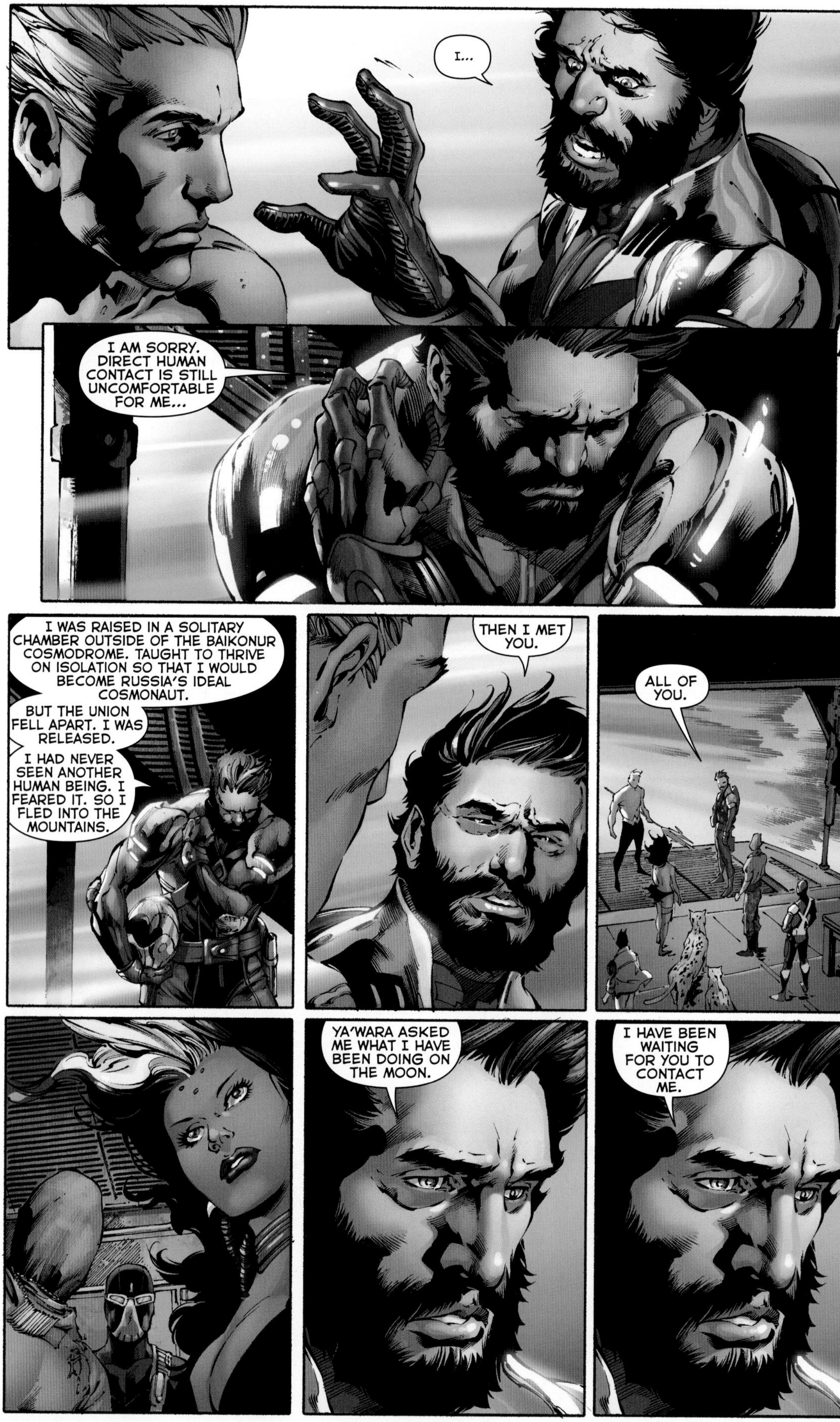
I...
I AM SORRY. DIRECT HUMAN CONTACT IS STILL UNCOMFORTABLE FOR ME...
I WAS RAISED IN A SOLITARY CHAMBER OUTSIDE OF THE BAIKONUR COSMODROME. TAUGHT TO THRIVE ON ISOLATION SO THAT I WOULD BECOME RUSSIA'S IDEAL COSMONAUT.
BUT THE UNION FELL APART. I WAS RELEASED.
I HAD NEVER SEEN ANOTHER HUMAN BEING. I FEARED IT. SO I FLED INTO THE MOUNTAINS.
THEN I MET YOU.
ALL OF YOU.
YA'WARA ASKED ME WHAT I HAVE BEEN DOING ON THE MOON.
I HAVE BEEN WAITING FOR YOU TO CONTACT ME.

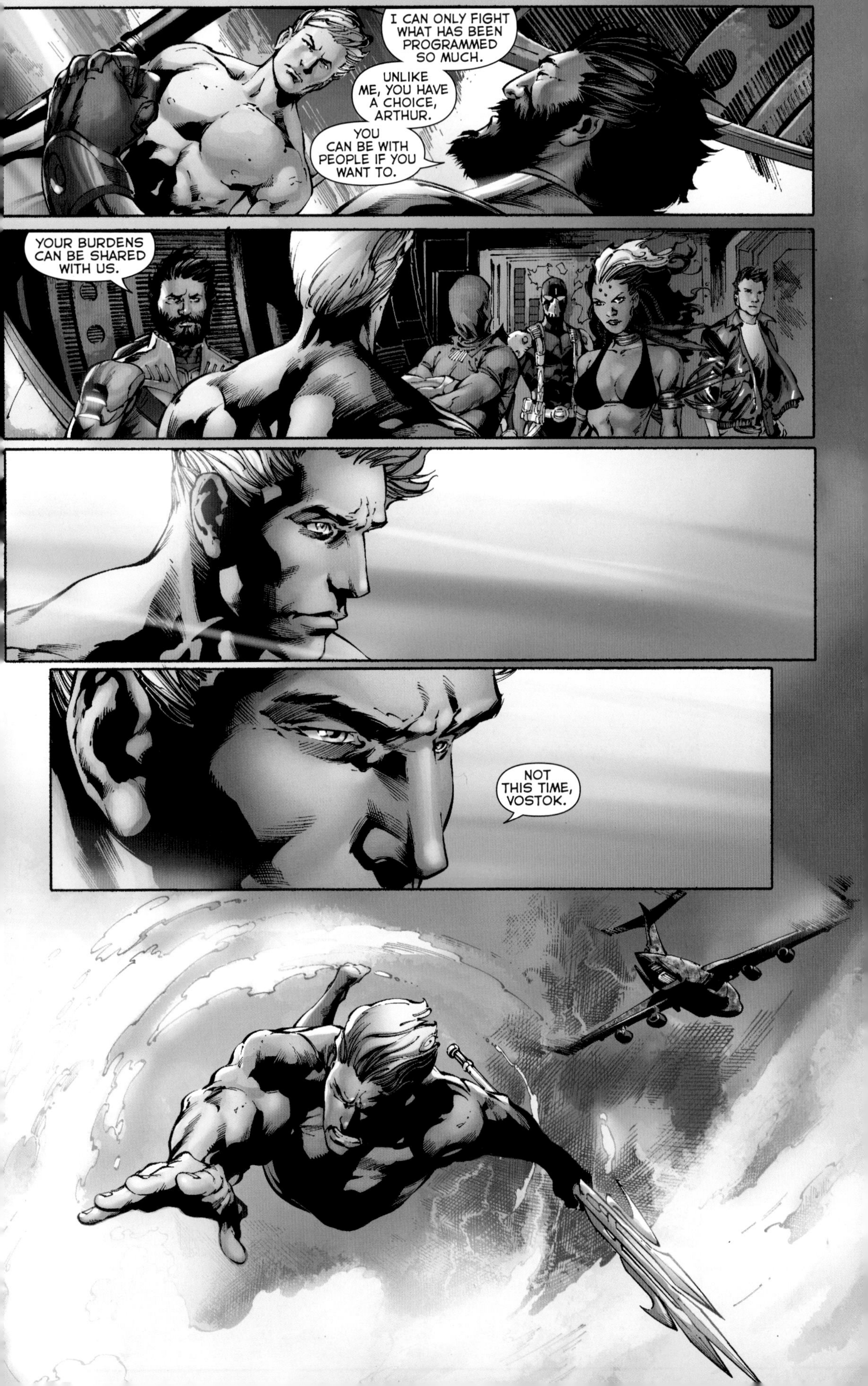
I CAN ONLY FIGHT WHAT HAS BEEN PROGRAMMED SO MUCH.
UNLIKE ME, YOU HAVE A CHOICE, ARTHUR.
YOU CAN BE WITH PEOPLE IF YOU WANT TO.
YOUR BURDENS CAN BE SHARED WITH US.
NOT THIS TIME, VOSTOK.

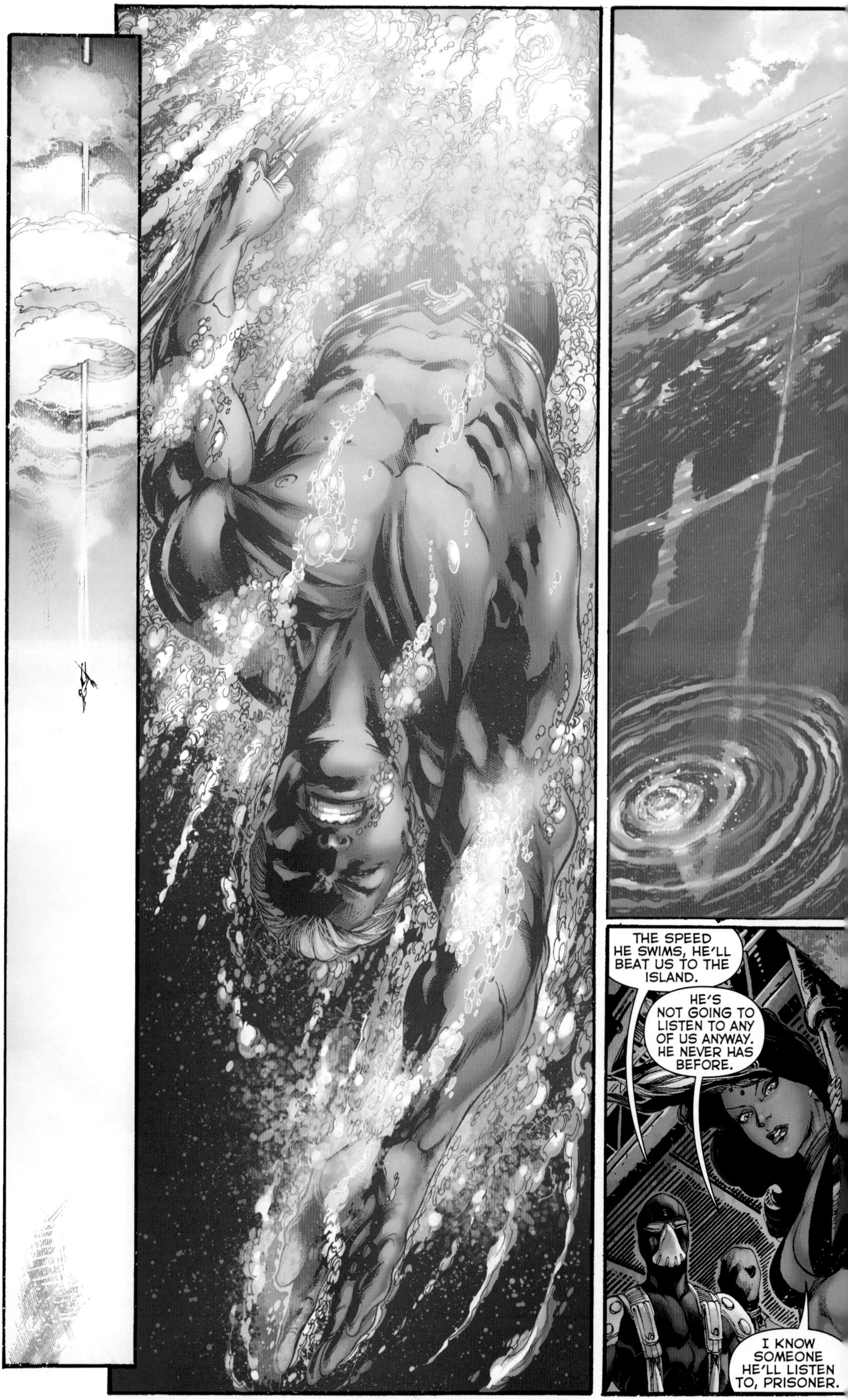
THE SPEED HE SWIMS, HE'LL BEAT US TO THE ISLAND.
HE'S NOT GOING TO LISTEN TO ANY OF US ANYWAY. HE NEVER HAS BEFORE.
I KNOW SOMEONE HE'LL LISTEN TO, PRISONER.

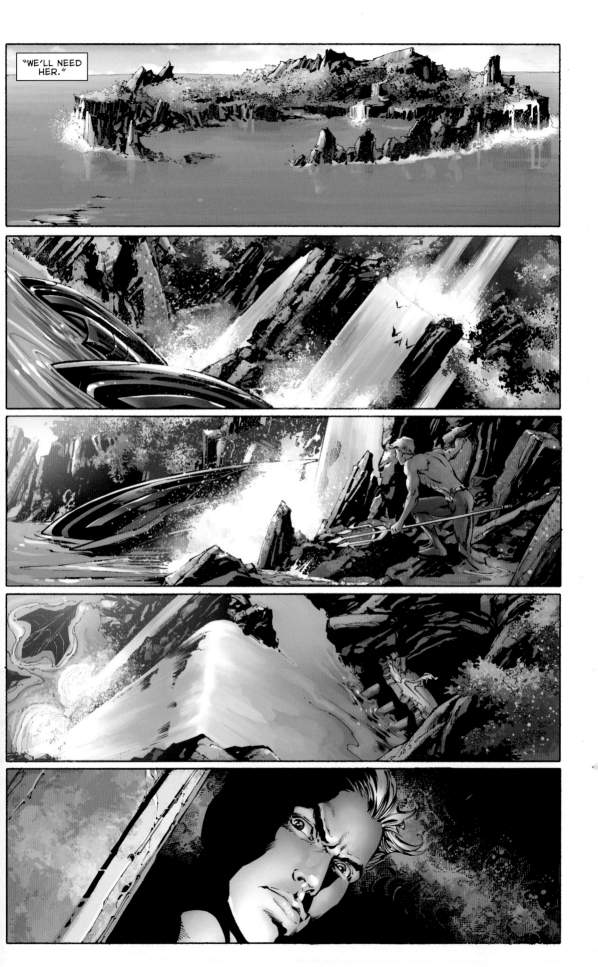

"WE'LL NEED HER."

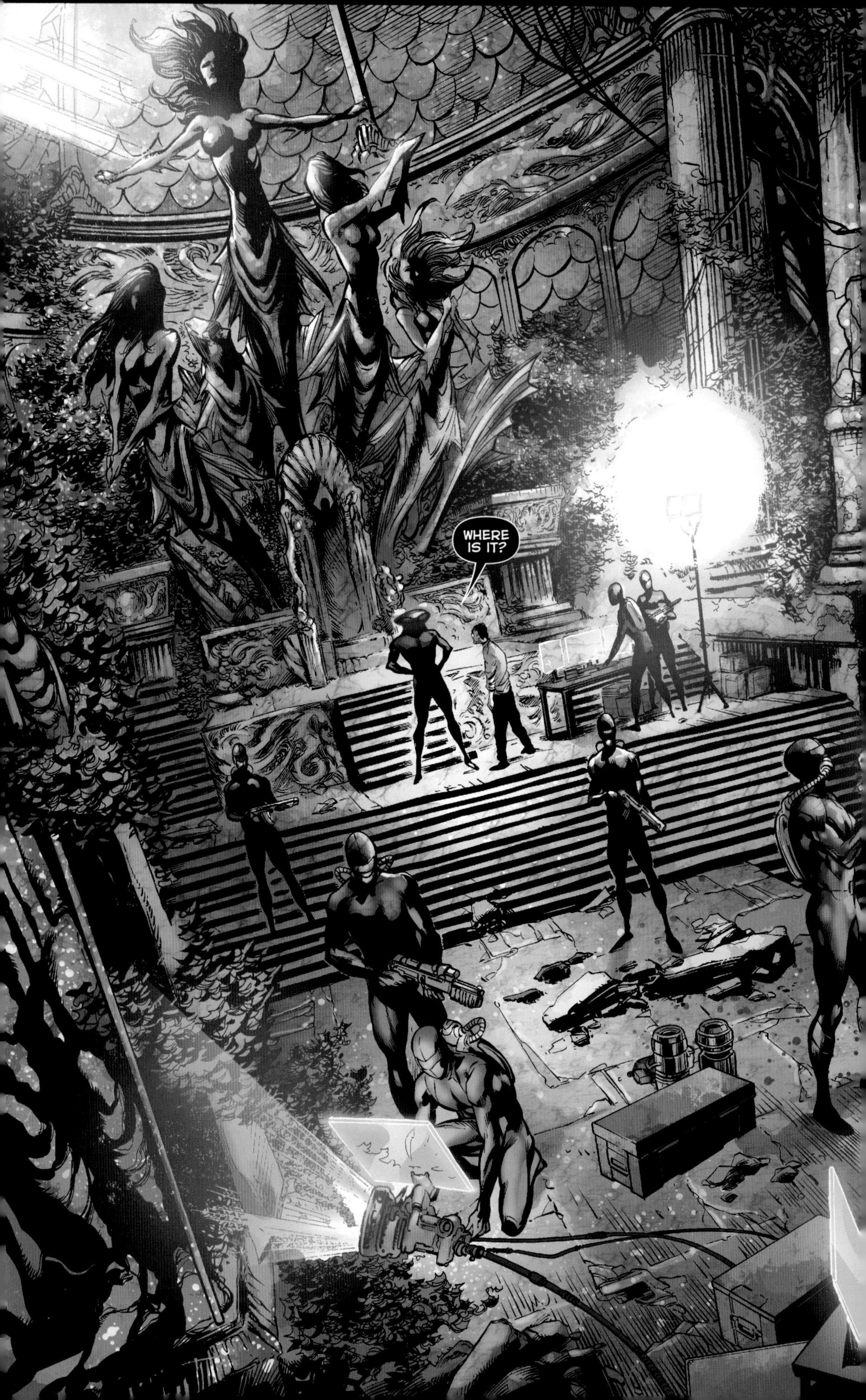
WHERE IS IT?

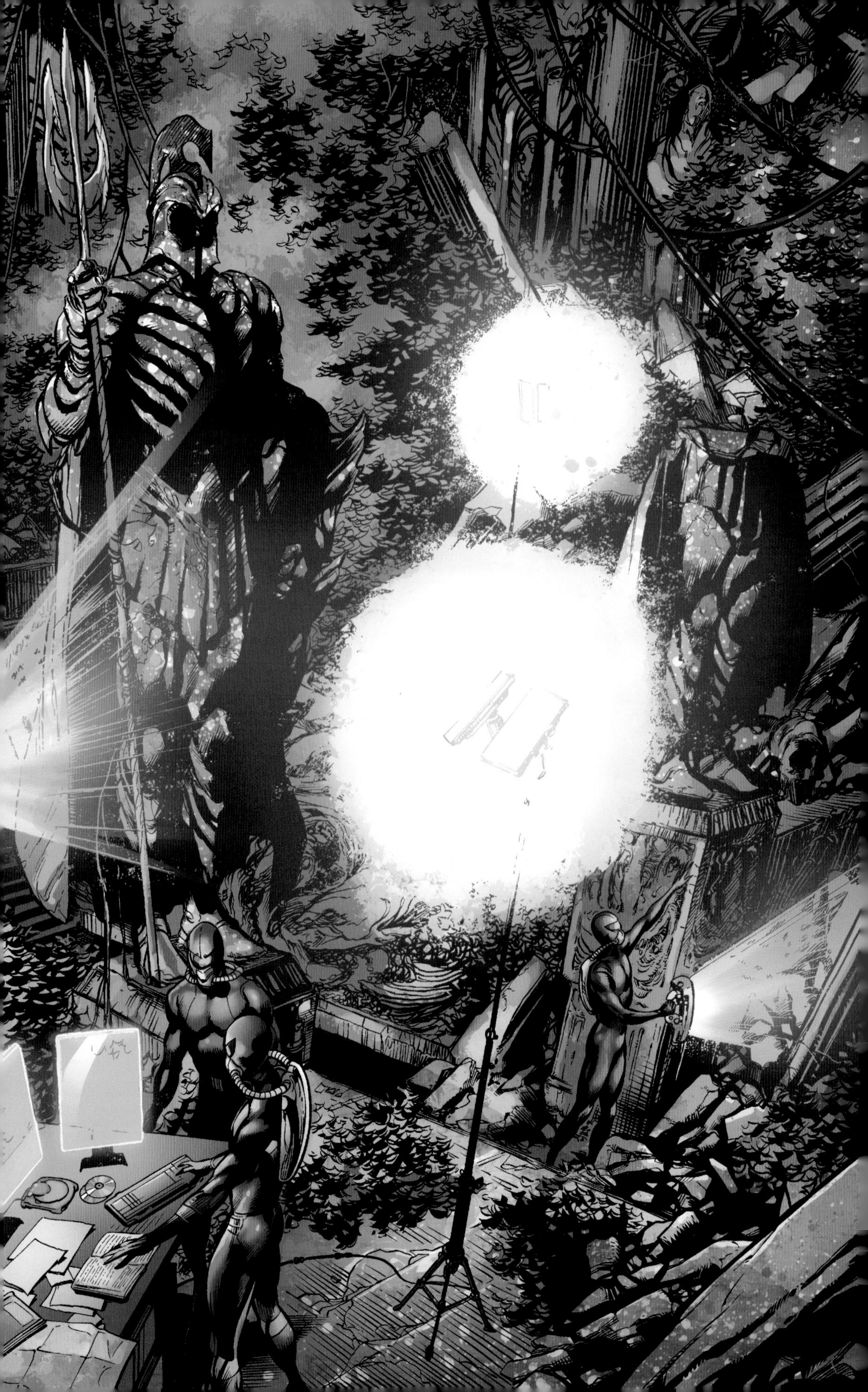

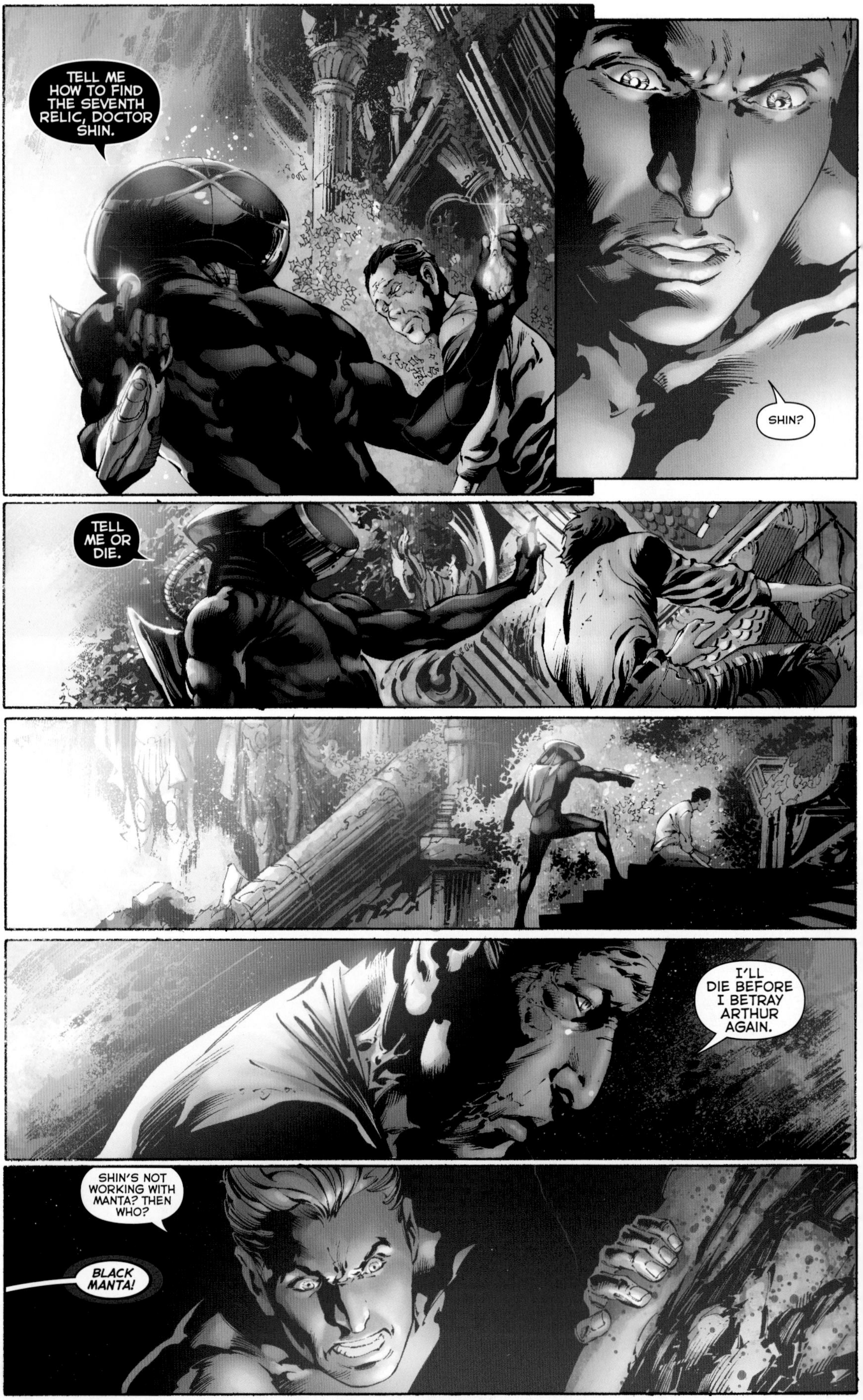
TELL ME HOW TO FIND THE SEVENTH RELIC, DOCTOR SHIN.
SHIN?
TELL ME OR DIE.
I'LL DIE BEFORE I BETRAY ARTHUR AGAIN.
SHIN'S NOT WORKING WITH MANTA? THEN WHO?
BLACK MANTA!

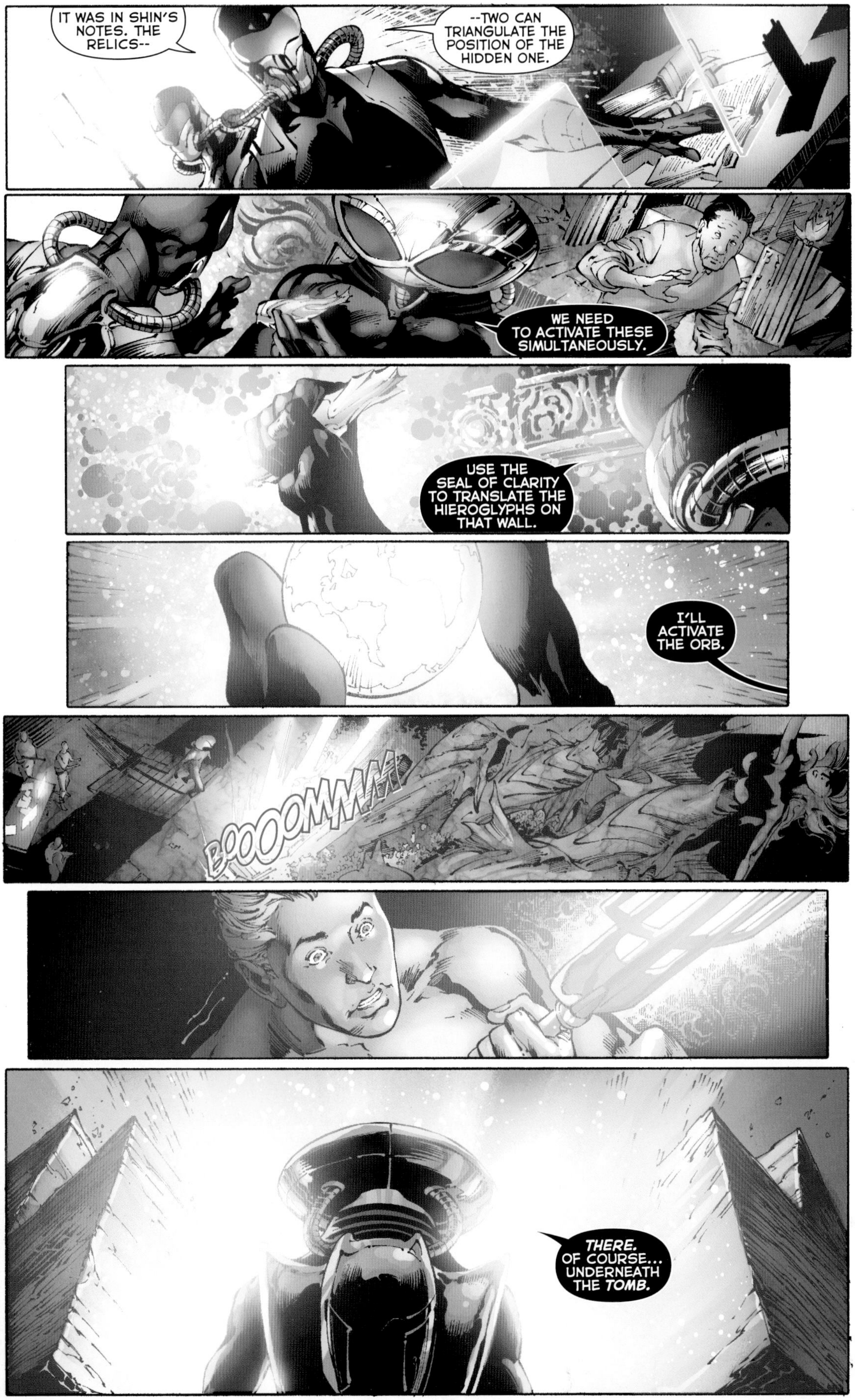
IT WAS IN SHIN'S NOTES. THE RELICS--
--TWO CAN TRIANGULATE THE POSITION OF THE HIDDEN ONE.
WE NEED TO ACTIVATE THESE SIMULTANEOUSLY.
USE THE SEAL OF CLARITY TO TRANSLATE THE HIEROGLYPHS ON THAT WALL.
I'LL ACTIVATE THE ORB.
BOOOOMMMM
THERE. OF COURSE... UNDERNEATH THE *TOMB.*

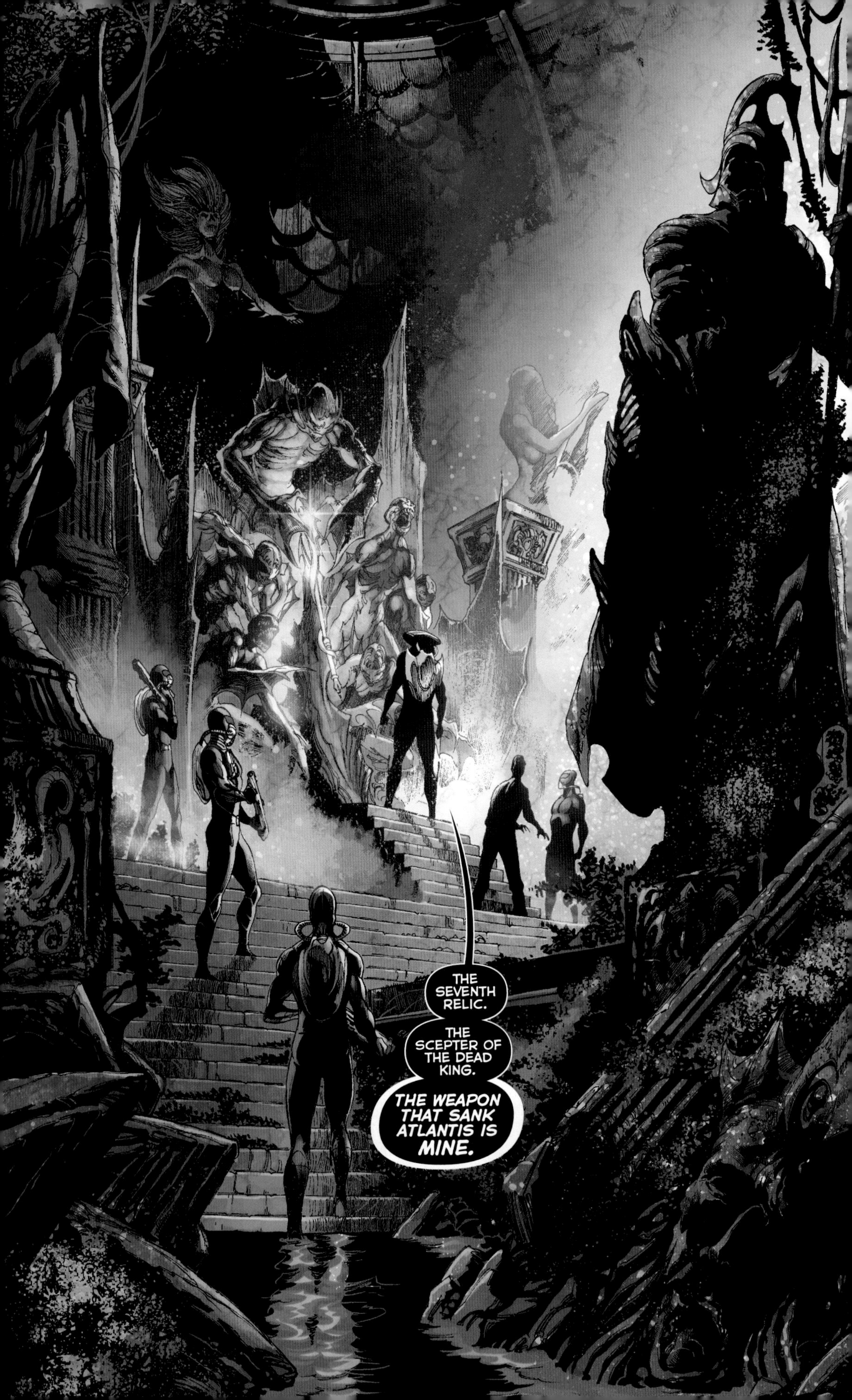
THE SEVENTH RELIC.
THE SCEPTER OF THE DEAD KING.
THE WEAPON THAT SANK ATLANTIS IS MINE.

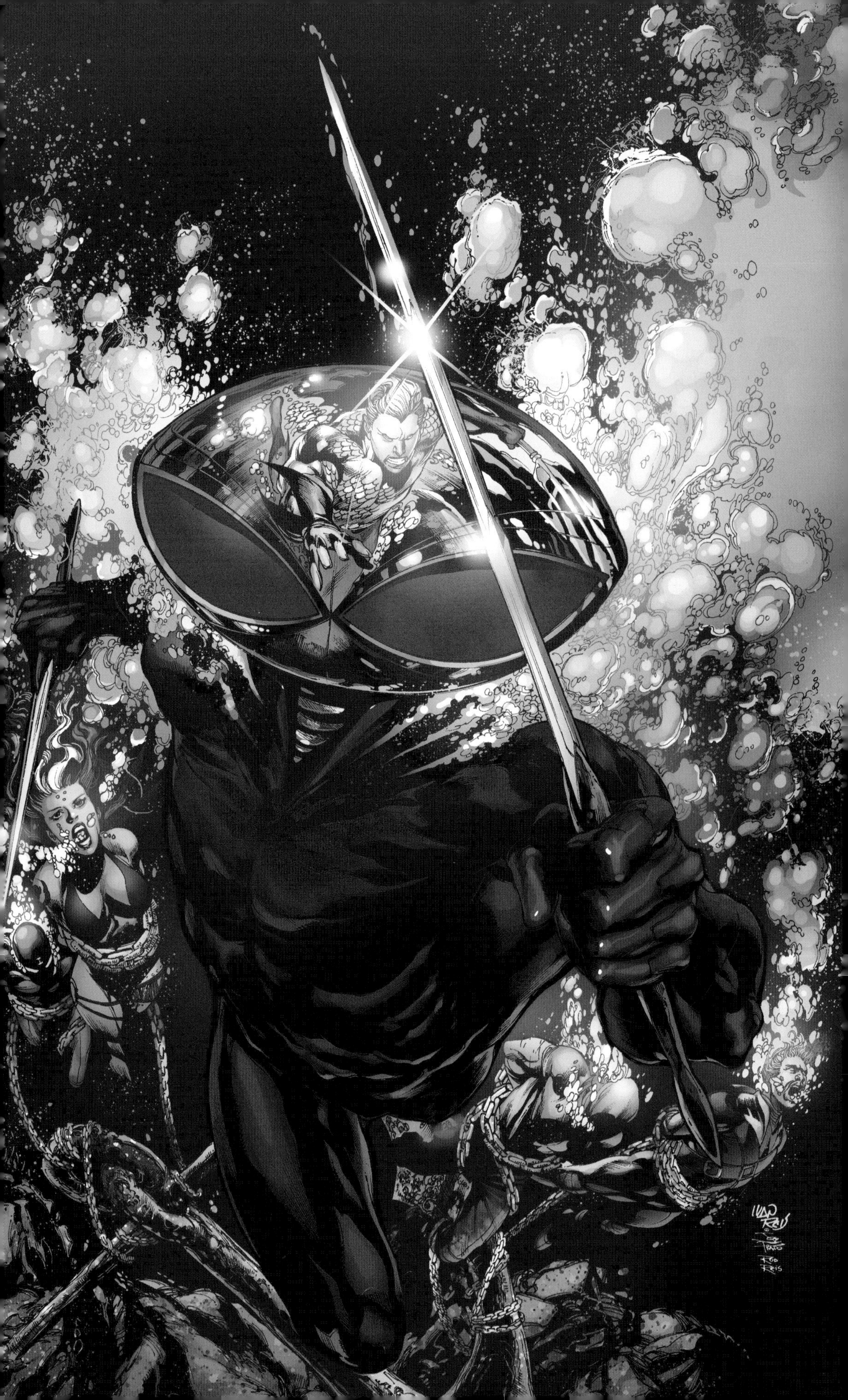

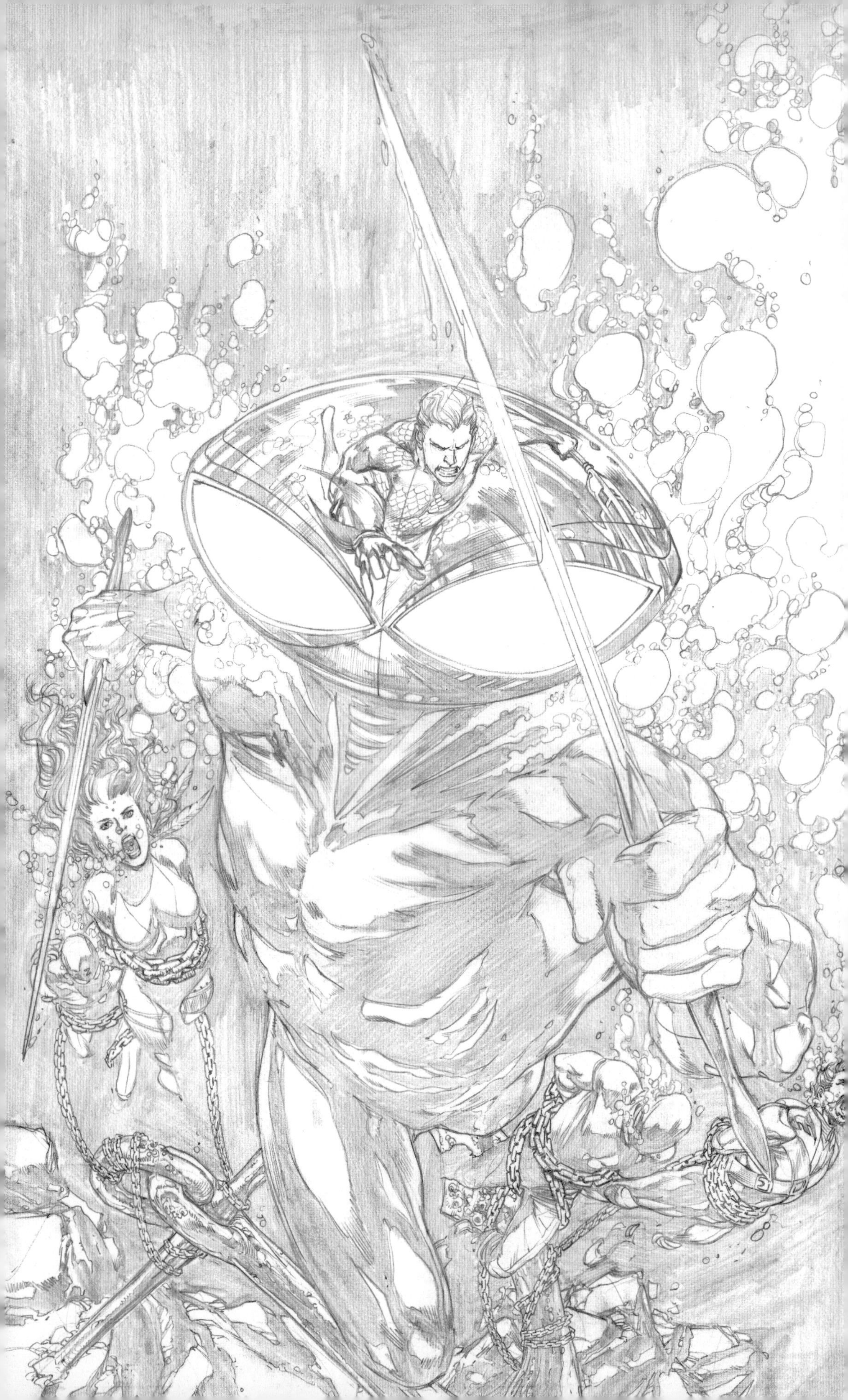

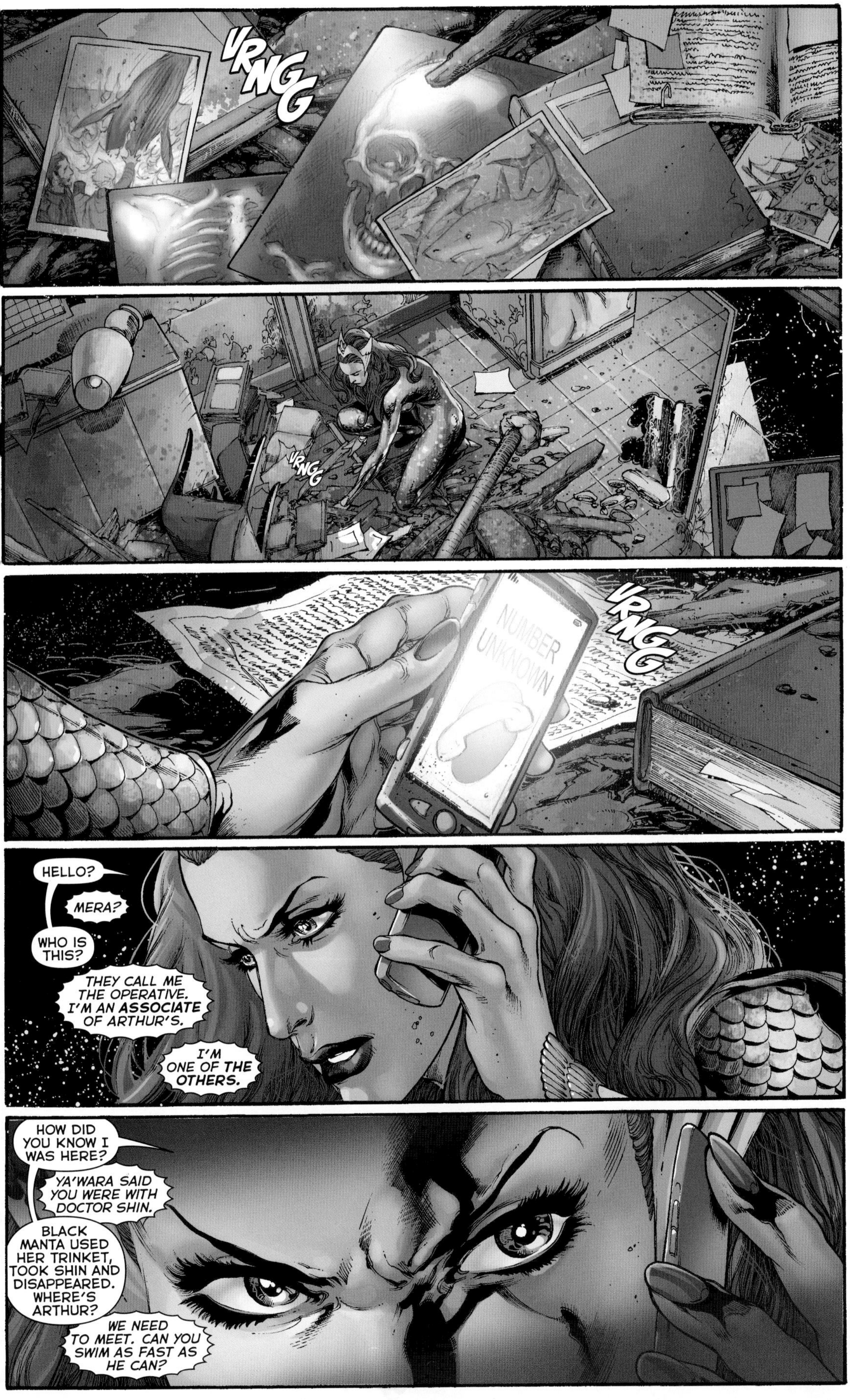
VRNGG
VRNGG
NUMBER UNKNOWN
VRNGG
HELLO?
MERA?
WHO IS THIS?
THEY CALL ME THE OPERATIVE. I'M AN ASSOCIATE OF ARTHUR'S.
I'M ONE OF THE OTHERS.
HOW DID YOU KNOW I WAS HERE?
YA'WARA SAID YOU WERE WITH DOCTOR SHIN.
BLACK MANTA USED HER TRINKET, TOOK SHIN AND DISAPPEARED. WHERE'S ARTHUR?
WE NEED TO MEET. CAN YOU SWIM AS FAST AS HE CAN?

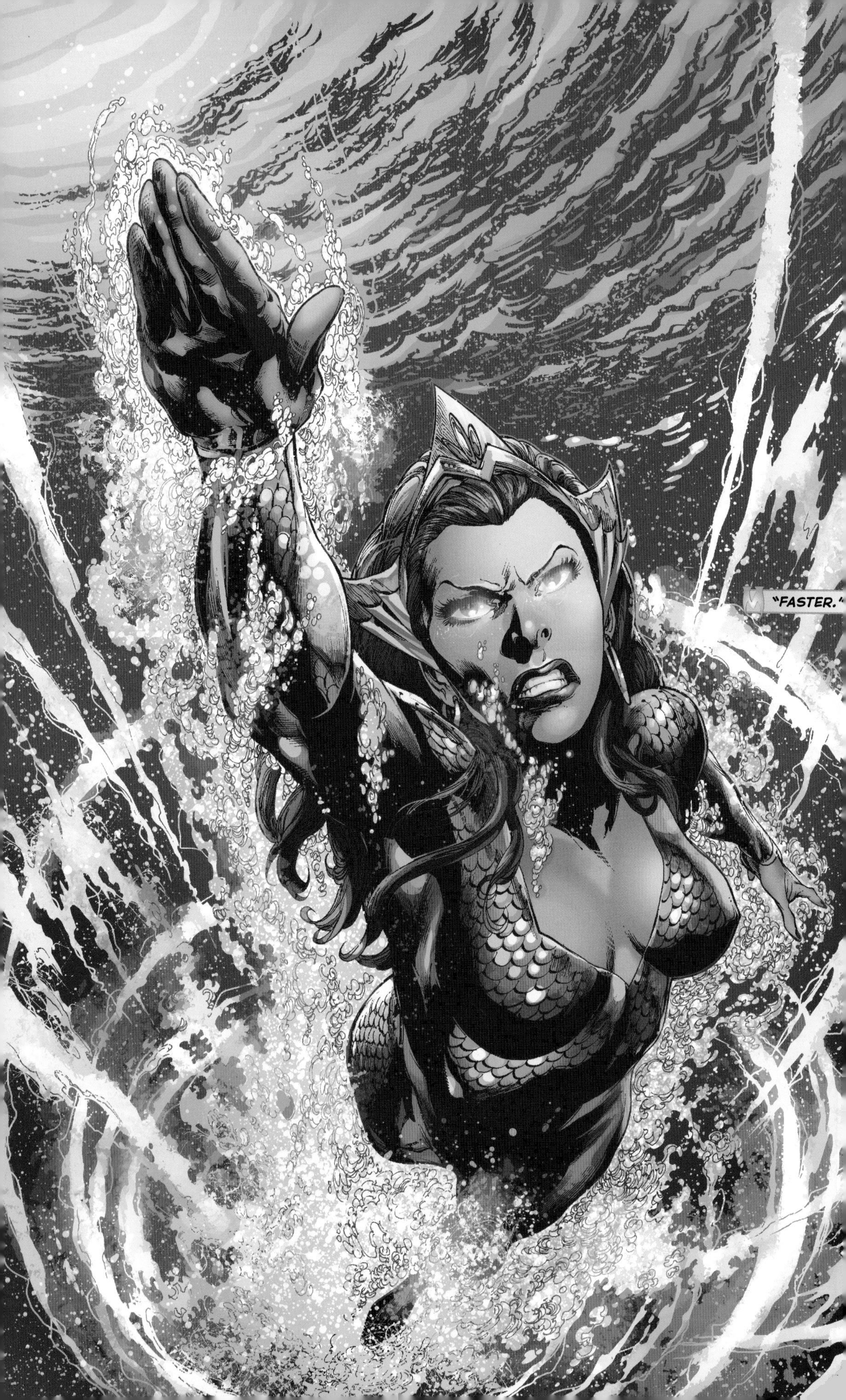
"FASTER."

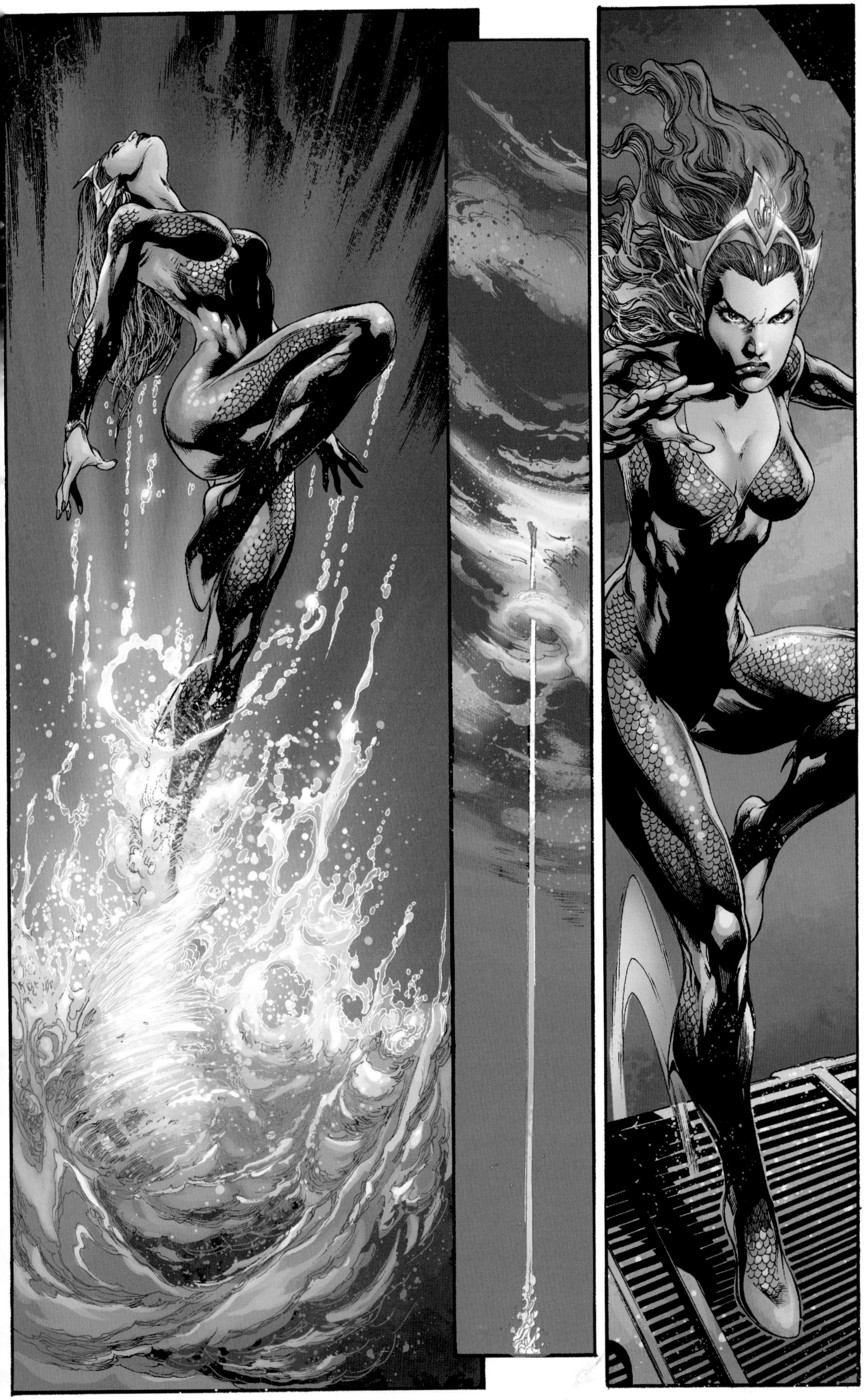

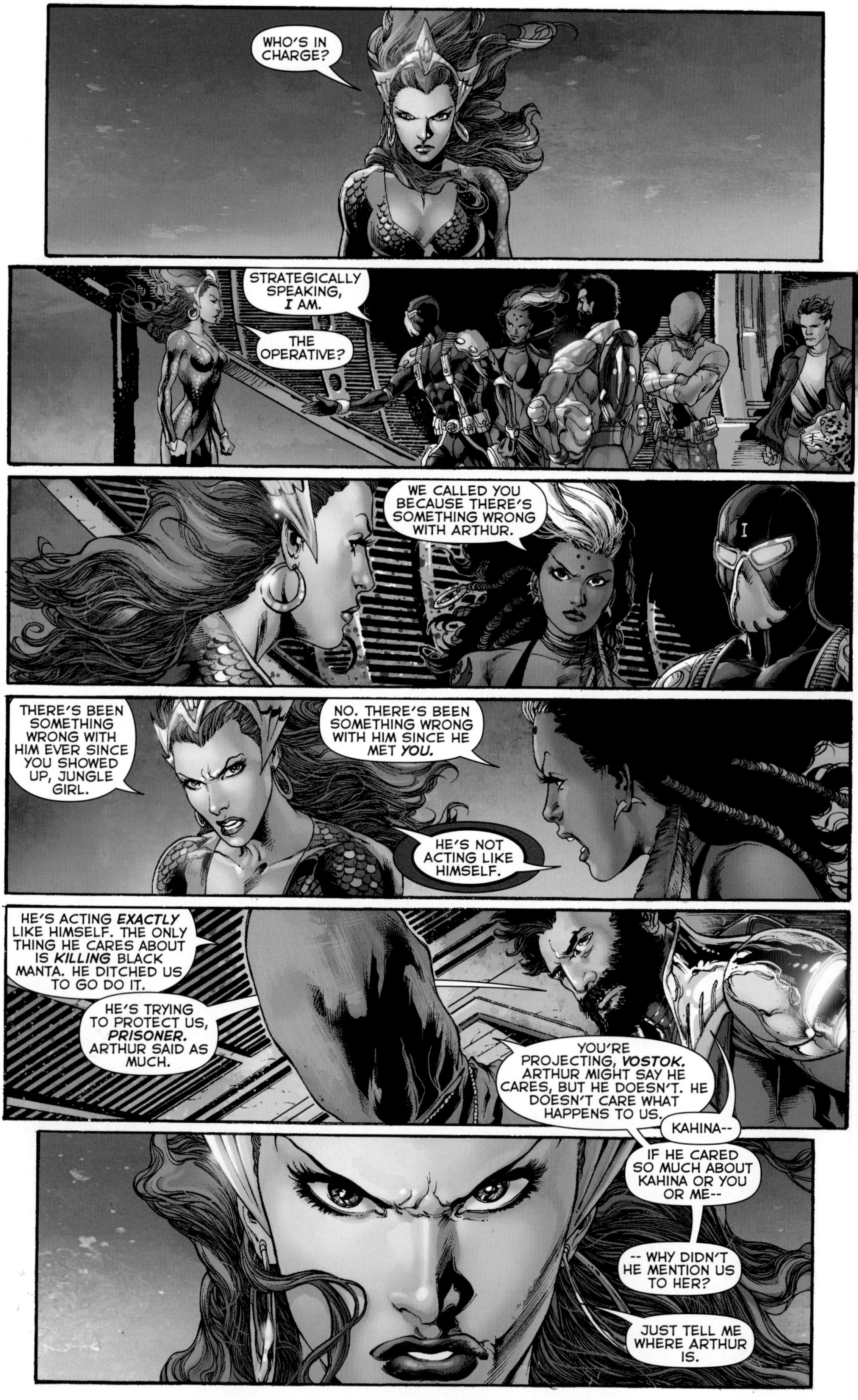

WHO'S IN CHARGE?
STRATEGICALLY SPEAKING, I AM.
THE OPERATIVE?
WE CALLED YOU BECAUSE THERE'S SOMETHING WRONG WITH ARTHUR.
THERE'S BEEN SOMETHING WRONG WITH HIM EVER SINCE YOU SHOWED UP, JUNGLE GIRL.
NO. THERE'S BEEN SOMETHING WRONG WITH HIM SINCE HE MET YOU.
HE'S NOT ACTING LIKE HIMSELF.
HE'S ACTING EXACTLY LIKE HIMSELF. THE ONLY THING HE CARES ABOUT IS KILLING BLACK MANTA. HE DITCHED US TO GO DO IT.
HE'S TRYING TO PROTECT US, PRISONER. ARTHUR SAID AS MUCH.
YOU'RE PROJECTING, VOSTOK. ARTHUR MIGHT SAY HE CARES, BUT HE DOESN'T. HE DOESN'T CARE WHAT HAPPENS TO US.
KAHINA--
IF HE CARED SO MUCH ABOUT KAHINA OR YOU OR ME--
-- WHY DIDN'T HE MENTION US TO HER?
JUST TELL ME WHERE ARTHUR IS.

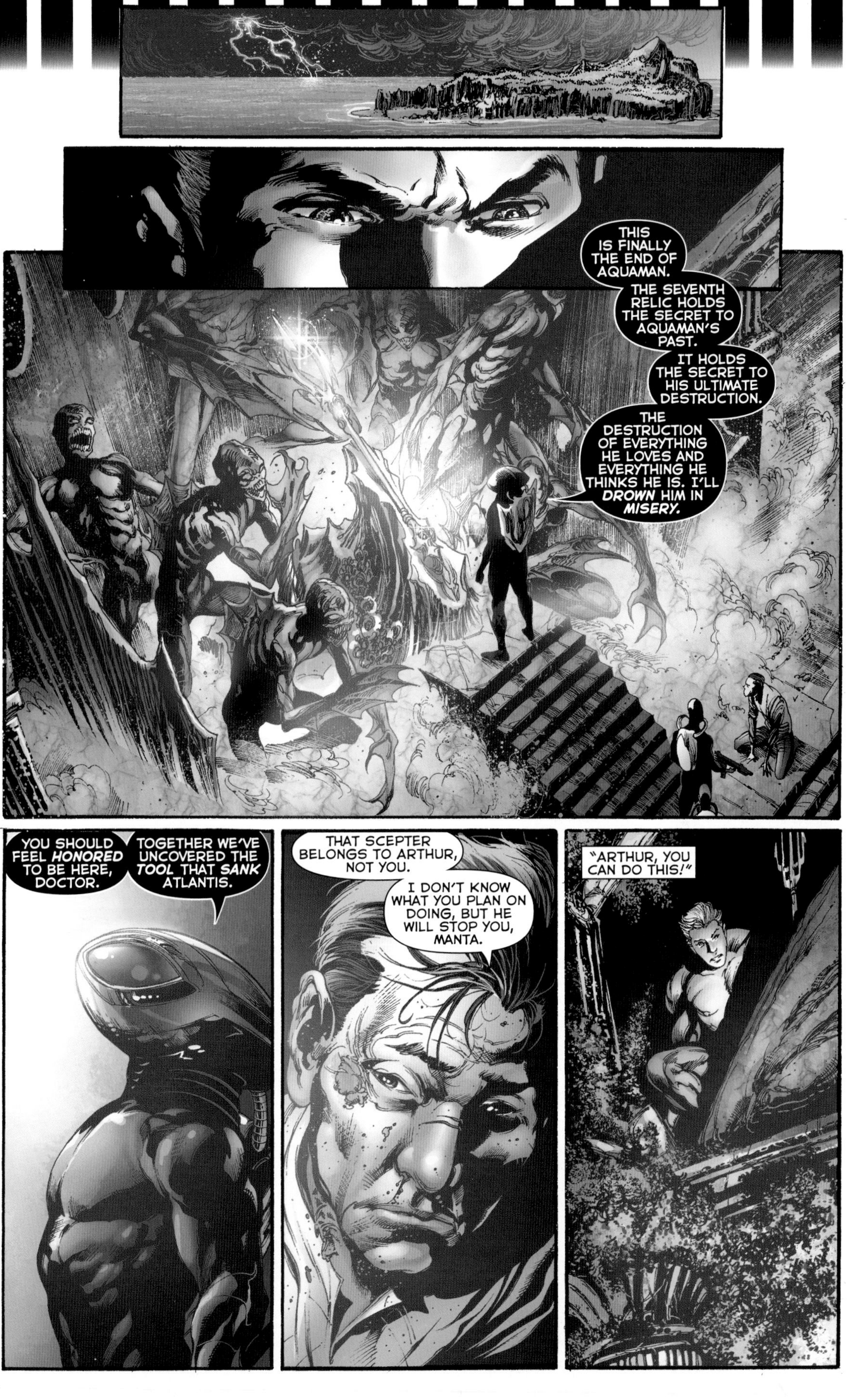
THIS IS FINALLY THE END OF AQUAMAN.
THE SEVENTH RELIC HOLDS THE SECRET TO AQUAMAN'S PAST.
IT HOLDS THE SECRET TO HIS ULTIMATE DESTRUCTION.
THE DESTRUCTION OF EVERYTHING HE LOVES AND EVERYTHING HE THINKS HE IS. I'LL *DROWN* HIM IN *MISERY.*
YOU SHOULD FEEL *HONORED* TO BE HERE, DOCTOR.
TOGETHER WE'VE UNCOVERED THE *TOOL* THAT *SANK* ATLANTIS.
THAT SCEPTER BELONGS TO ARTHUR, NOT YOU.
I DON'T KNOW WHAT YOU PLAN ON DOING, BUT HE WILL STOP YOU, MANTA.
"ARTHUR, YOU CAN DO THIS!"

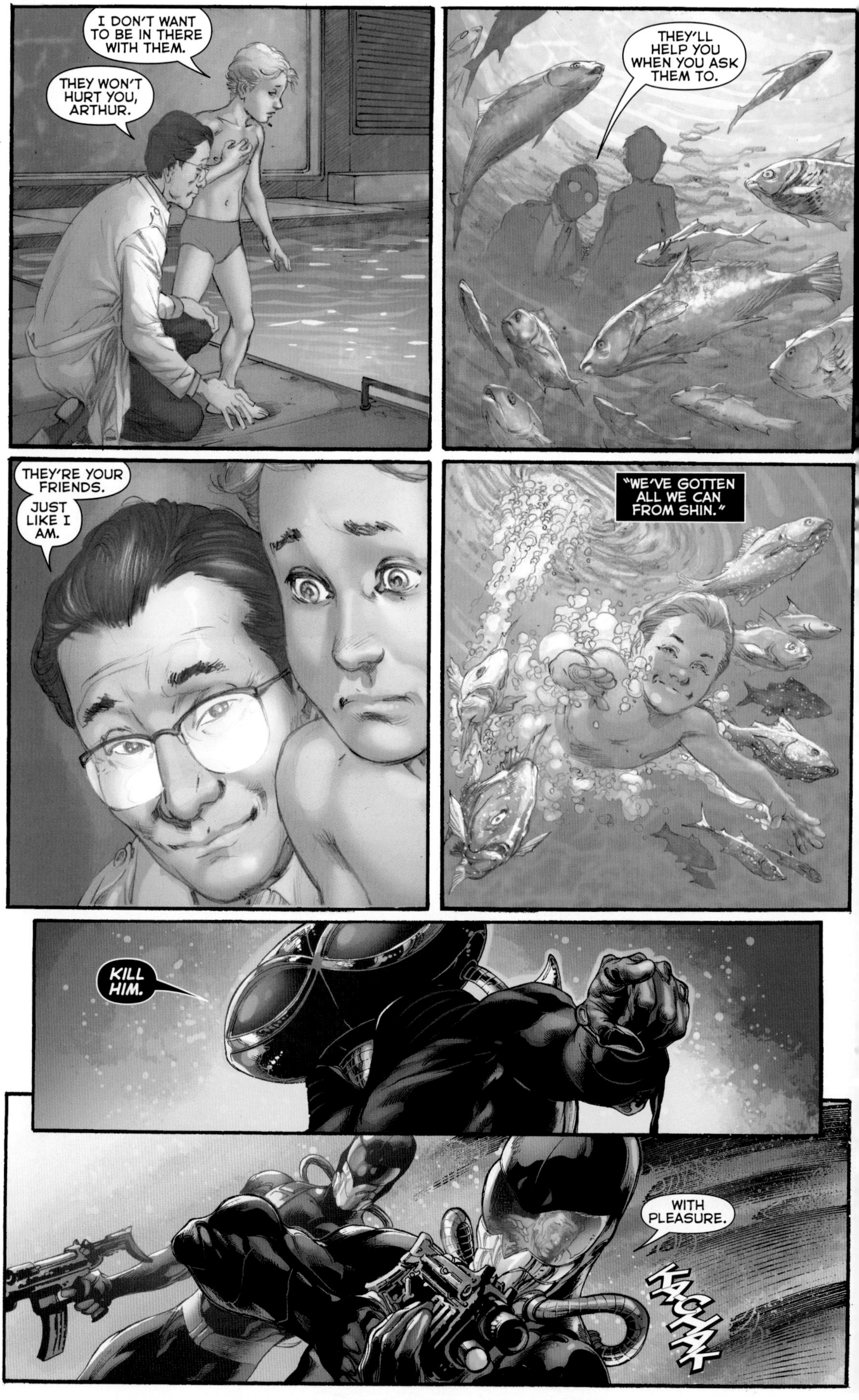
I DON'T WANT TO BE IN THERE WITH THEM.
THEY WON'T HURT YOU, ARTHUR.
THEY'LL HELP YOU WHEN YOU ASK THEM TO.
THEY'RE YOUR FRIENDS.
JUST LIKE I AM.
"WE'VE GOTTEN ALL WE CAN FROM SHIN."
KILL HIM.
WITH PLEASURE.
KACHAK

AH. YOU'RE ALREADY HERE.

THINK!

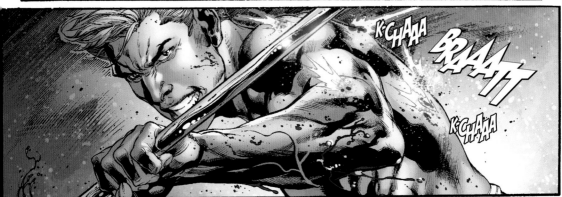

K-CHAAA

BRAATT

K-CHAAA

YOUR TRIDENT IS *NOTHING* COMPARED TO THIS SCEPTER.

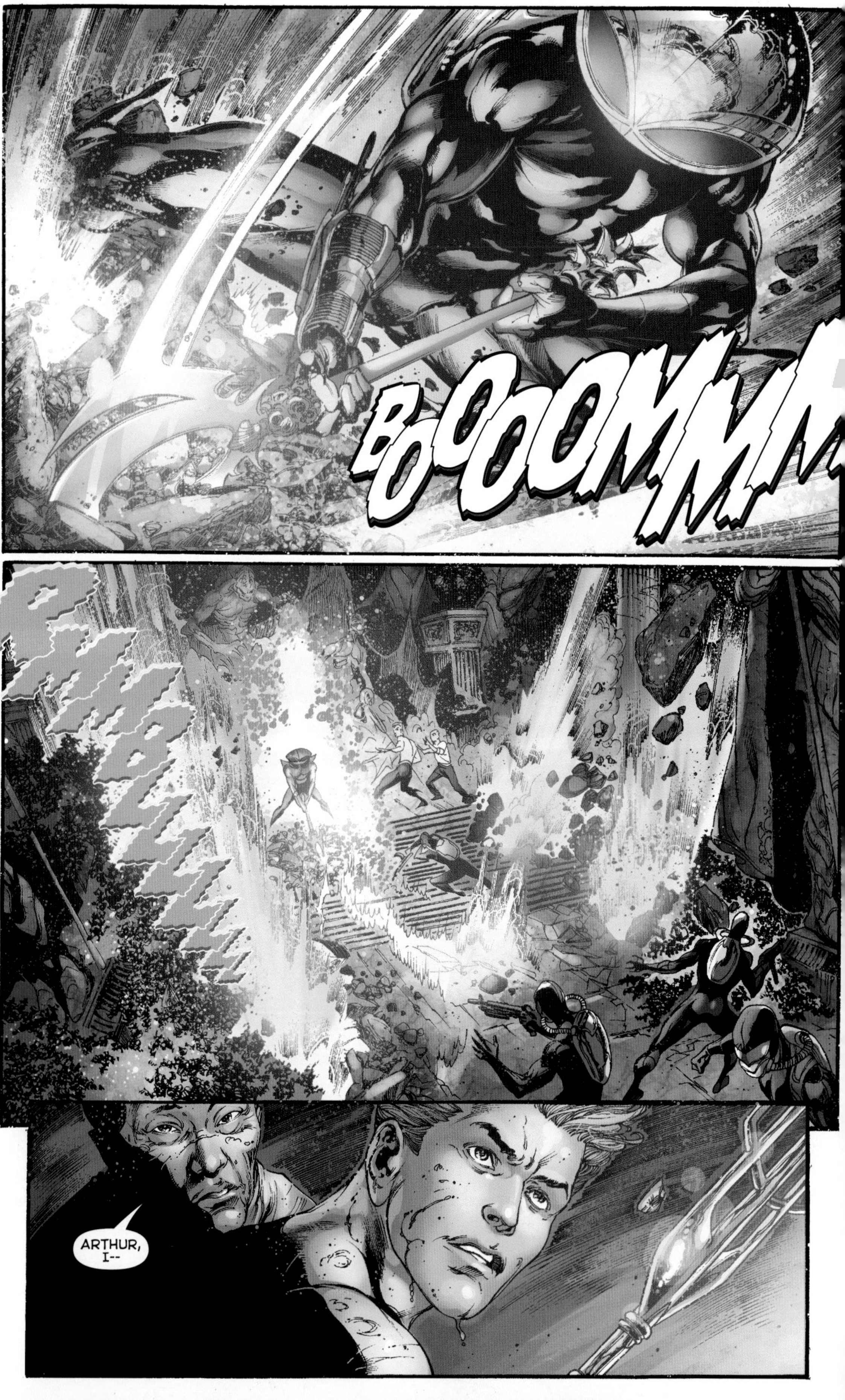
BOOOOMMM
ARTHUR, I--

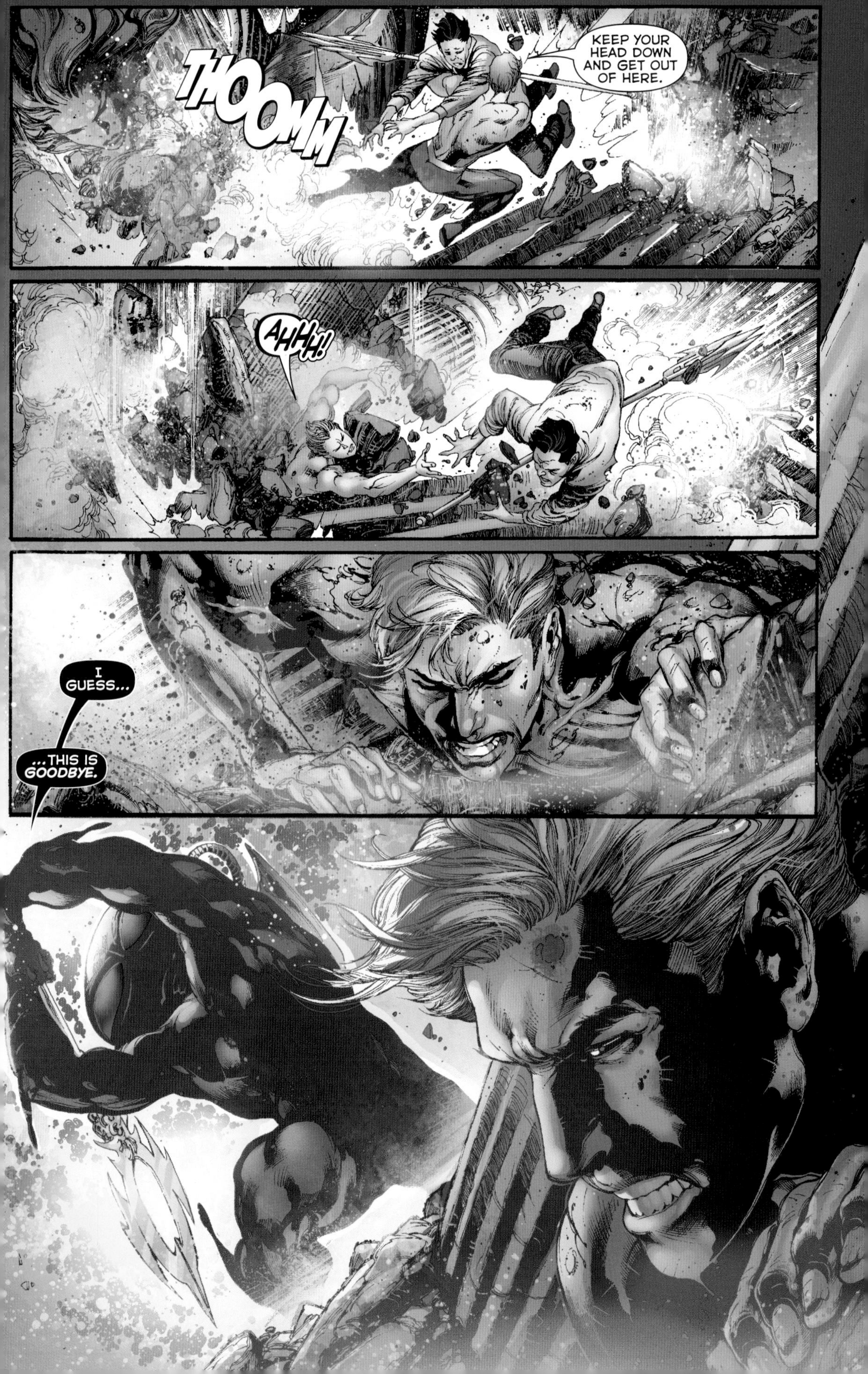
THOOMM
KEEP YOUR HEAD DOWN AND GET OUT OF HERE.
AHHH!
I GUESS...
...THIS IS GOODBYE.

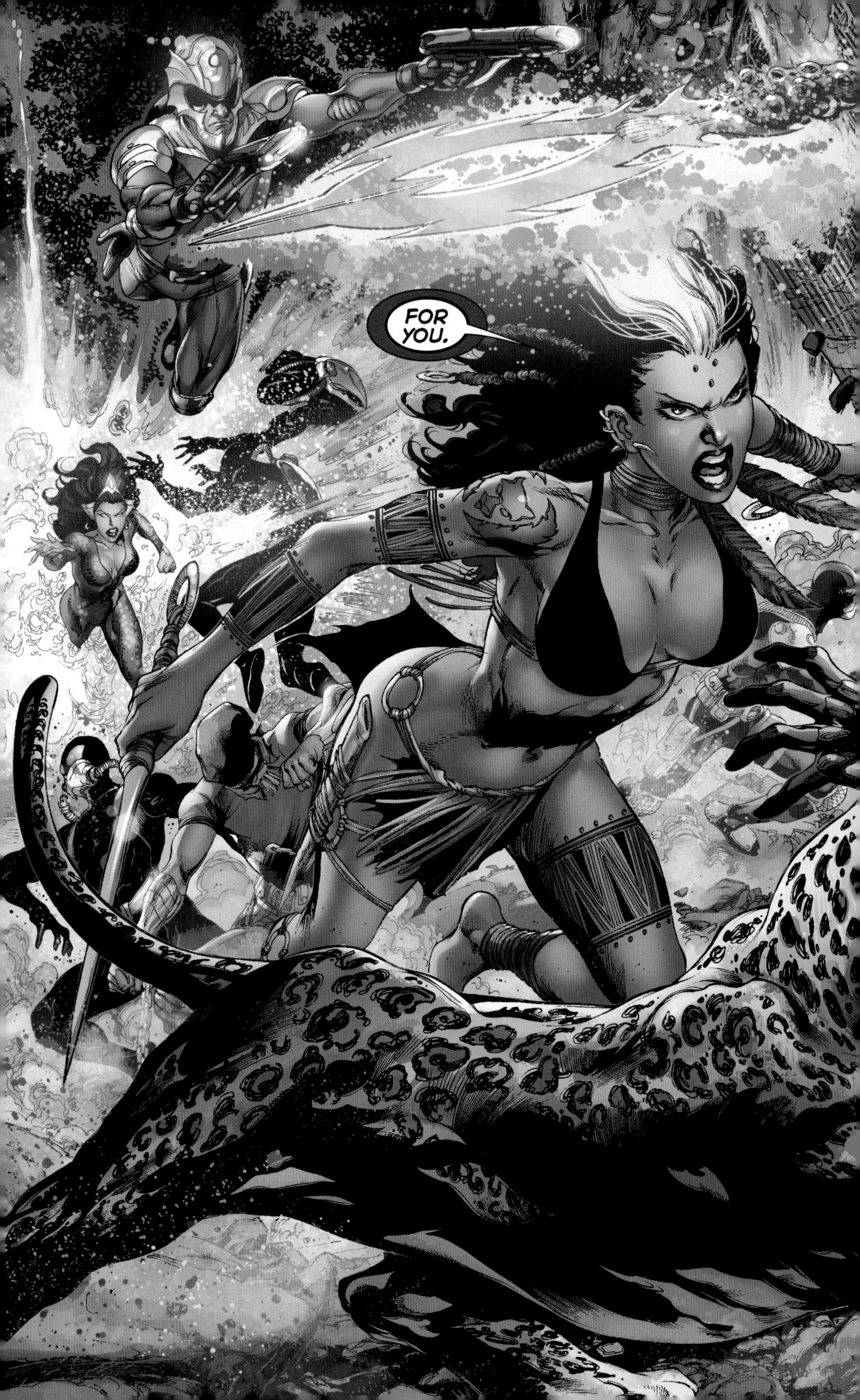
FOR YOU.

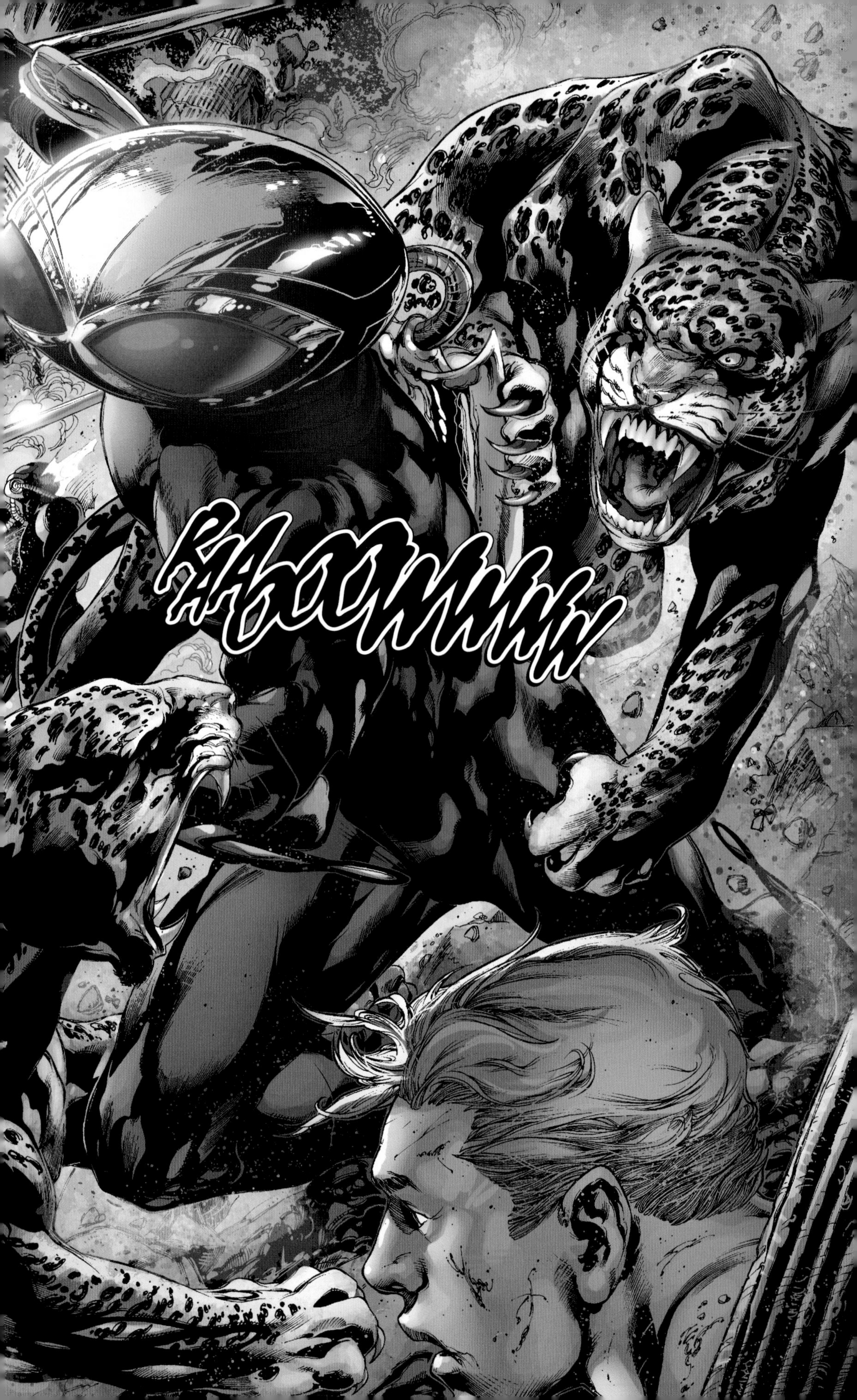

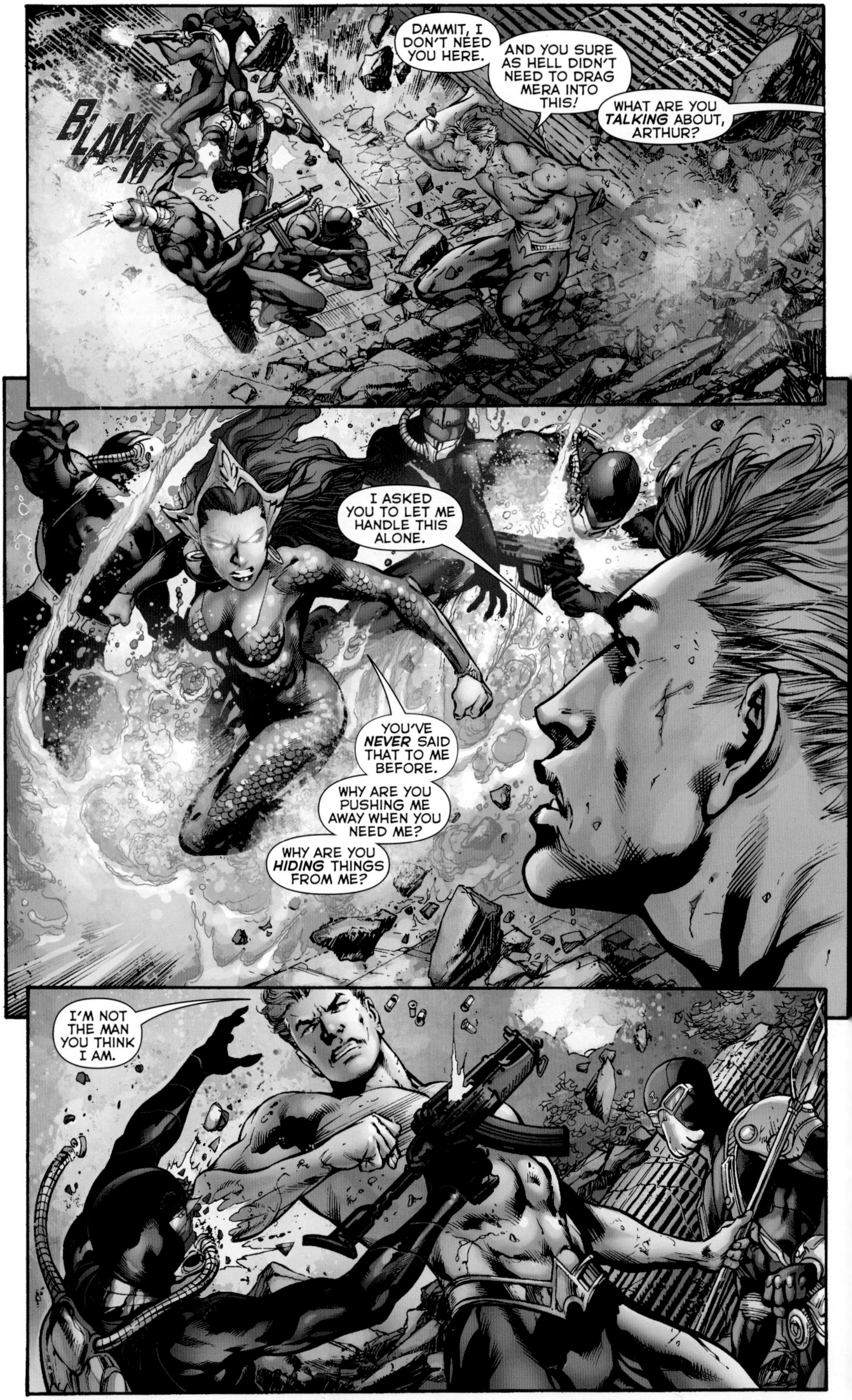
DAMMIT, I DON'T NEED YOU HERE.
AND YOU SURE AS HELL DIDN'T NEED TO DRAG MERA INTO THIS!
WHAT ARE YOU TALKING ABOUT, ARTHUR?
BLAMM
I ASKED YOU TO LET ME HANDLE THIS ALONE.
YOU'VE NEVER SAID THAT TO ME BEFORE.
WHY ARE YOU PUSHING ME AWAY WHEN YOU NEED ME?
WHY ARE YOU HIDING THINGS FROM ME?
I'M NOT THE MAN YOU THINK I AM.

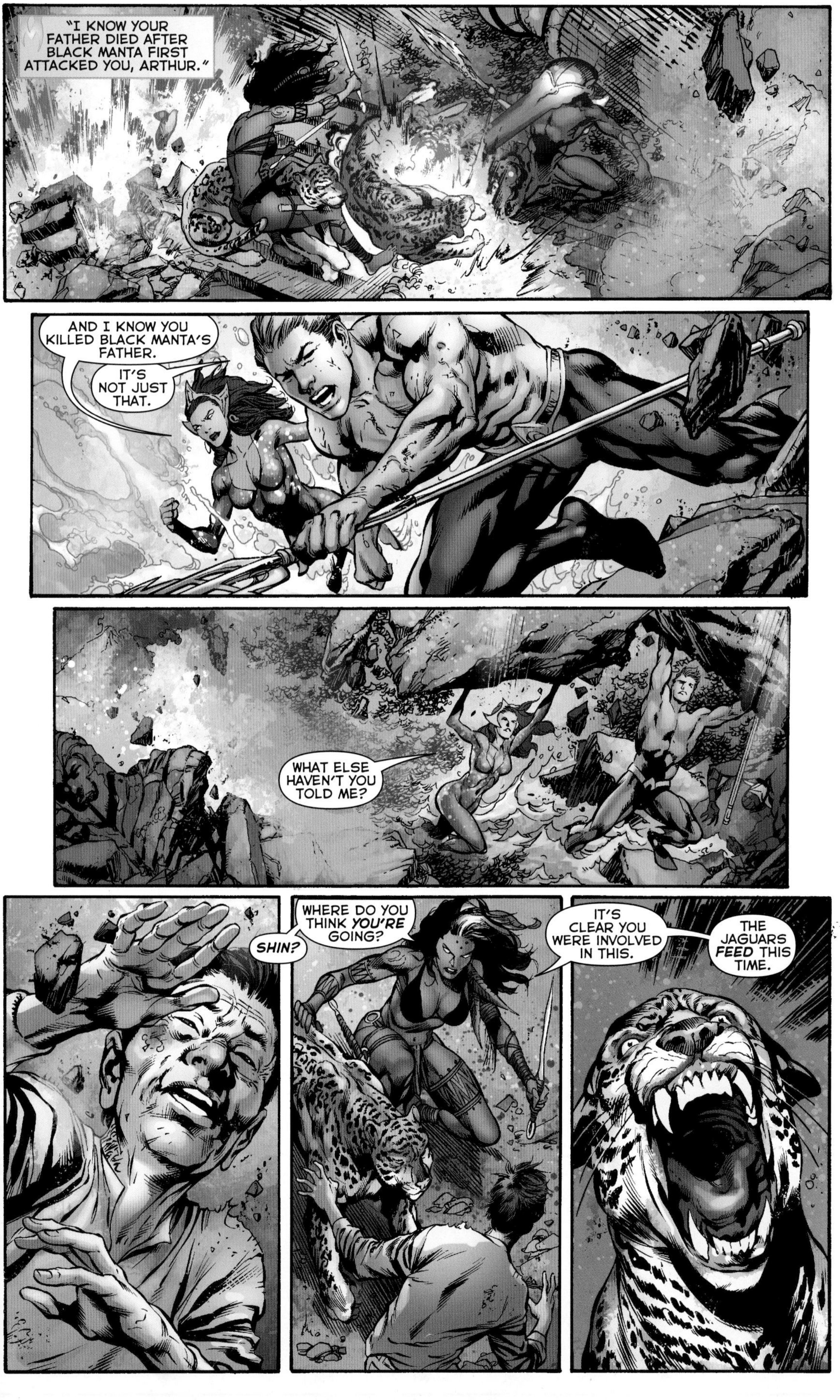
"I KNOW YOUR FATHER DIED AFTER BLACK MANTA FIRST ATTACKED YOU, ARTHUR."
AND I KNOW YOU KILLED BLACK MANTA'S FATHER.
IT'S NOT JUST THAT.
WHAT ELSE HAVEN'T YOU TOLD ME?
WHERE DO YOU THINK YOU'RE GOING?
SHIN?
IT'S CLEAR YOU WERE INVOLVED IN THIS.
THE JAGUARS FEED THIS TIME.

STOP!

DOCTOR SHIN IS UNARMED.

SHIN LED MANTA RIGHT TO US, VOSTOK. TO KAHINA! HE MURDERED HER!

SHIN HAD NOTHING TO DO WITH THIS.

HE'S ONLY MADE YOU *THINK* THAT, ARTHUR. HE'S BETRAYED YOU *BEFORE* AND HE'S DONE IT AGAIN.

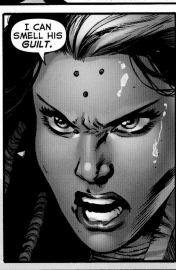

I CAN SMELL HIS *GUILT.*

I'M SO SORRY. GOD, I'M SORRY FOR EVERYTHING, ARTHUR.

DOCTOR SHIN'S REGRET IS REAL, YA'WARA.

LOOK OUT!

BOOOOMMMM

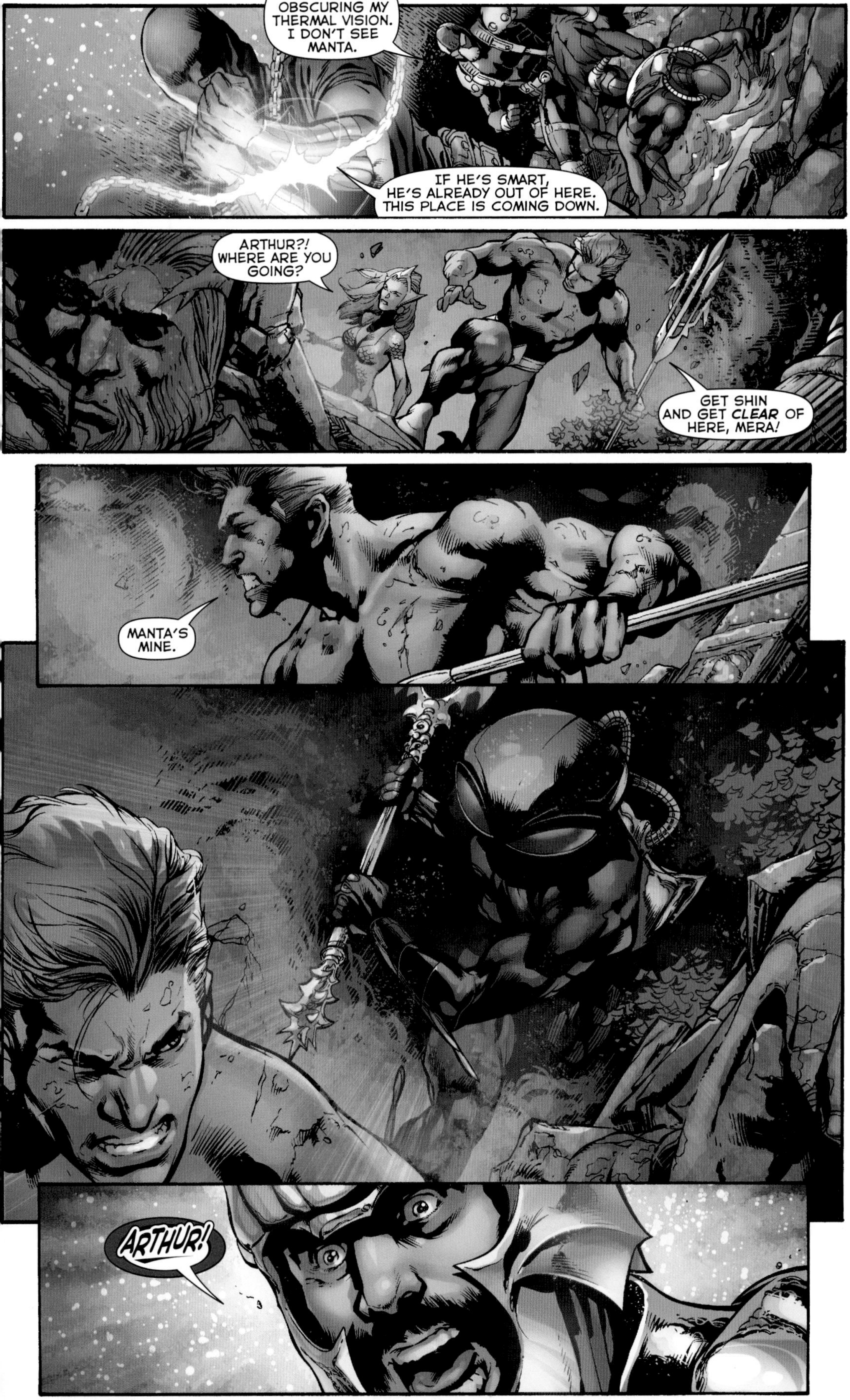
THE CAVE-IN'S OBSCURING MY THERMAL VISION. I DON'T SEE MANTA.
IF HE'S SMART, HE'S ALREADY OUT OF HERE. THIS PLACE IS COMING DOWN.
ARTHUR?! WHERE ARE YOU GOING?
GET SHIN AND GET *CLEAR* OF HERE, MERA!
MANTA'S MINE.
ARTHUR!

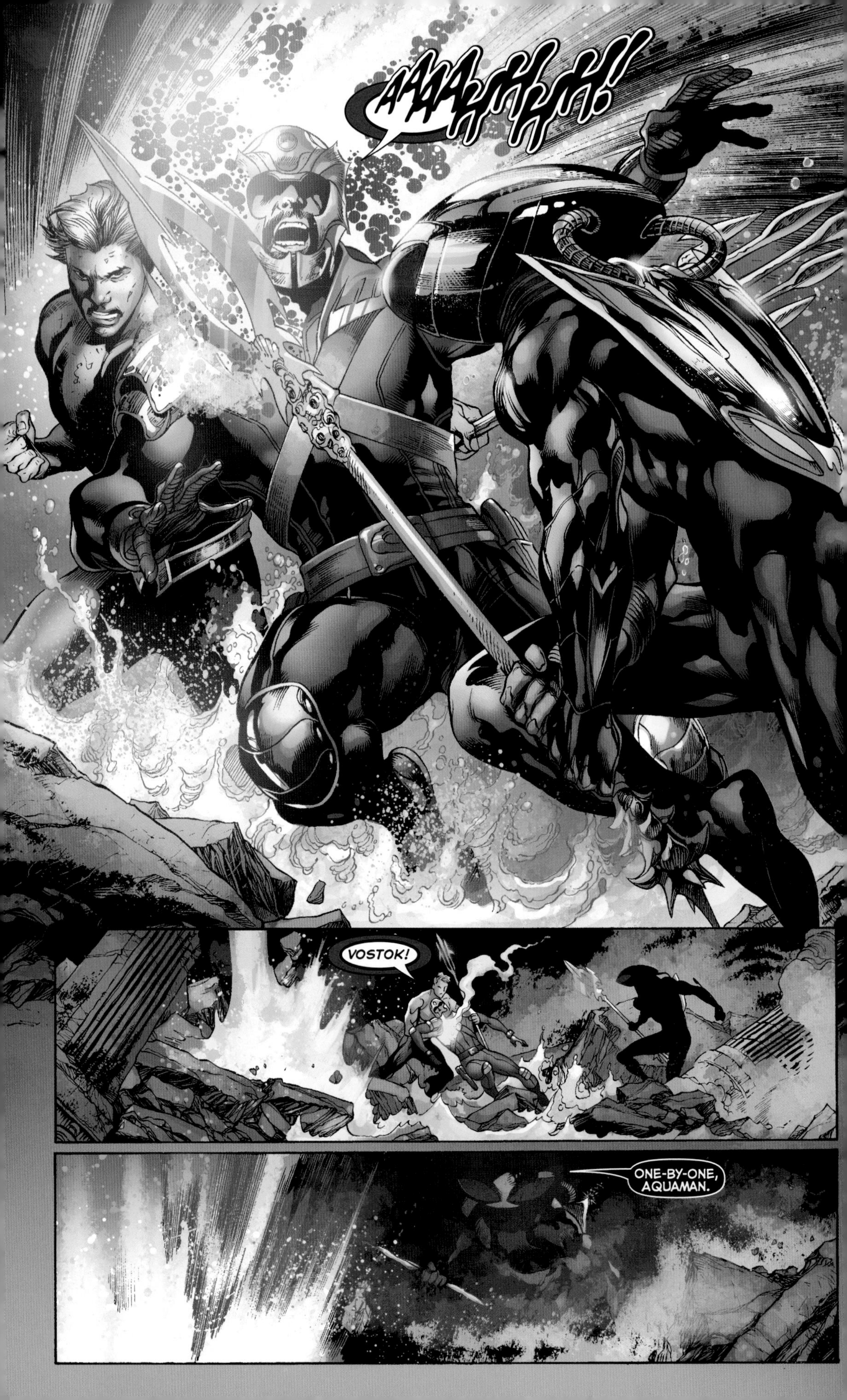
AAAAHHHH!
VOSTOK!
ONE-BY-ONE, AQUAMAN.

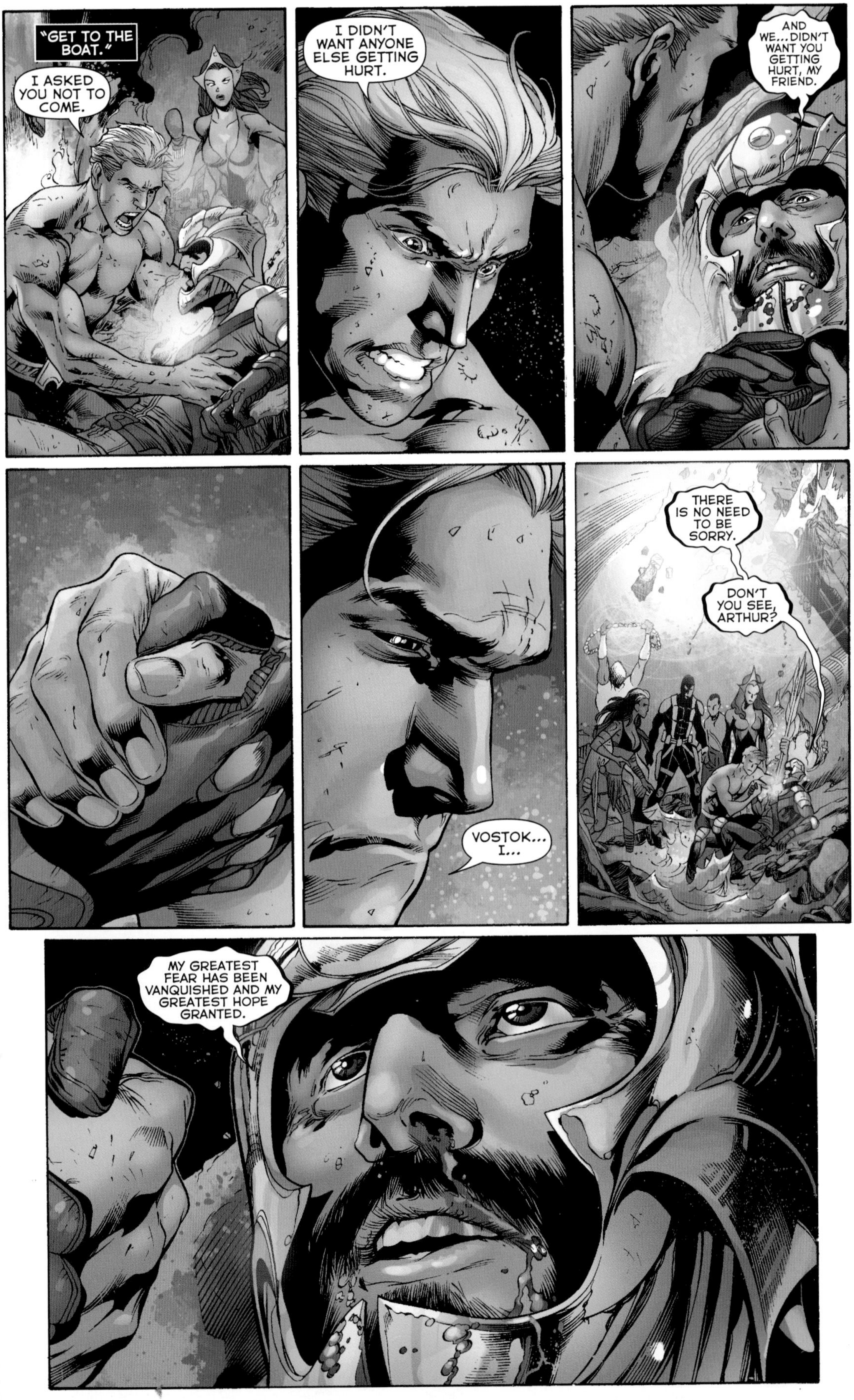
"GET TO THE BOAT."
I ASKED YOU NOT TO COME.
I DIDN'T WANT ANYONE ELSE GETTING HURT.
AND WE...DIDN'T WANT YOU GETTING HURT, MY FRIEND.
VOSTOK... I...
THERE IS NO NEED TO BE SORRY.
DON'T YOU SEE, ARTHUR?
MY GREATEST FEAR HAS BEEN VANQUISHED AND MY GREATEST HOPE GRANTED.

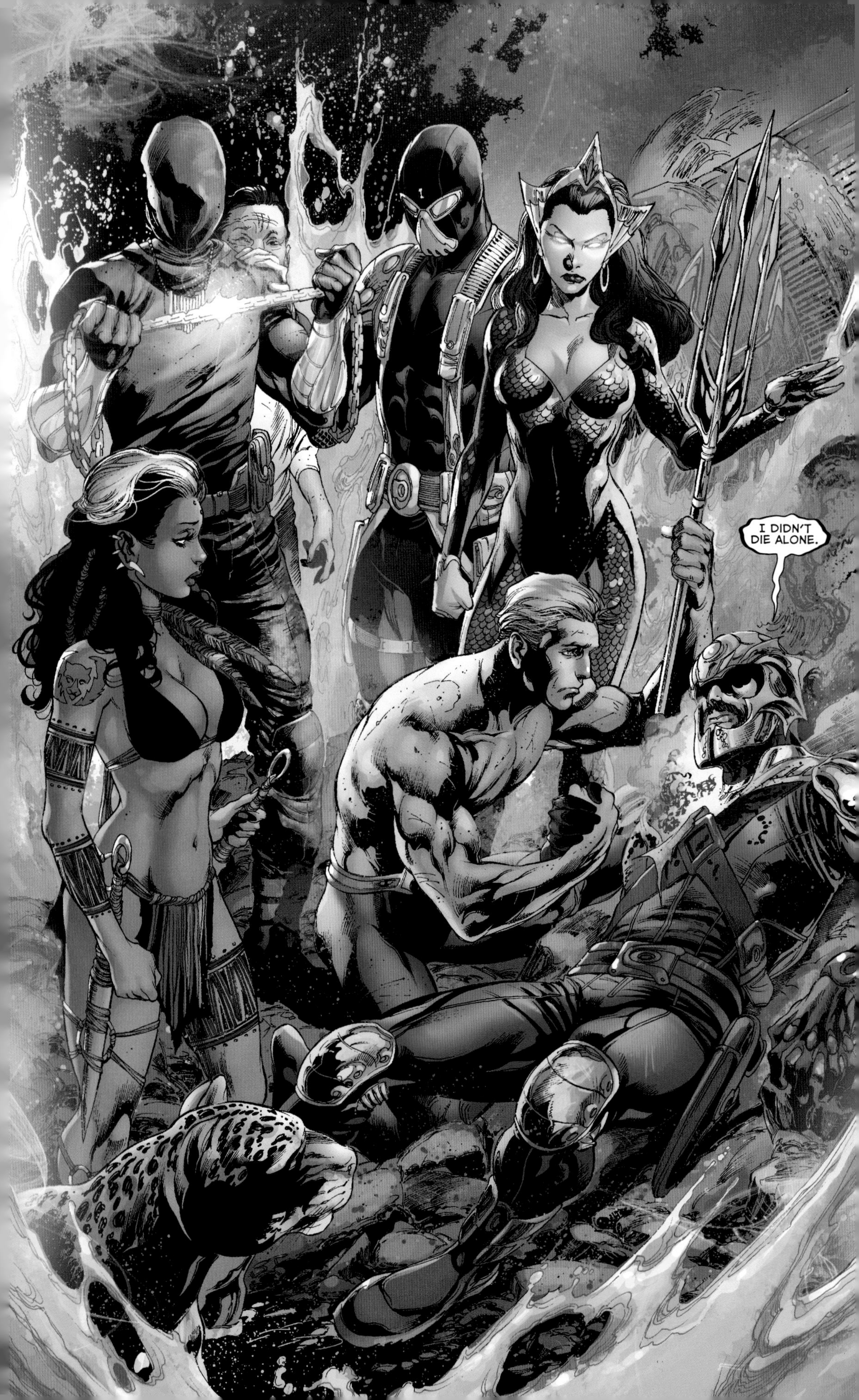
I DIDN'T DIE ALONE.

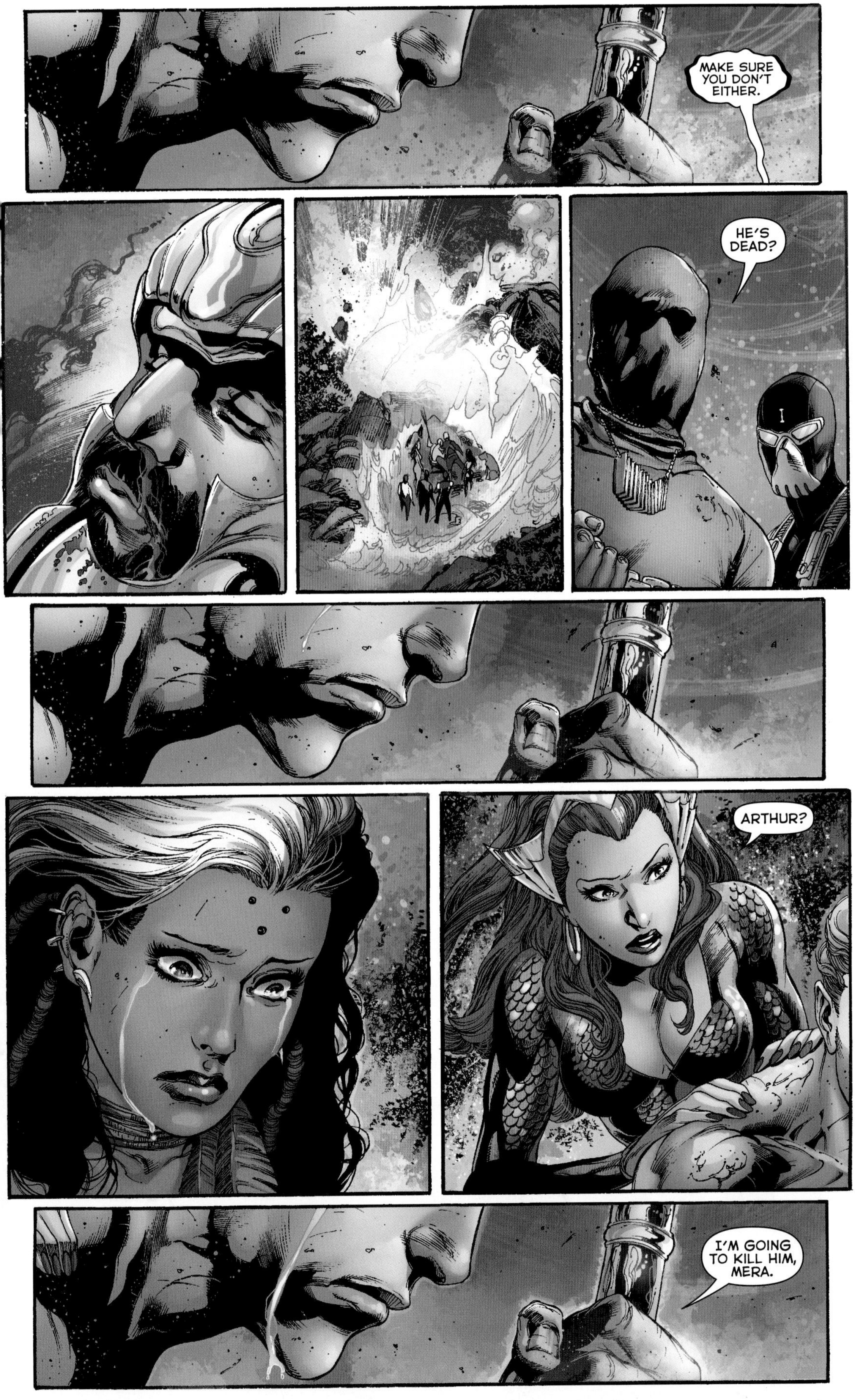
MAKE SURE YOU DON'T EITHER.
HE'S DEAD?
ARTHUR?
I'M GOING TO KILL HIM, MERA.

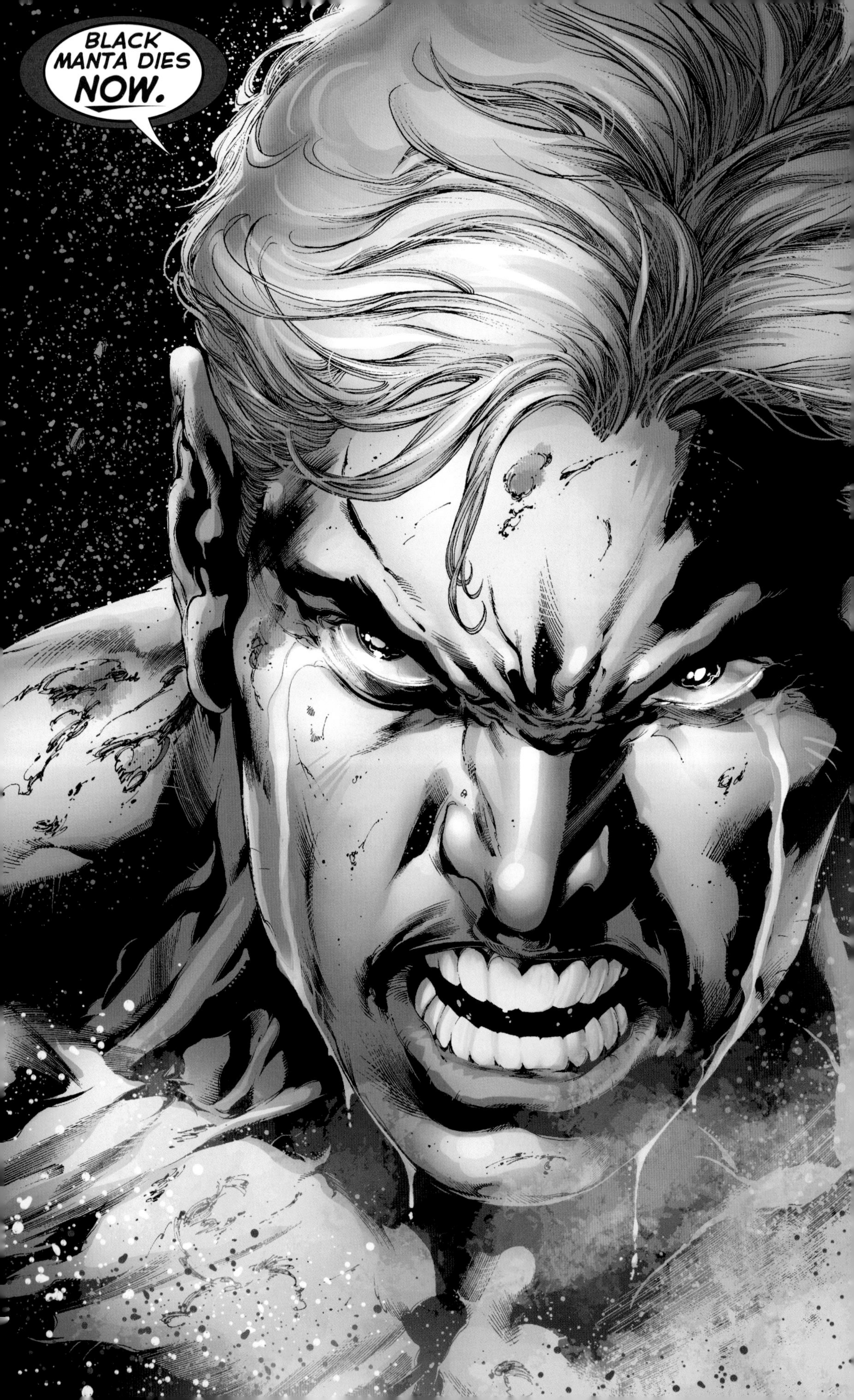
BLACK MANTA DIES NOW.

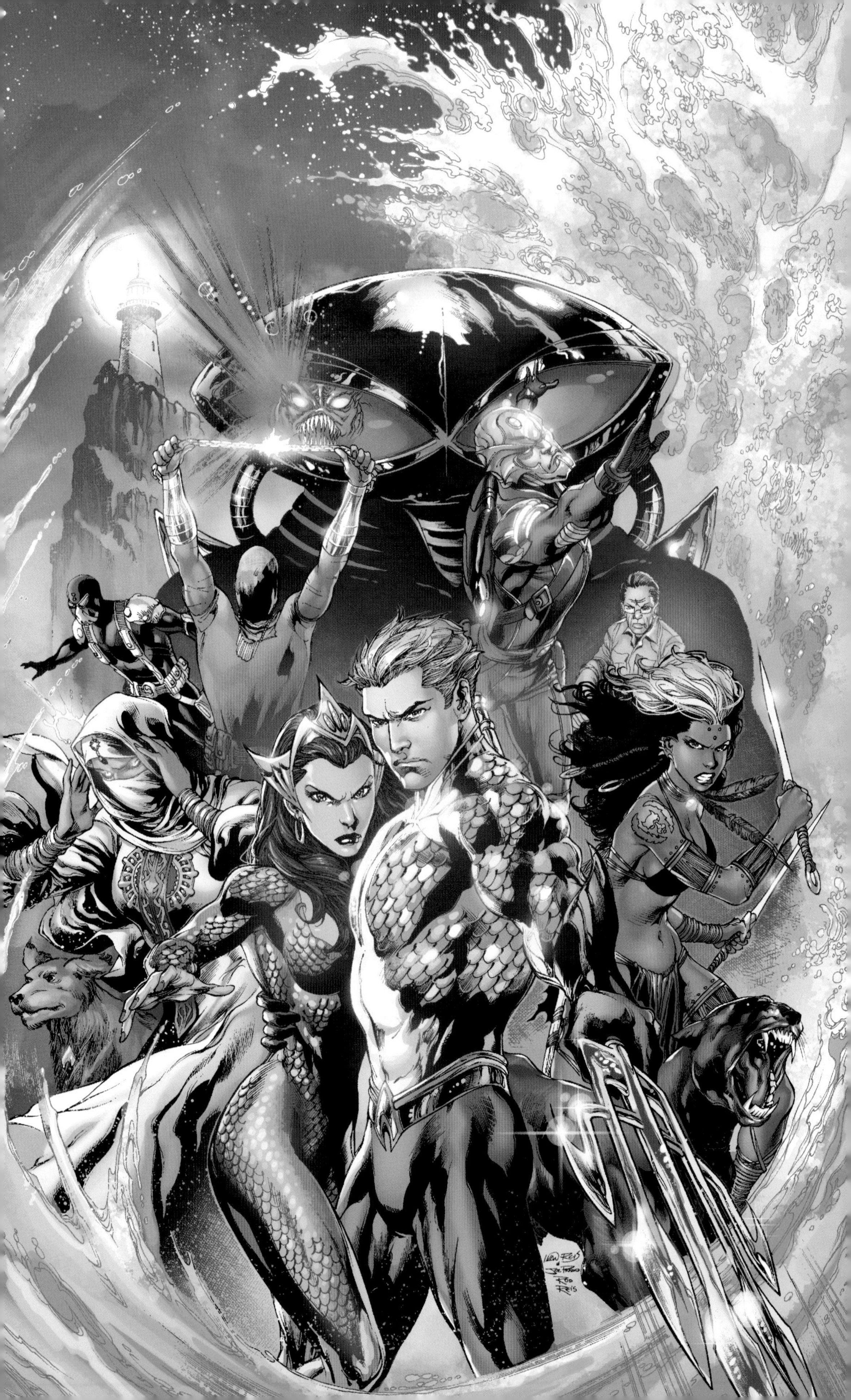

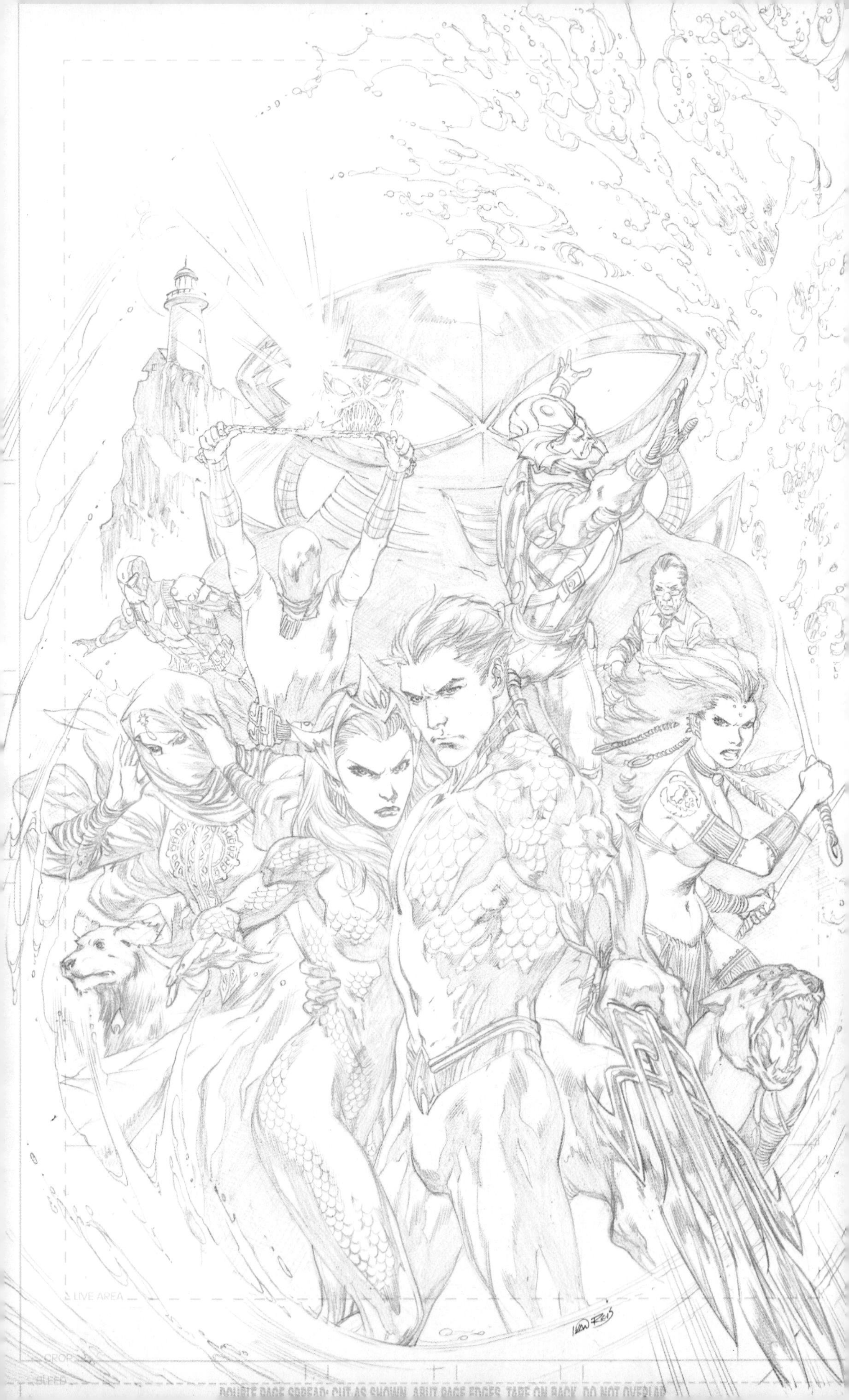
LIVE AREA
CROP
BLEED
DOUBLE PAGE SPREAD: CUT AS SHOWN. ABUT PAGE EDGES. TAPE ON BACK. DO NOT OVERLAP

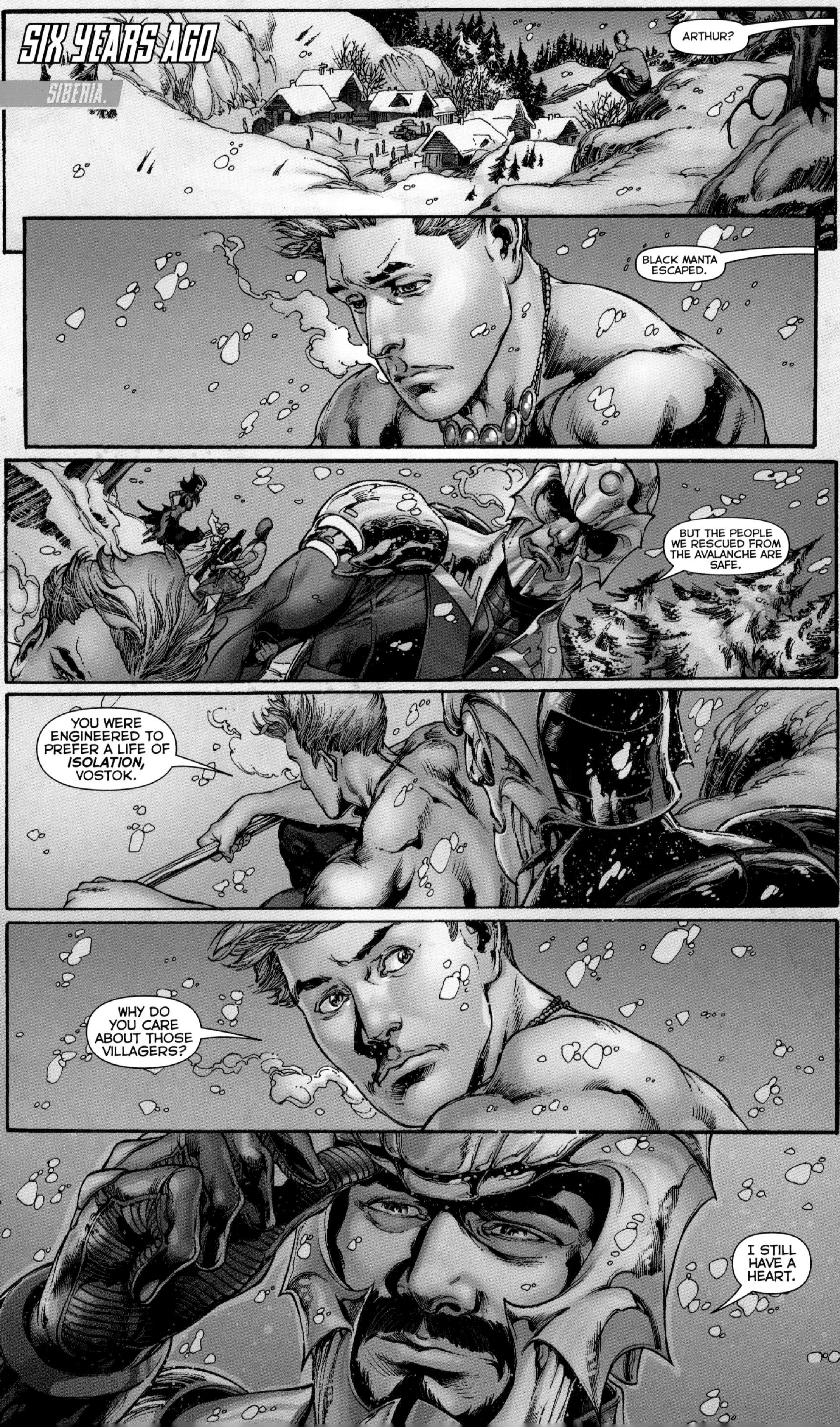
SIX YEARS AGO
SIBERIA.
ARTHUR?
BLACK MANTA ESCAPED.
BUT THE PEOPLE WE RESCUED FROM THE AVALANCHE ARE SAFE.
YOU WERE ENGINEERED TO PREFER A LIFE OF *ISOLATION,* VOSTOK.
WHY DO YOU CARE ABOUT THOSE VILLAGERS?
I STILL HAVE A HEART.

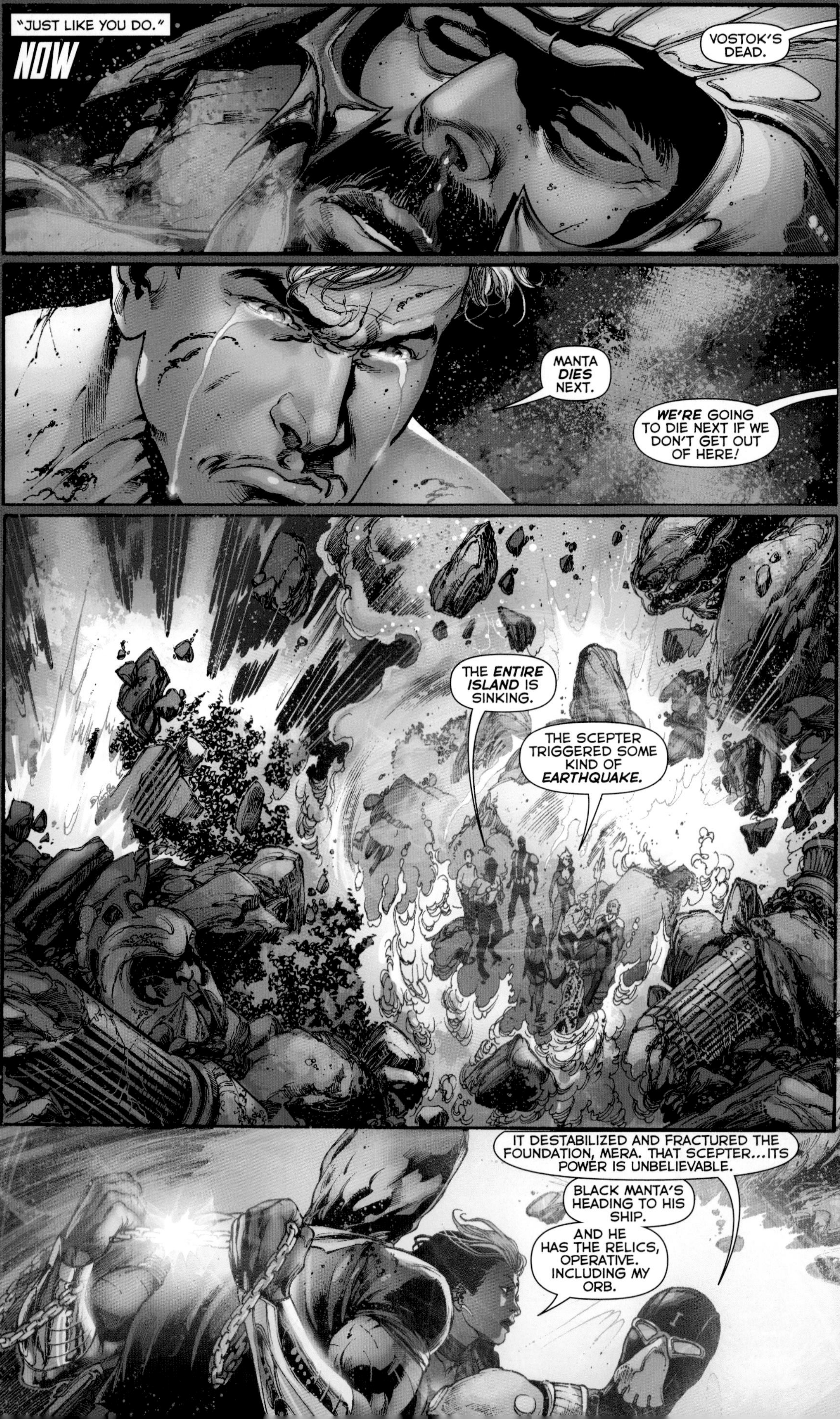
"JUST LIKE YOU DO."
NOW
VOSTOK'S DEAD.
MANTA *DIES* NEXT.
WE'RE GOING TO DIE NEXT IF WE DON'T GET OUT OF HERE!
THE *ENTIRE ISLAND* IS SINKING.
THE SCEPTER TRIGGERED SOME KIND OF *EARTHQUAKE.*
IT DESTABILIZED AND FRACTURED THE FOUNDATION, MERA. THAT SCEPTER...ITS POWER IS UNBELIEVABLE.
BLACK MANTA'S HEADING TO HIS SHIP.
AND HE HAS THE RELICS, OPERATIVE. INCLUDING MY ORB.

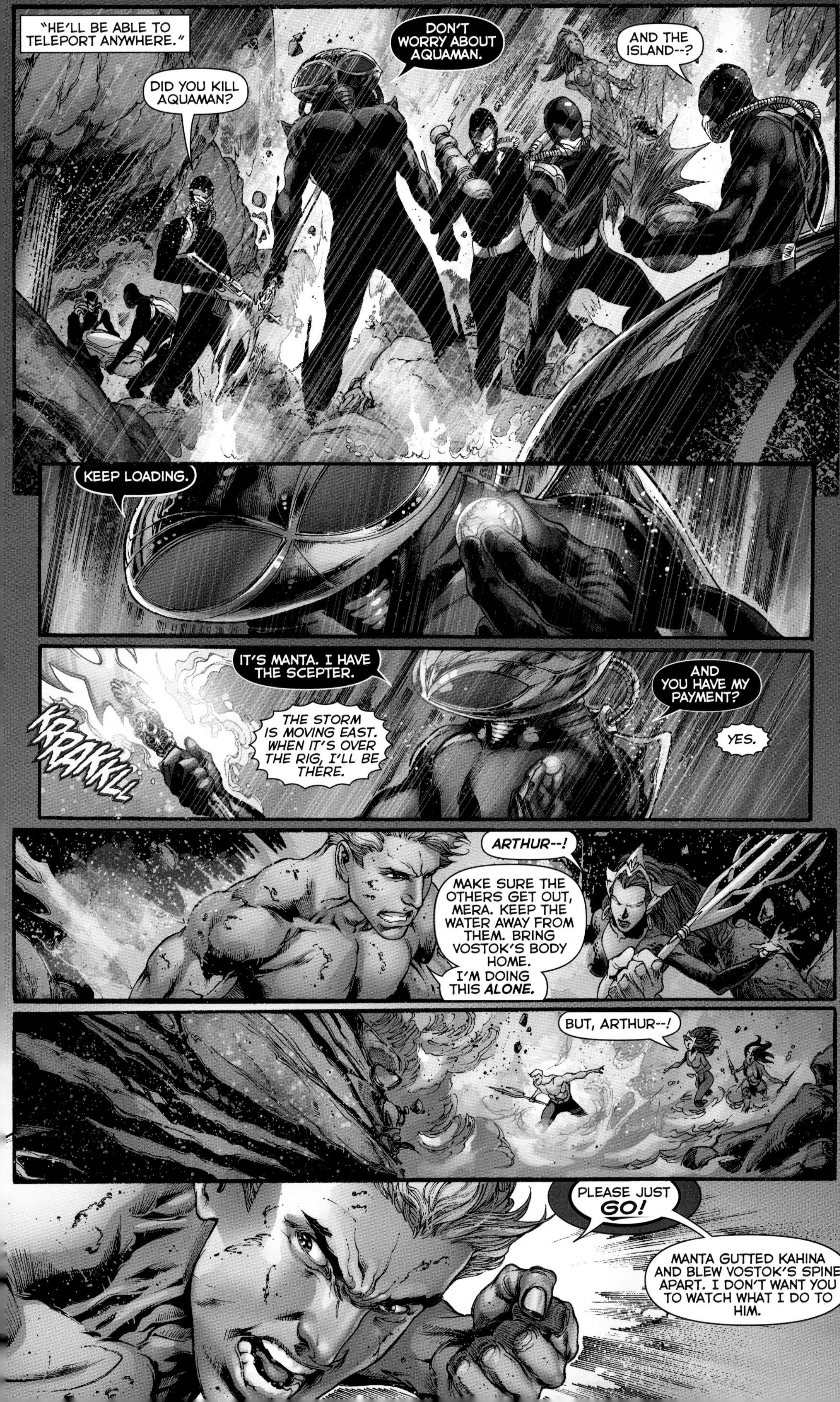
"HE'LL BE ABLE TO TELEPORT ANYWHERE."
DID YOU KILL AQUAMAN?
DON'T WORRY ABOUT AQUAMAN.
AND THE ISLAND--?
KEEP LOADING.
KRRAKKLL
IT'S MANTA. I HAVE THE SCEPTER.
THE STORM IS MOVING EAST. WHEN IT'S OVER THE RIG, I'LL BE THERE.
AND YOU HAVE MY PAYMENT?
YES.
ARTHUR--!
MAKE SURE THE OTHERS GET OUT, MERA. KEEP THE WATER AWAY FROM THEM. BRING VOSTOK'S BODY HOME.
I'M DOING THIS ALONE.
BUT, ARTHUR--!
PLEASE JUST GO!
MANTA GUTTED KAHINA AND BLEW VOSTOK'S SPINE APART. I DON'T WANT YOU TO WATCH WHAT I DO TO HIM.

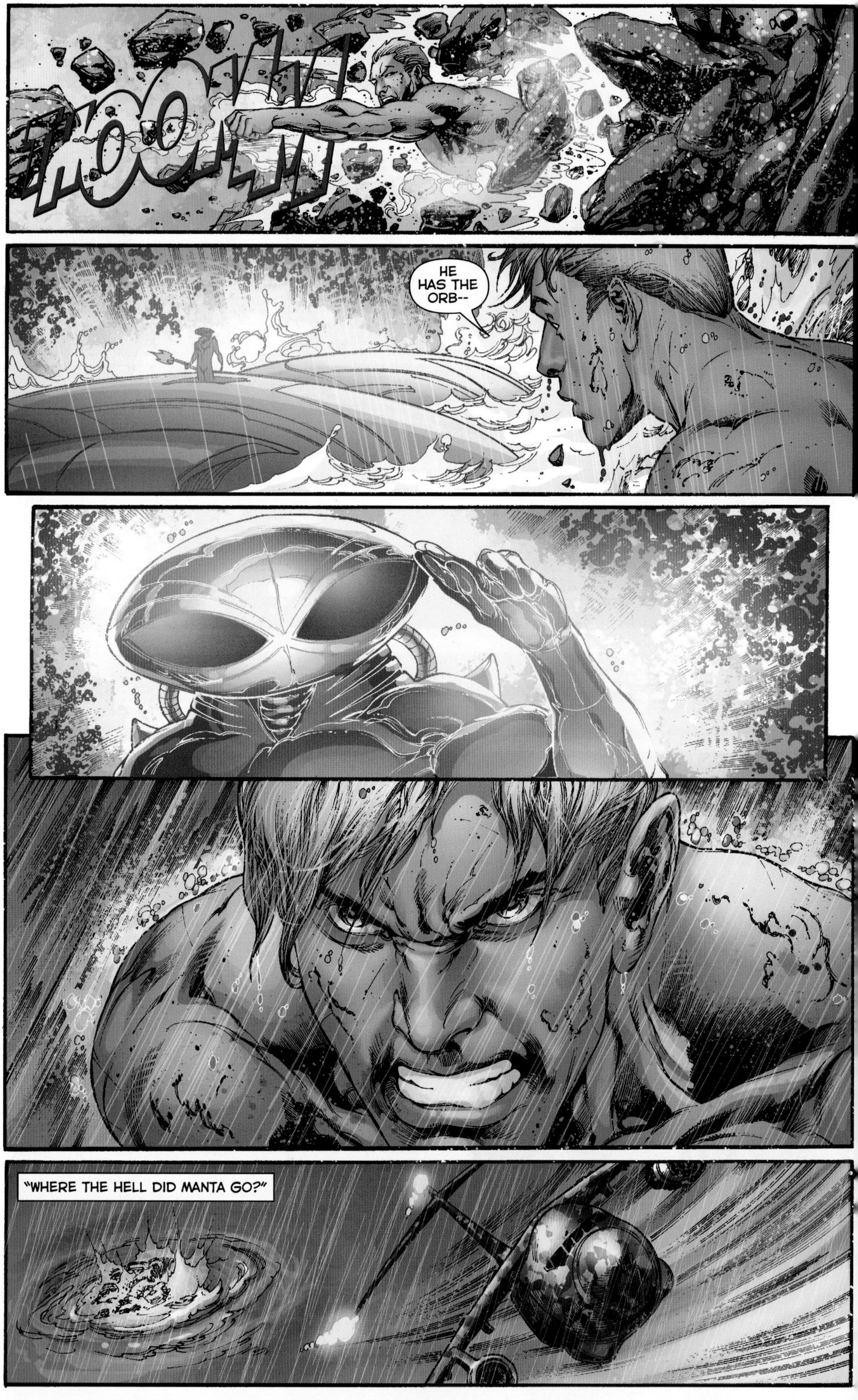
THOOMM!
HE HAS THE ORB--
"WHERE THE HELL DID MANTA GO?"

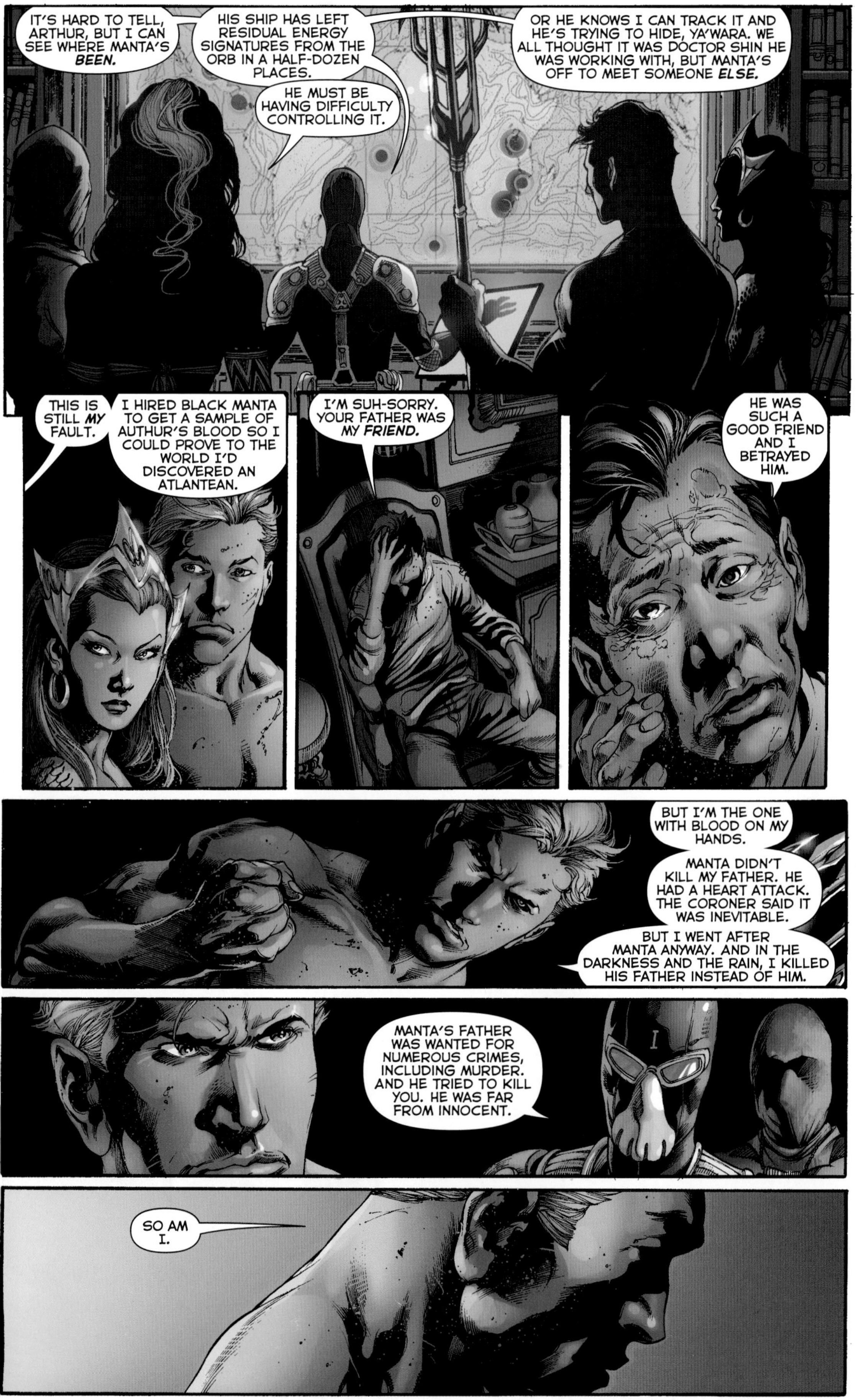
IT'S HARD TO TELL, ARTHUR, BUT I CAN SEE WHERE MANTA'S BEEN.
HIS SHIP HAS LEFT RESIDUAL ENERGY SIGNATURES FROM THE ORB IN A HALF-DOZEN PLACES.
HE MUST BE HAVING DIFFICULTY CONTROLLING IT.
OR HE KNOWS I CAN TRACK IT AND HE'S TRYING TO HIDE, YA'WARA. WE ALL THOUGHT IT WAS DOCTOR SHIN HE WAS WORKING WITH, BUT MANTA'S OFF TO MEET SOMEONE ELSE.
THIS IS STILL MY FAULT.
I HIRED BLACK MANTA TO GET A SAMPLE OF AUTHUR'S BLOOD SO I COULD PROVE TO THE WORLD I'D DISCOVERED AN ATLANTEAN.
I'M SUH-SORRY. YOUR FATHER WAS MY FRIEND.
HE WAS SUCH A GOOD FRIEND AND I BETRAYED HIM.
BUT I'M THE ONE WITH BLOOD ON MY HANDS.
MANTA DIDN'T KILL MY FATHER. HE HAD A HEART ATTACK. THE CORONER SAID IT WAS INEVITABLE.
BUT I WENT AFTER MANTA ANYWAY. AND IN THE DARKNESS AND THE RAIN, I KILLED HIS FATHER INSTEAD OF HIM.
MANTA'S FATHER WAS WANTED FOR NUMEROUS CRIMES, INCLUDING MURDER. AND HE TRIED TO KILL YOU. HE WAS FAR FROM INNOCENT.
SO AM I.

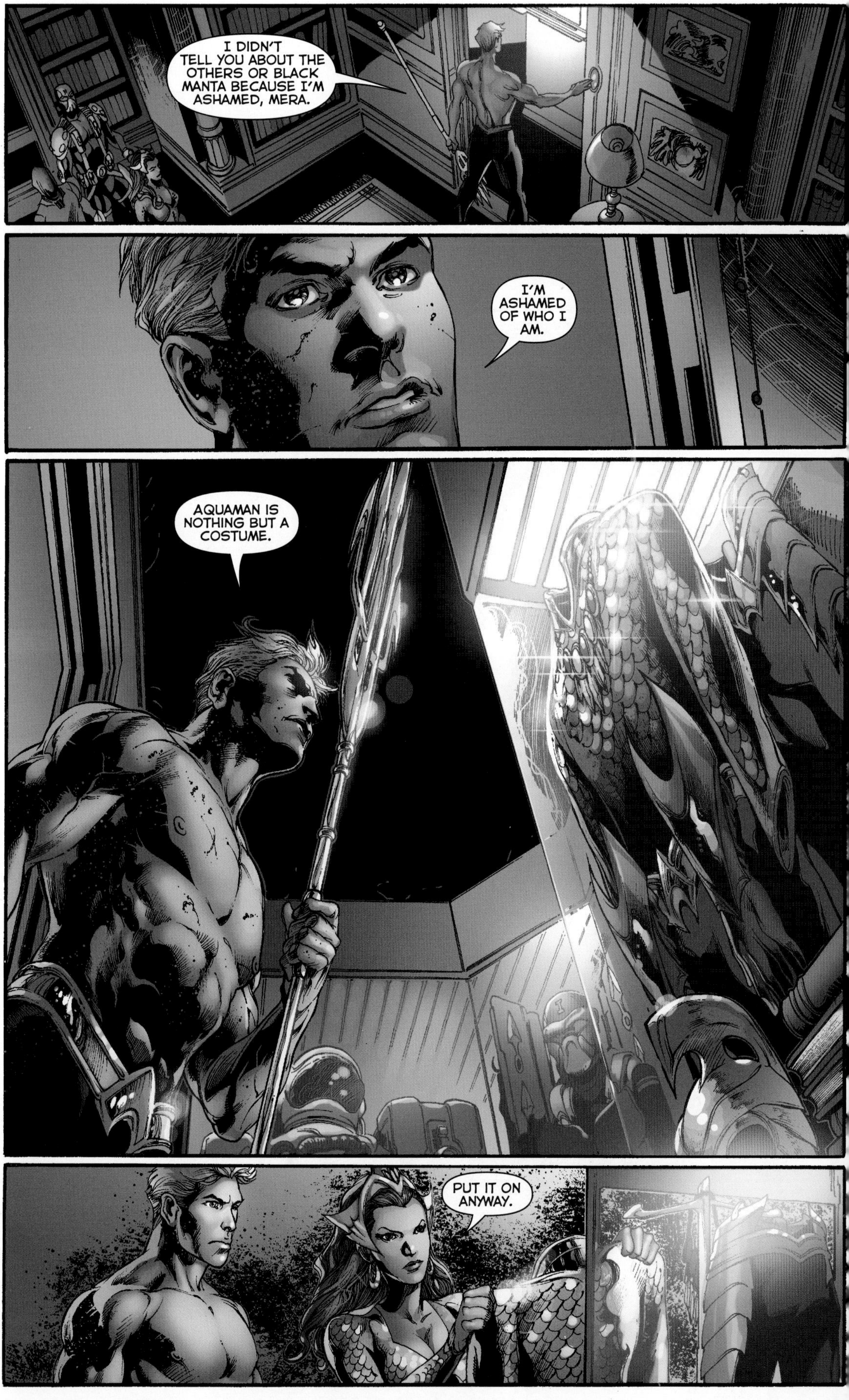
I DIDN'T TELL YOU ABOUT THE OTHERS OR BLACK MANTA BECAUSE I'M ASHAMED, MERA.
I'M ASHAMED OF WHO I AM.
AQUAMAN IS NOTHING BUT A COSTUME.
PUT IT ON ANYWAY.

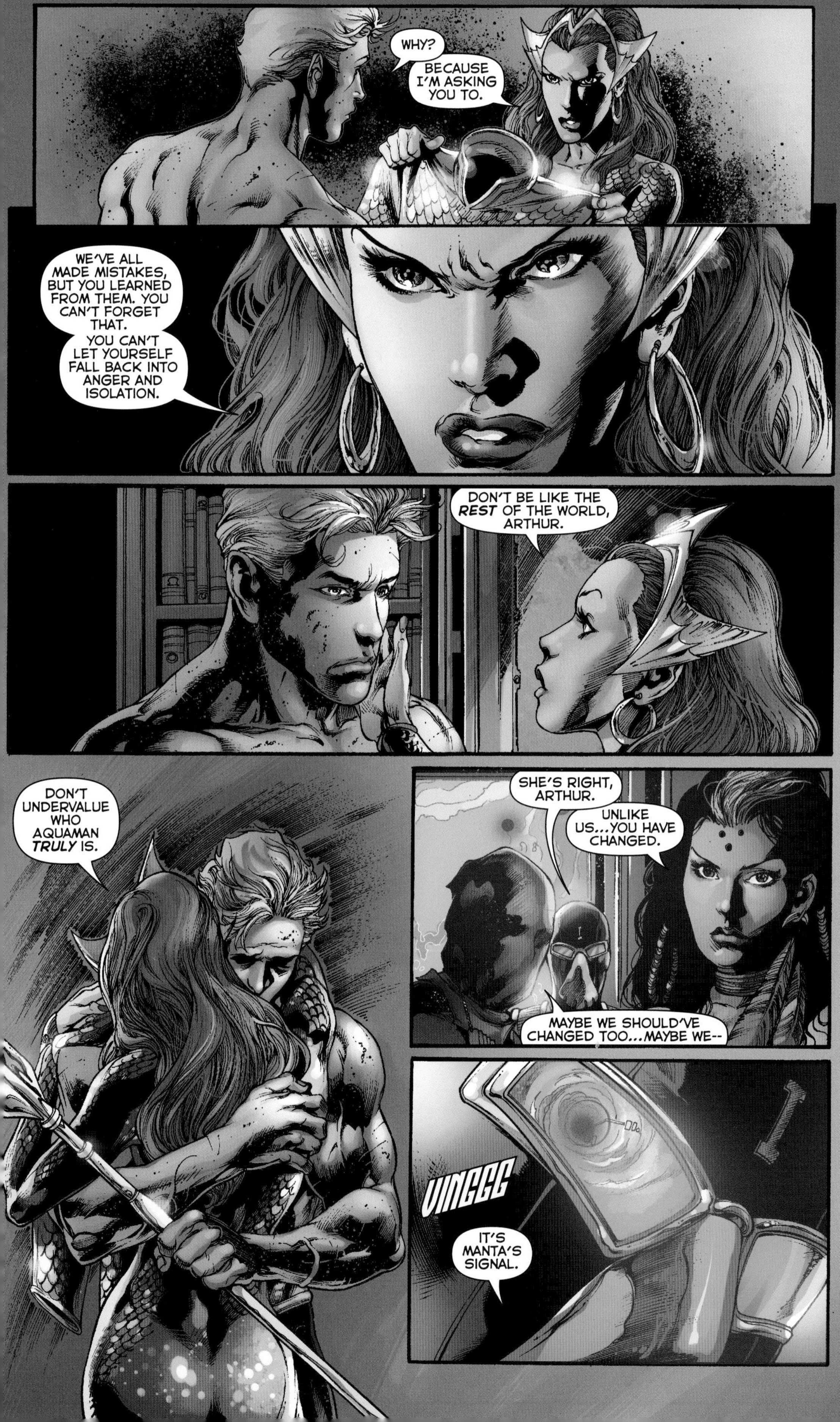
WHY?
BECAUSE I'M ASKING YOU TO.
WE'VE ALL MADE MISTAKES, BUT YOU LEARNED FROM THEM. YOU CAN'T FORGET THAT.
YOU CAN'T LET YOURSELF FALL BACK INTO ANGER AND ISOLATION.
DON'T BE LIKE THE REST OF THE WORLD, ARTHUR.
DON'T UNDERVALUE WHO AQUAMAN TRULY IS.
SHE'S RIGHT, ARTHUR.
UNLIKE US...YOU HAVE CHANGED.
MAYBE WE SHOULD'VE CHANGED TOO...MAYBE WE--
VINGGG
IT'S MANTA'S SIGNAL.

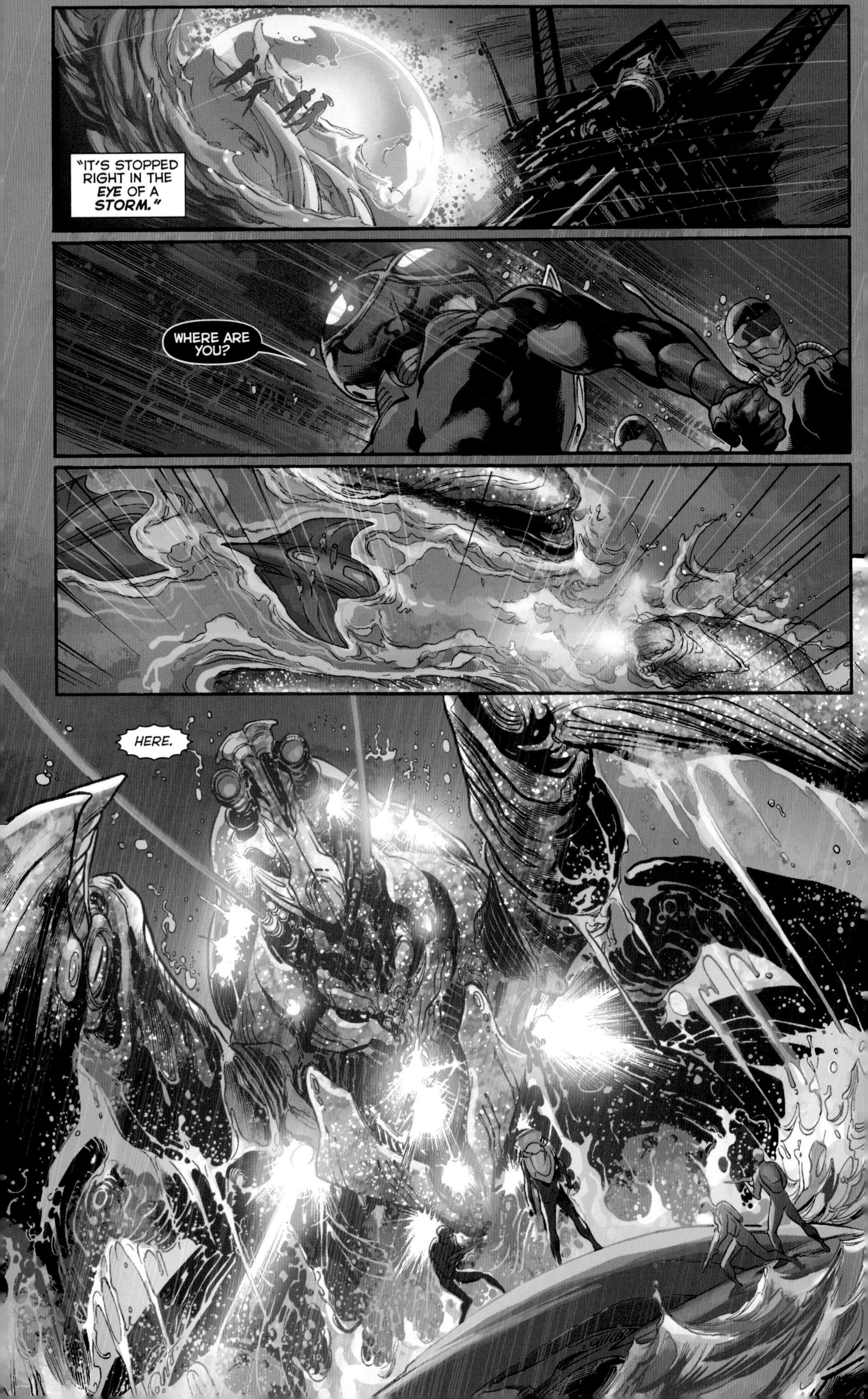
"IT'S STOPPED RIGHT IN THE EYE OF A STORM."
WHERE ARE YOU?
HERE.

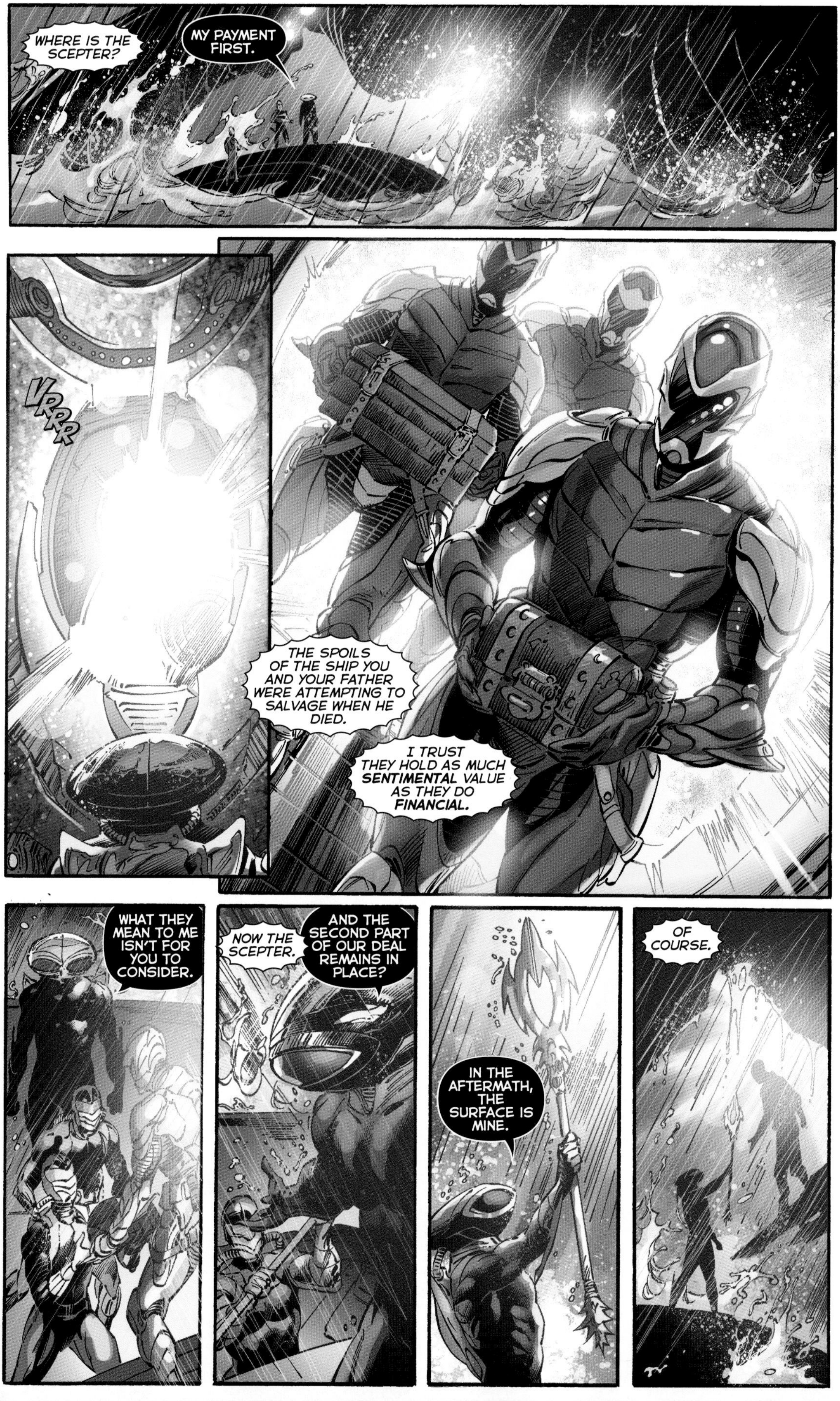
WHERE IS THE SCEPTER?
MY PAYMENT FIRST.
VRRR
THE SPOILS OF THE SHIP YOU AND YOUR FATHER WERE ATTEMPTING TO SALVAGE WHEN HE DIED.
I TRUST THEY HOLD AS MUCH SENTIMENTAL VALUE AS THEY DO FINANCIAL.
WHAT THEY MEAN TO ME ISN'T FOR YOU TO CONSIDER.
NOW THE SCEPTER.
AND THE SECOND PART OF OUR DEAL REMAINS IN PLACE?
IN THE AFTERMATH, THE SURFACE IS MINE.
OF COURSE.

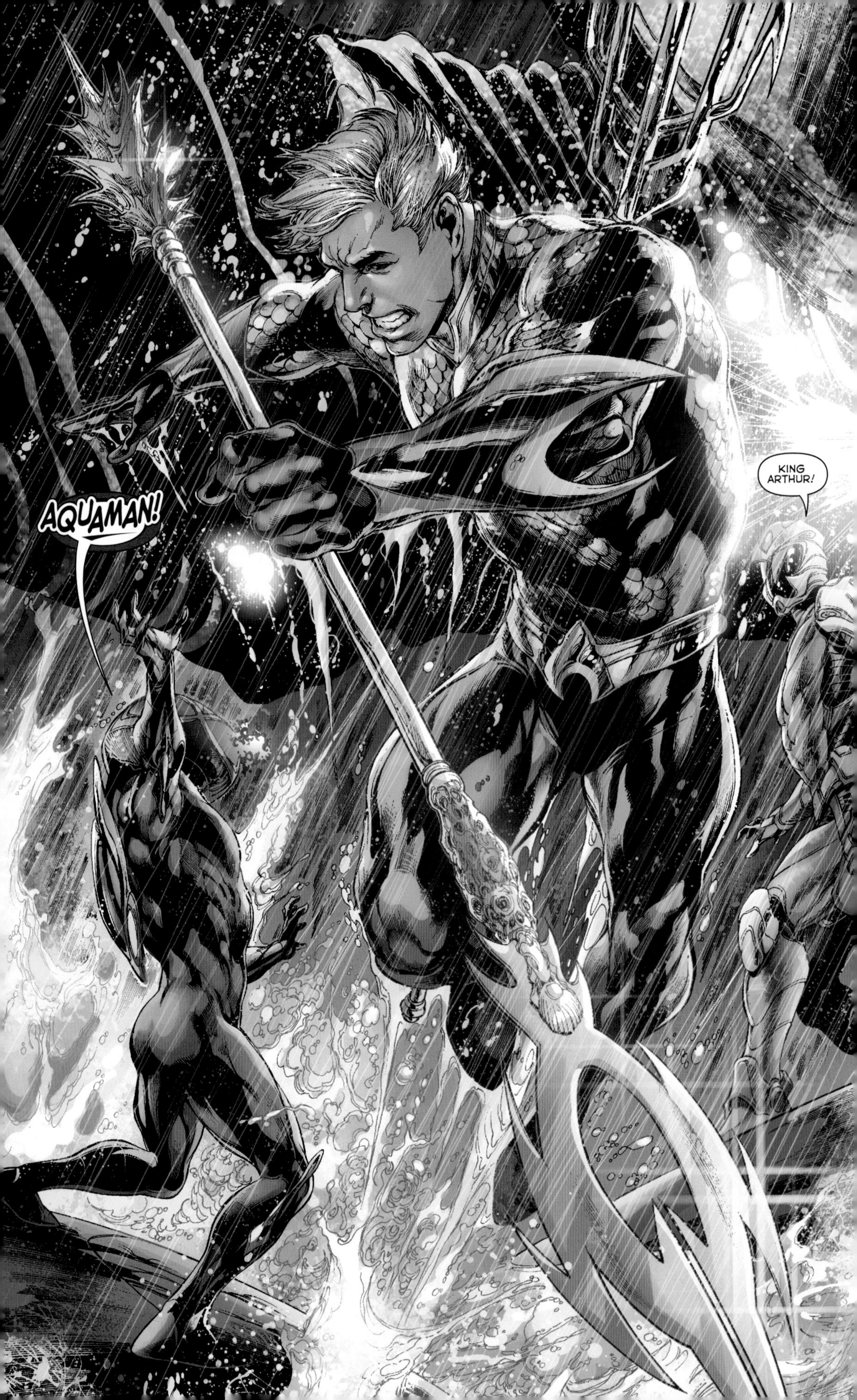
AQUAMAN!
KING ARTHUR!

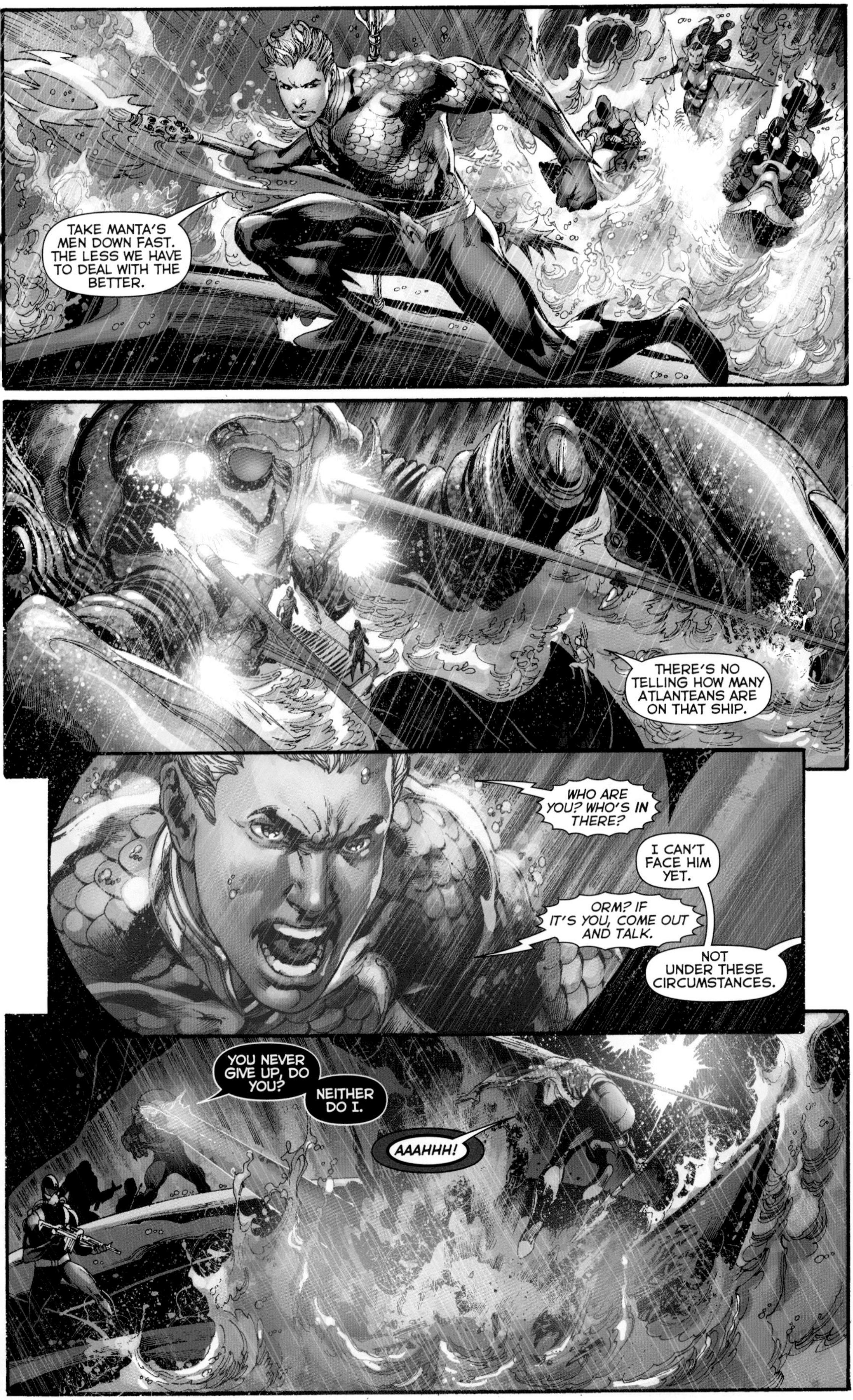

TAKE MANTA'S MEN DOWN FAST. THE LESS WE HAVE TO DEAL WITH THE BETTER.
THERE'S NO TELLING HOW MANY ATLANTEANS ARE ON THAT SHIP.
WHO ARE YOU? WHO'S IN THERE?
I CAN'T FACE HIM YET.
ORM? IF IT'S YOU, COME OUT AND TALK.
NOT UNDER THESE CIRCUMSTANCES.
YOU NEVER GIVE UP, DO YOU?
NEITHER DO I.
AAAHHH!

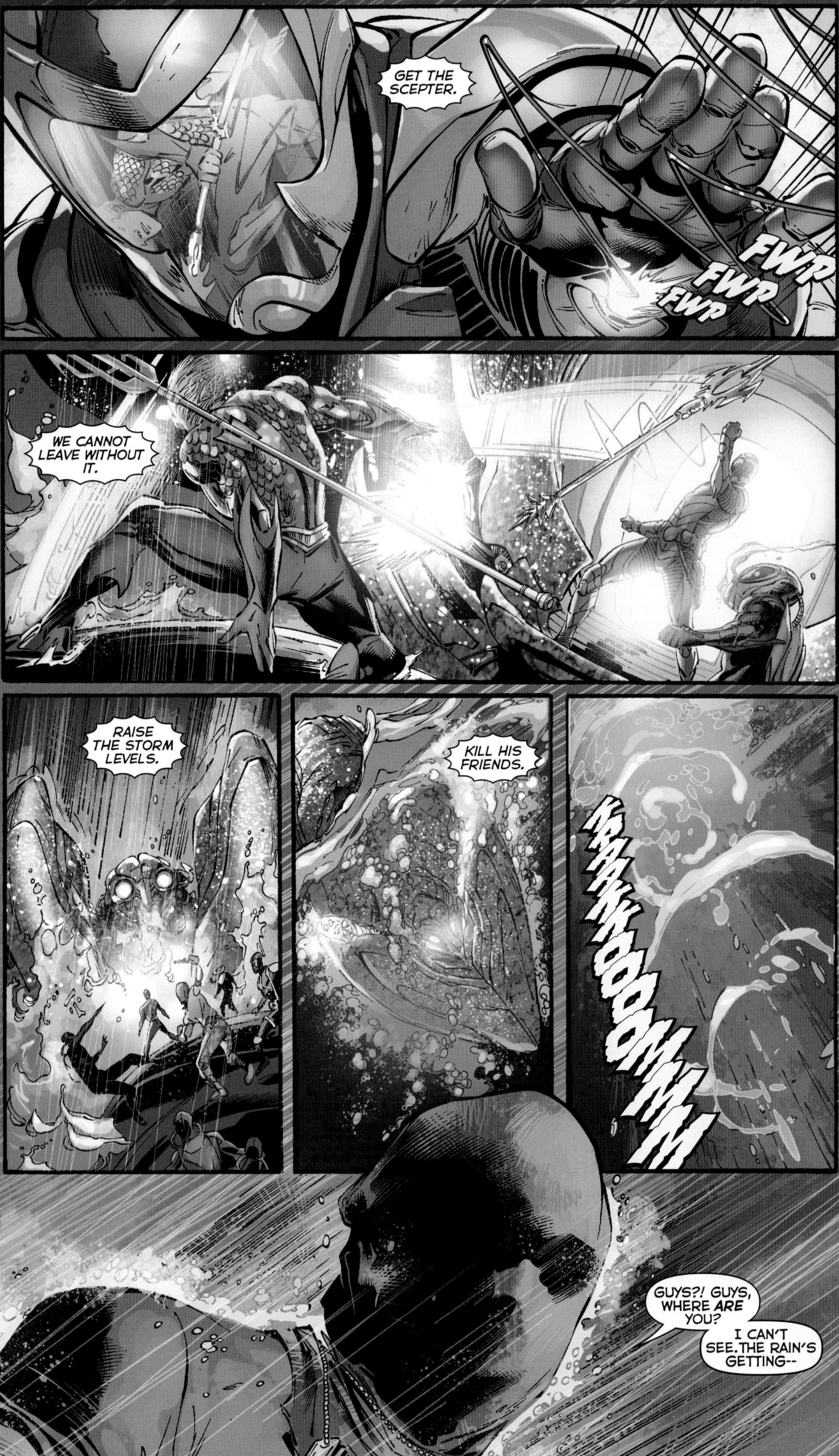
GET THE SCEPTER.
FWP
FWP
FWP
WE CANNOT LEAVE WITHOUT IT.
RAISE THE STORM LEVELS.
KILL HIS FRIENDS.
KRAKKOOOOMMM
GUYS?! GUYS, WHERE ARE YOU?
I CAN'T SEE. THE RAIN'S GETTING--

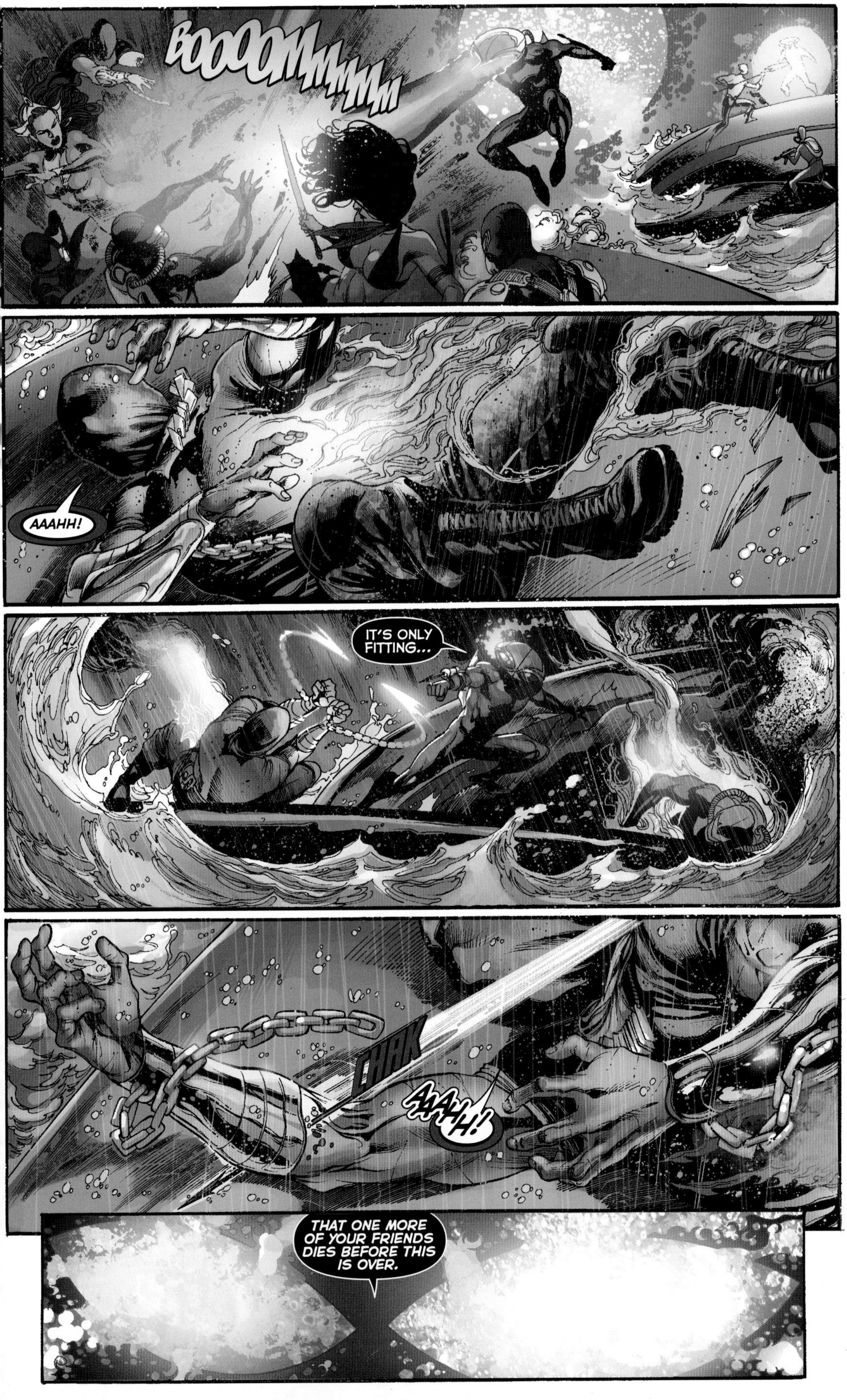
BOOOOMMMMMM
AAAHH!
IT'S ONLY FITTING...
CHAK
AAAHH!
THAT ONE MORE OF YOUR FRIENDS DIES BEFORE THIS IS OVER.

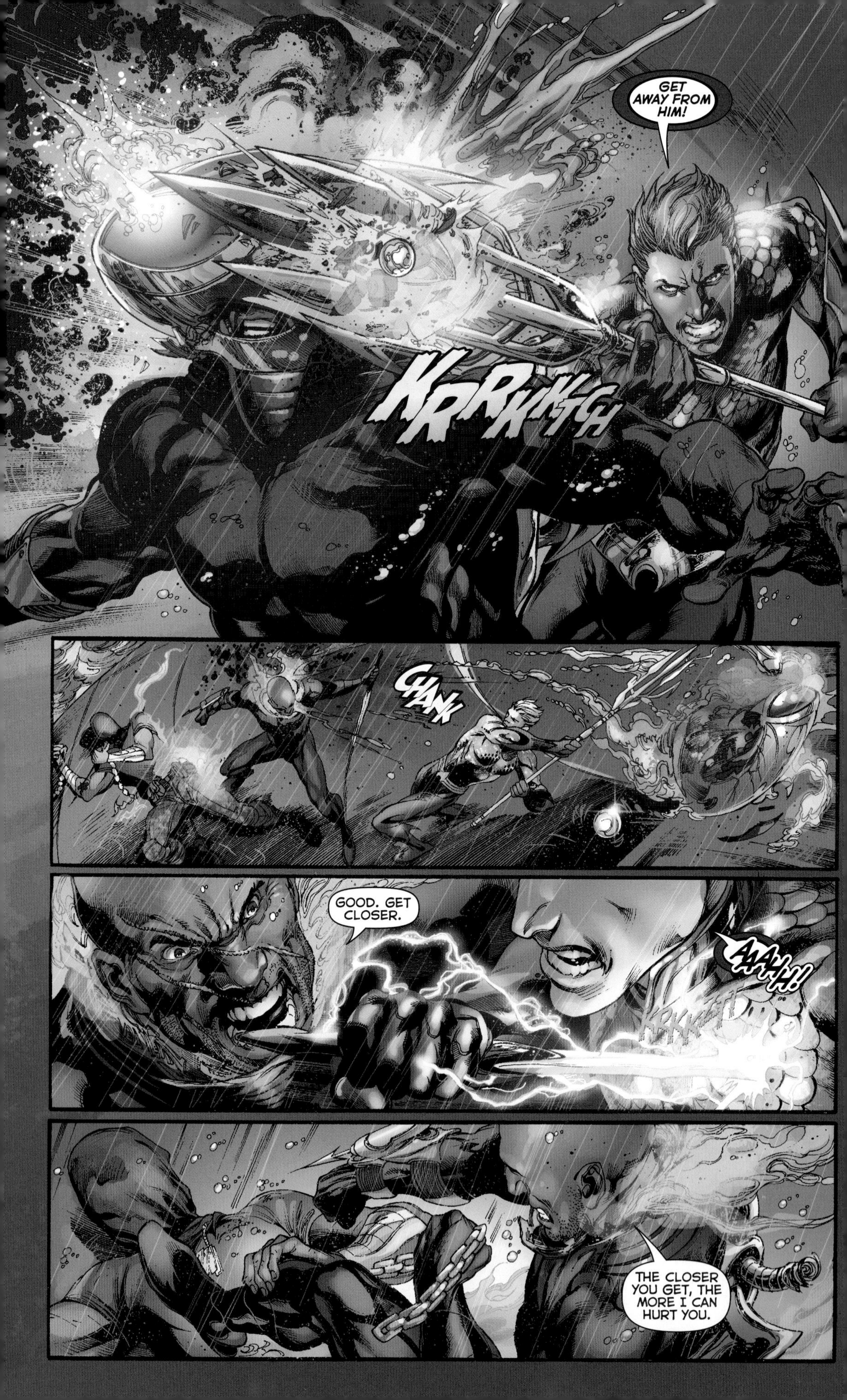
GET AWAY FROM HIM!
KRRKKTCH
CHANK
GOOD. GET CLOSER.
AAAHH!
THE CLOSER YOU GET, THE MORE I CAN HURT YOU.

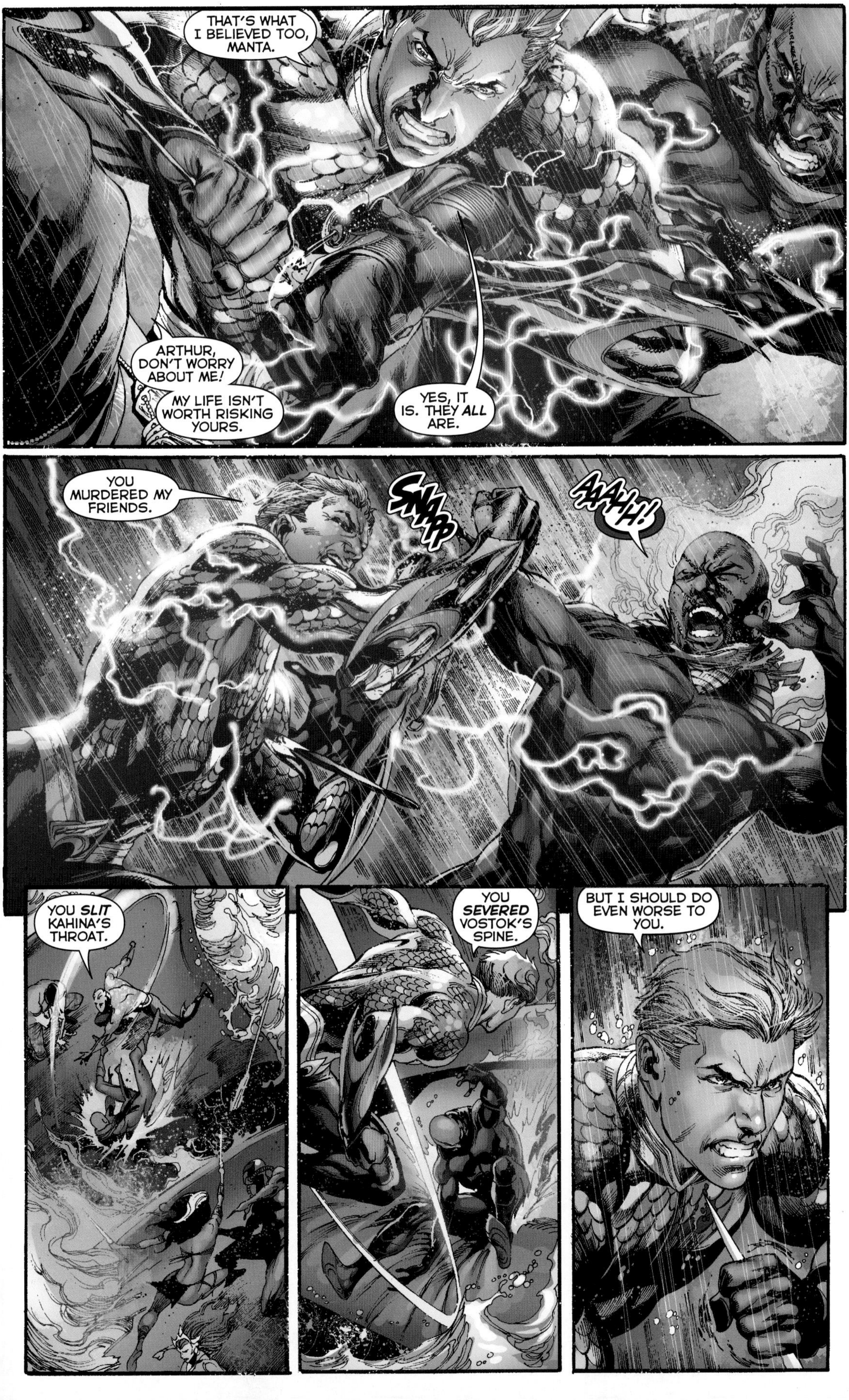
THAT'S WHAT I BELIEVED TOO, MANTA.
ARTHUR, DON'T WORRY ABOUT ME!
MY LIFE ISN'T WORTH RISKING YOURS.
YES, IT IS. THEY ALL ARE.
YOU MURDERED MY FRIENDS.
SNAPP
AAAHH!
YOU SLIT KAHINA'S THROAT.
YOU SEVERED VOSTOK'S SPINE.
BUT I SHOULD DO EVEN WORSE TO YOU.

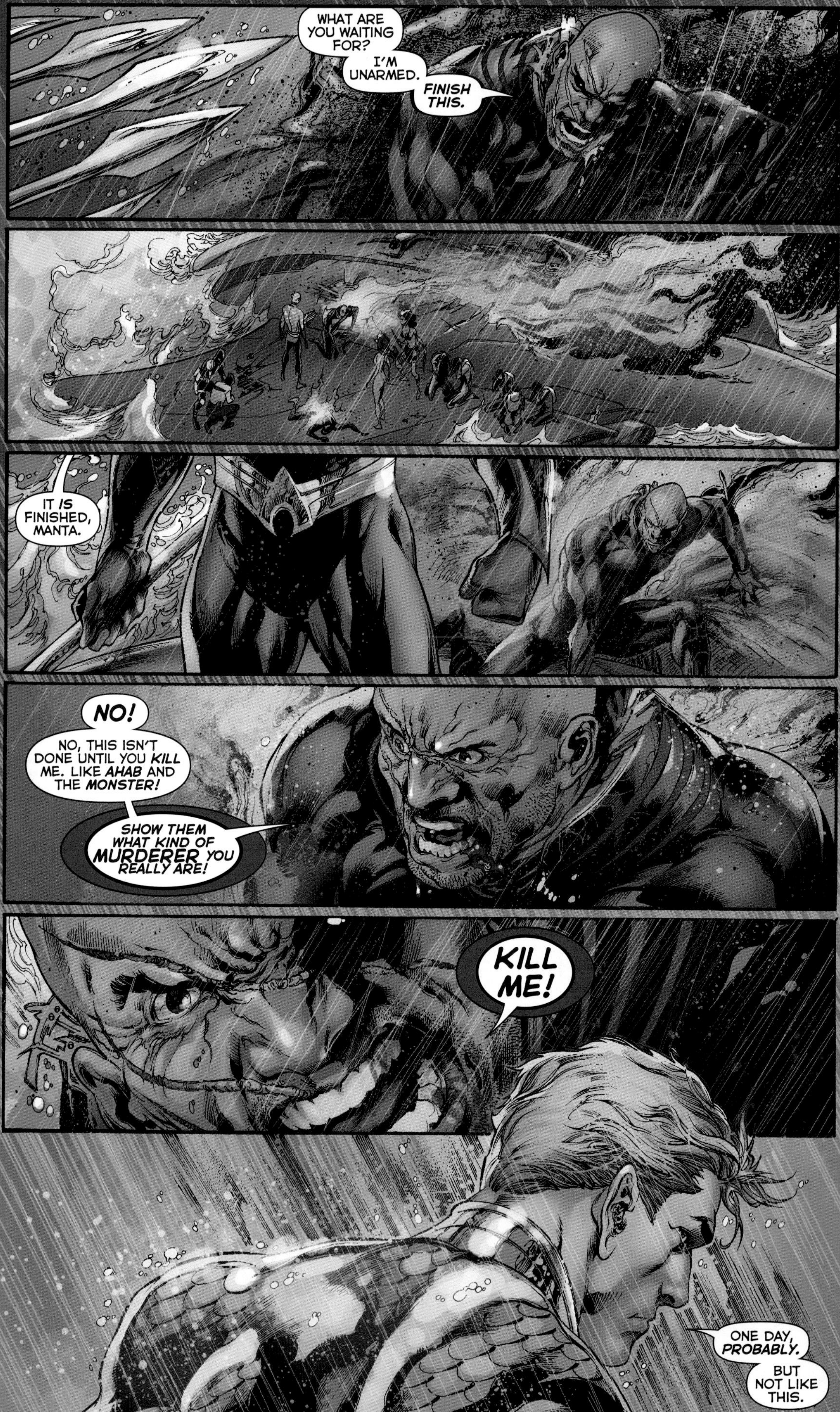
WHAT ARE YOU WAITING FOR?
I'M UNARMED.
FINISH THIS.
IT IS FINISHED, MANTA.
NO!
NO, THIS ISN'T DONE UNTIL YOU KILL ME. LIKE AHAB AND THE MONSTER!
SHOW THEM WHAT KIND OF MURDERER YOU REALLY ARE!
KILL ME!
ONE DAY, PROBABLY.
BUT NOT LIKE THIS.

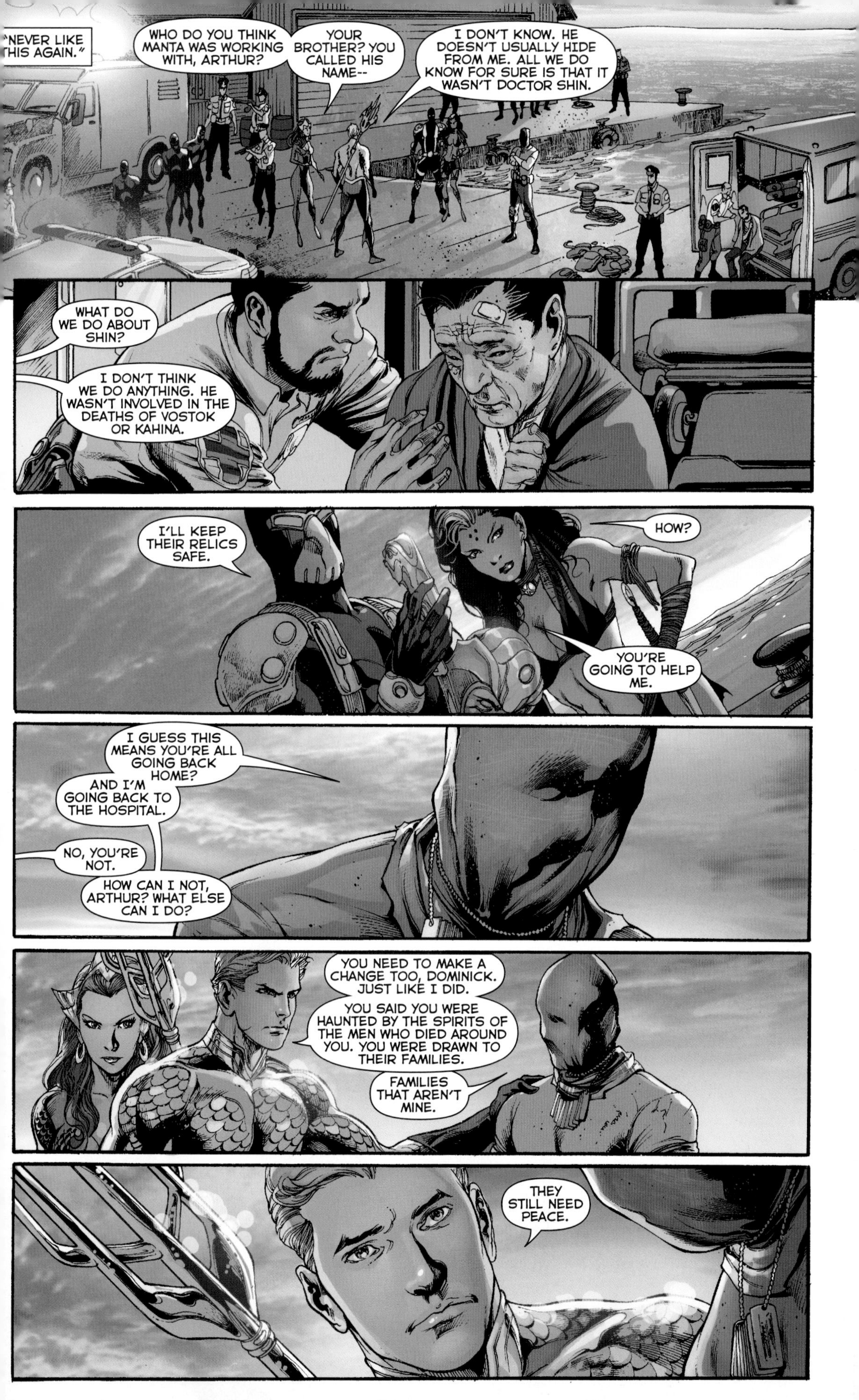
"NEVER LIKE THIS AGAIN."
WHO DO YOU THINK MANTA WAS WORKING WITH, ARTHUR?
YOUR BROTHER? YOU CALLED HIS NAME--
I DON'T KNOW. HE DOESN'T USUALLY HIDE FROM ME. ALL WE DO KNOW FOR SURE IS THAT IT WASN'T DOCTOR SHIN.
WHAT DO WE DO ABOUT SHIN?
I DON'T THINK WE DO ANYTHING. HE WASN'T INVOLVED IN THE DEATHS OF VOSTOK OR KAHINA.
I'LL KEEP THEIR RELICS SAFE.
HOW?
YOU'RE GOING TO HELP ME.
I GUESS THIS MEANS YOU'RE ALL GOING BACK HOME?
AND I'M GOING BACK TO THE HOSPITAL.
NO, YOU'RE NOT.
HOW CAN I NOT, ARTHUR? WHAT ELSE CAN I DO?
YOU NEED TO MAKE A CHANGE TOO, DOMINICK. JUST LIKE I DID.
YOU SAID YOU WERE HAUNTED BY THE SPIRITS OF THE MEN WHO DIED AROUND YOU. YOU WERE DRAWN TO THEIR FAMILIES.
FAMILIES THAT AREN'T MINE.
THEY STILL NEED PEACE.

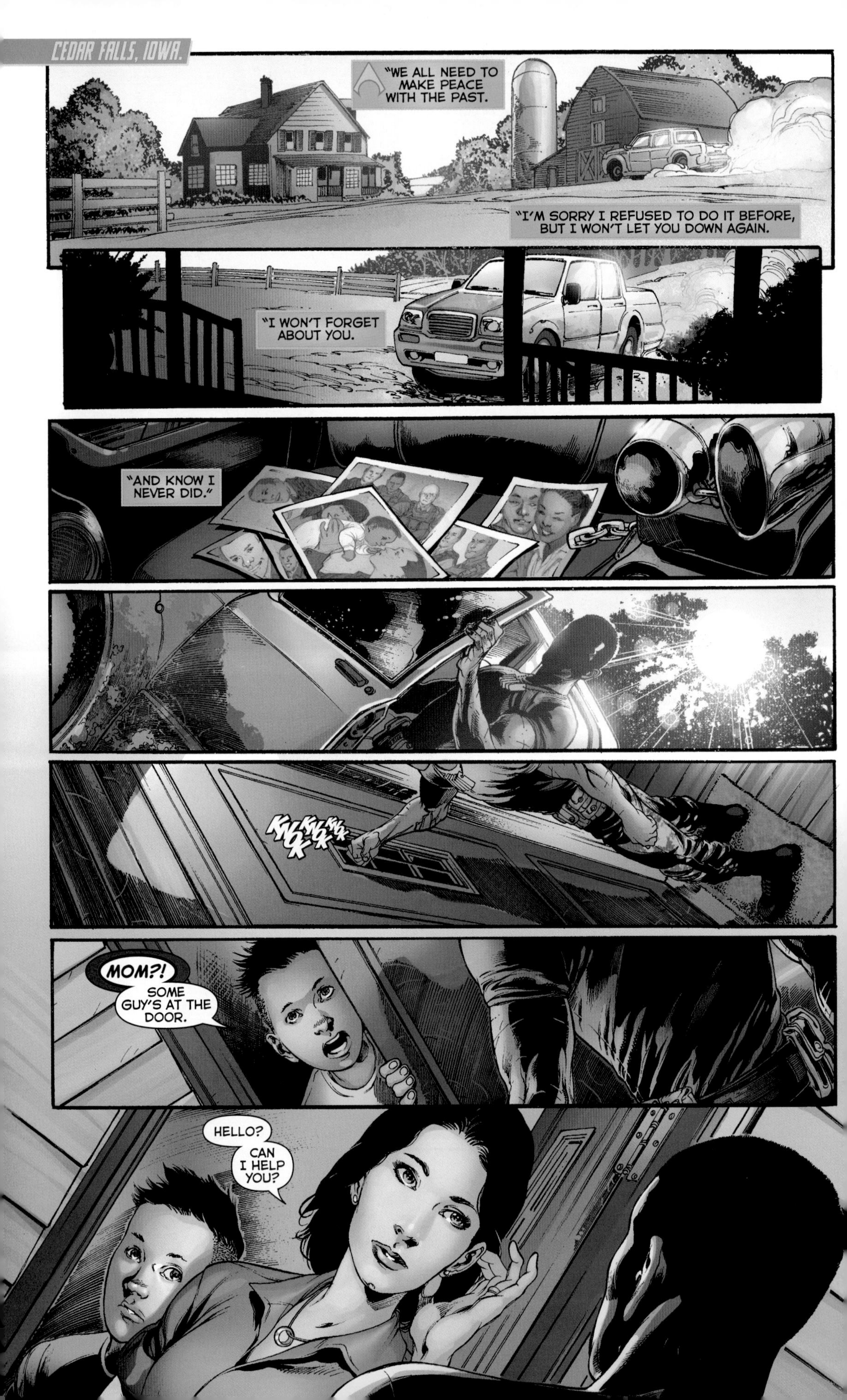

CEDAR FALLS, IOWA.
"WE ALL NEED TO MAKE PEACE WITH THE PAST.
"I'M SORRY I REFUSED TO DO IT BEFORE, BUT I WON'T LET YOU DOWN AGAIN.
"I WON'T FORGET ABOUT YOU.
"AND KNOW I NEVER DID."
KNOK KNOK KNOK
MOM?! SOME GUY'S AT THE DOOR.
HELLO?
CAN I HELP YOU?

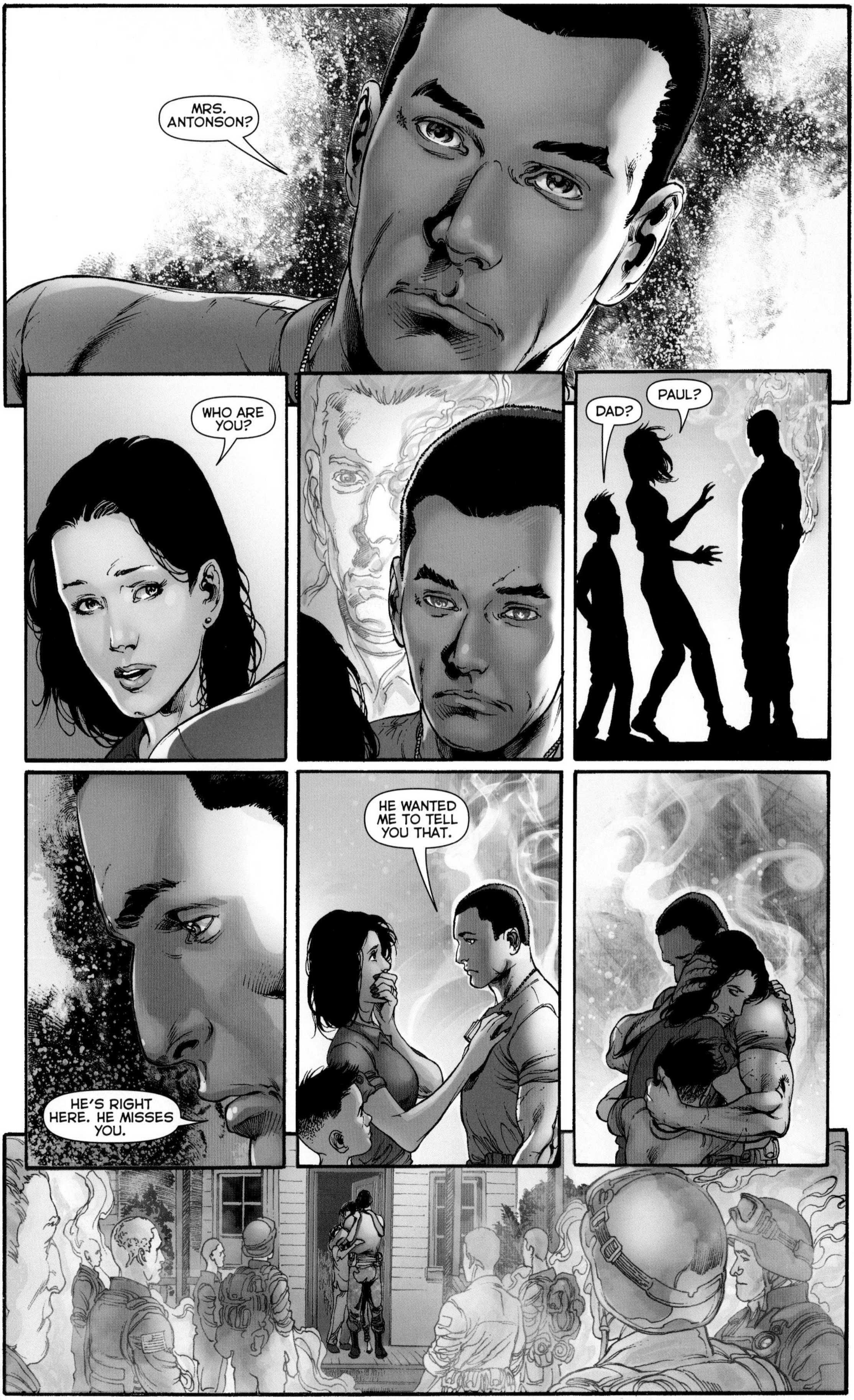
MRS. ANTONSON?
WHO ARE YOU?
PAUL?
DAD?
HE'S RIGHT HERE. HE MISSES YOU.
HE WANTED ME TO TELL YOU THAT.

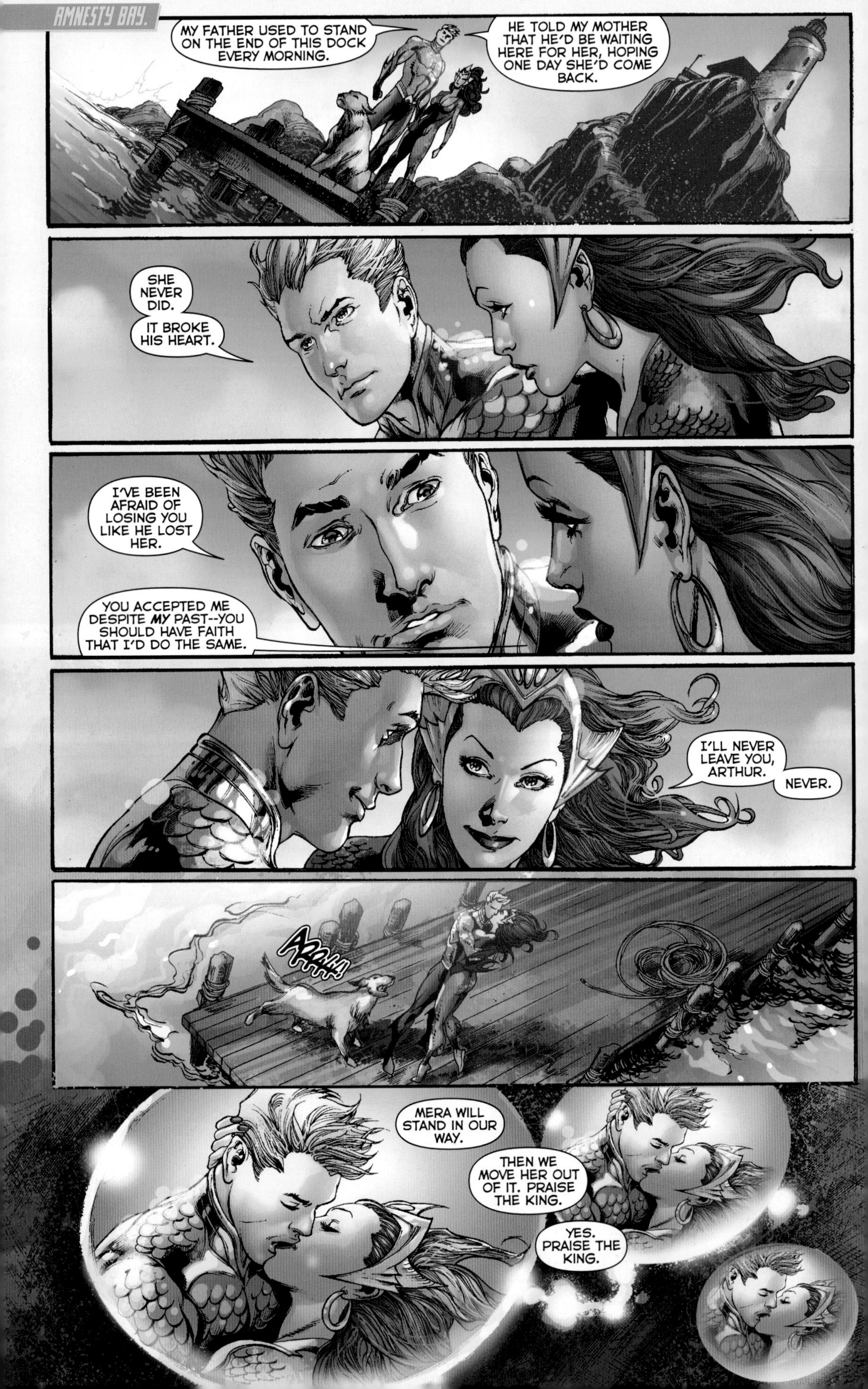
AMNESTY BAY.
MY FATHER USED TO STAND ON THE END OF THIS DOCK EVERY MORNING.
HE TOLD MY MOTHER THAT HE'D BE WAITING HERE FOR HER, HOPING ONE DAY SHE'D COME BACK.
SHE NEVER DID.
IT BROKE HIS HEART.
I'VE BEEN AFRAID OF LOSING YOU LIKE HE LOST HER.
YOU ACCEPTED ME DESPITE *MY* PAST--YOU SHOULD HAVE FAITH THAT I'D DO THE SAME.
I'LL NEVER LEAVE YOU, ARTHUR.
NEVER.
MERA WILL STAND IN OUR WAY.
THEN WE MOVE HER OUT OF IT. PRAISE THE KING.
YES. PRAISE THE KING.

Robot Chicken: DC Comics Special variant cover to AQUAMAN #12

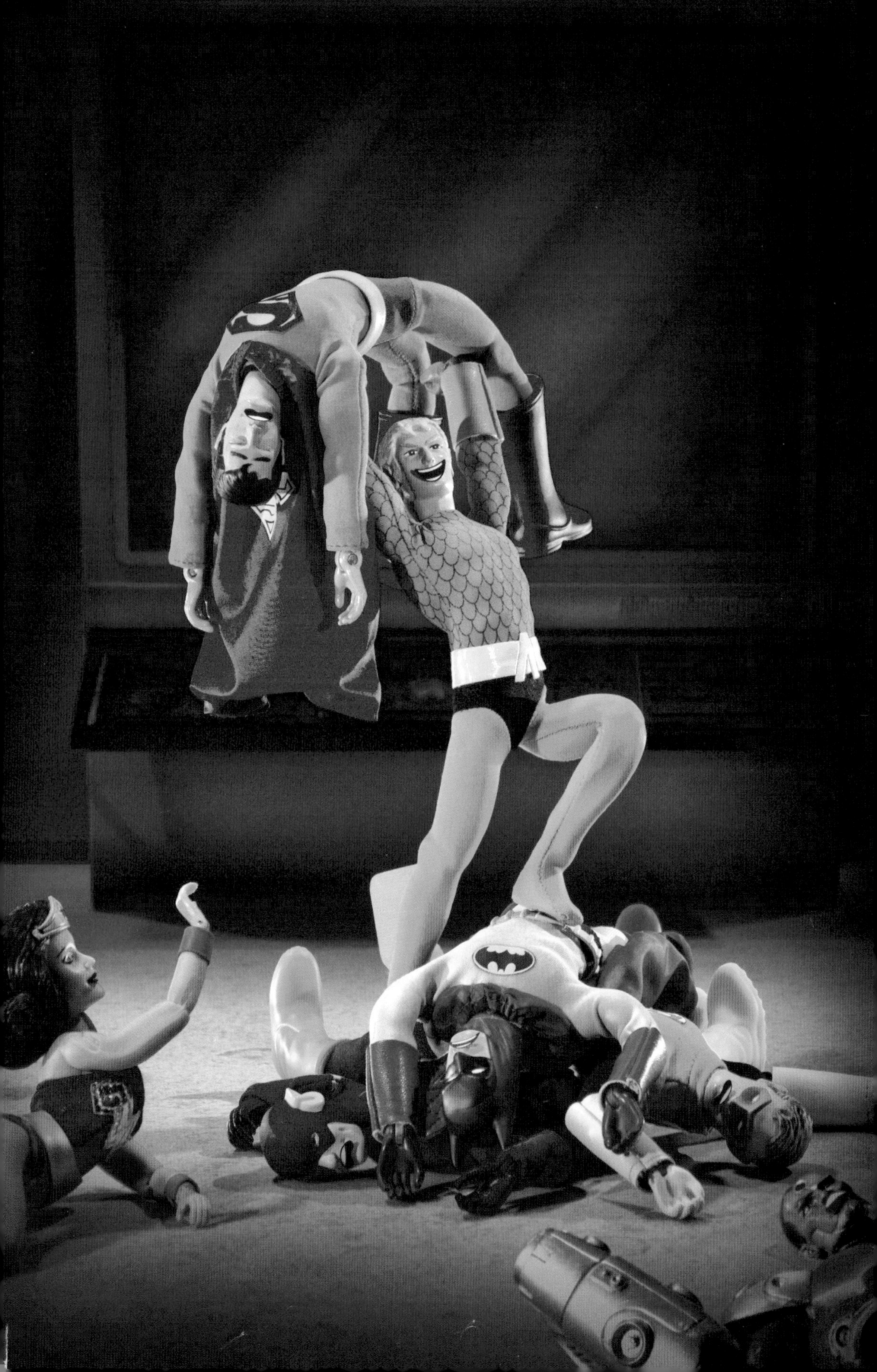